Magazine Journalism Today

ANTHONY DAVIS

Focal Press

Focal Press
An imprint of Butterworth-Heinemann
Linacre House, Jordan Hill, Oxford OX2 8DP
225 Wildwood Avenue, Woburn, MA 01801-2041
A division of Reed Educational and Professional Publishing Ltd

℞ A member of the Reed Elsevier plc group

OXFORD   BOSTON   JOHANNESBURG
MELBOURNE   NEW DELHI   SINGAPORE

First published 1998
Reprinted 1992, 1994
Revised reprint 1995
Reprinted 1998

© Anthony Davis 1988

British Library Cataloguing in Publication Data
David, Anthony, *1927-*
  Magazine journalism today
  1. Great Britain, Magazines. Journalism
  I. Title
  070'.023'41

ISBN 0 7506 0728 9

Printed and bound in Great Britain
by MPG Books Ltd, Bodmin, Cornwall

CONTENTS

7 Presentation 79

Word counting – Typefaces – Type sizes – Column widths – Justified, unjustified – Picture selection and retouching – Sizing pictures – Picture cropping – Design – Bleed offs – Picture balance – Headings – Boxes and panels – Typebreakers – Captions, continuations and rules – Final layout – Computerized layouts

8 Sub-editing 120

Duties of a sub – House style – Trade names – Marking copy – Marking for type – Headline writing – Straplines and standfirsts –Bylines – Captions and credits – Final work – Subbing on screen

9 An ABC of magazine contents 137

Advice columns – Backgrounders – Book adaptations – Campaigns – Competitions – Contents pages – Covers – Diaries – Do-it-yourself features – Fiction – Horoscopes – In Our Next Issue – Letters pages – Lists – Make-overs – Merchandising – Opinion columns – Quizzes – Reviews – Strips – Supplements – Surveys

10 Printing and production 170

Typesetting – The paste-up process – Half tones – Colour separations – Colour proofing – Proof reading – Proof marks – The working dummy – Printing – Desktop publishing – Laser printing – Types of paper – Finishing

11 Post production 188

Correspondence – Market research – Pressure groups – The Press Council – Libel – Official secrets – Breach of confidence – Contempt of court – Copyright – The journalist's code

12 A career guide 201

Pre-entry courses for graduates – Post A-level courses – The editorial training scheme – Block release courses – Other courses – Job hunting – The curriculum vitae – Women in magazine journalism – Job interviews – Contracts of employment – Early days – The expenses system – Union membership

13 The role of the freelance 212

The good and the bad – Setting up as a freelance – Freelance routine – Money matters – Contracts – Tax problems – Treatment of freelances

ACKNOWLEDGEMENTS

Many people gave me help in the preparation of this book, but I am particularly grateful to:

David Longbottom, Executive Director of the Periodicals Training Council, his predecessor, Ron Sumption, Jean Silvan Evans of the Centre for Journalism at University College, Cardiff, and Anthony Cox of the Department of Journalism and Business Studies at the London College of Printing, for information on journalistic training;

John Cunningham, Mike Hills and Bert Husk, my colleagues on different magazines over many years, for advice regarding some of the practicalities of periodical journalism;

Tom Hickman, a former colleague, for suggesting the book to me, and F. W. (Freddie) Hodgson, general editor of the series of which it is part, for much-appreciated encouragement and counselling during the writing of it;

and the following organizations and magazine publishers who gave permission for reproduction of material as illustrations: *Bella, Camera Weekly, Cosmopolitan, Elle, Hyway Printing Services Limited, Sunday, Sunday Express Magazine, Time, TVTimes, Woman, Woman's Own, You Magazine/Mail on Sunday.*

INTRODUCTION

There are many books about careers in journalism – on newspapers and in radio and television – but none devoted to magazine journalism, which is strange, given the number of periodicals published in this country and the fact that every year, on average, 5000 young people write to the Periodicals Training Council, which organizes training in the industry in Britain, inquiring about careers on magazines. This book is intended for all these, and for students of journalism and those with ambitions to freelance or to start their own magazines.

It sets out the processes by which a magazine is produced and the variety of skills required. There is, of course, a big difference between working on a mass selling magazine with a large and highly paid staff of specialists, and on a minority interest magazine with a small staff of jacks of all trades, but the work of, say, designing pages is the same whether done by an artist required to do nothing else, or by a sub-editor who also writes features and may even take photographs. The skills needed are the same whether they are divided between specialist members of large teams or are all embodied in one or two persons – and new computer-based technology has made it possible for publications to be written, designed, sub-edited, and even typeset and printed by one person.

That is one reason why this book roughly follows the progression of magazine production from the planning stage and commissioning of material to publication and distribution. Traditional ways of carrying out some of the processes described are being simplified by the use of computers, and there are likely to be further developments in the next decade.

1 THE MAGAZINE WORLD

Most magazines are sold over counters, though many are posted to subscribers and others are given away. In size they range from as few as 16 pages to more than 300, and from the pocketable to ones which open out into posters. They include magazines as popular as *Radio Times* and *TV Times*, each selling more than 1 million copies weekly, and others as esoteric as *Soil Survey and Land Evaluation* (published three times a year with a circulation of 300) and *Solar and Wind Technology* (six times a year, circulation 600). Specialized subjects range alphabetically from accident prevention and accountancy to Zionism and zoology.

Their diversity is recognized in the annual awards of the Periodical Publishers Association made to the magazine editor, consumer writer, technical writer, designer, consumer periodical and business periodical of the year. In one recent year awards and commendations went to journalists on magazines as disparate as *Country Living*, *Woman's Own*, *Bird Life*, *Crops*, *Business*, *New Society*, *Big Farm Weekly*, *Flight International*, *Network*, *Photography*, *Here's Health*, *Saga*, *Chat*, *Running*, *The Spectator*, *Motor*, *Child Education*, *Medeconomics*, *Reader's Digest*, *Architects' Journal*, *World of Interiors* and *Hardware Trade Journal*.

How many magazines there are is arguable, because there is no universally accepted definition of a magazine other than it should contain articles or stories by different authors, and that it should be published at regular intervals, which can be any period longer than a day, according to some, and not less than a week in the view of others. One media directory lists more than 7600 different periodicals published in the United Kingdom; another recognizes more than 8900, but some of these are essentially trade newspapers and have a tabloid newspaper format, while what most readers understand by a magazine is a publication with a colour cover and stapled or stitched pages.

But the magazine industry is a continually evolving one. In a typical year, in response to trends and fashions, the major companies that dominate magazine publishing in Britain close or merge around 10 per cent of their titles and launch about the same number of new ones. Others are also started, resulting in some 200 new titles every year. The number of periodicals continues to grow, and new technology making production cheaper means the number is likely to expand further.

The first magazines

Less hasty than newspapers, more timely than books, periodicals developed alongside the first printed newspapers in the seventeenth century. 'Serials', as they were then widely known, grew out of publishers' book lists and led, in Paris in 1665, to the *Journal des Sçavans*, a weekly 12-page digest of important books, bibliographies and obituaries of writers, and in England in 1682 to *Weekly Memorials for the Ingenious*, which consisted of eight pages of extracts from, and reviews of, books, with occasional woodcut illustrations.

Then in Paris in 1672 *Le Mercure Galant* introduced gossip for the smart set in the form of a letter to a woman who had supposedly left the city for the provinces, a formula imitated in England in 1692 by *The Gentleman's Journal or the Monthly Miscellany*, 'a Letter to a gentleman in the country, consisting of News, History, Philosophy, Poetry, Musick, Translations, etc.' It had 64 pages, mostly written by the editor, Peter Anthony Motteux, though Henry Purcell contributed an original composition every month. From its third issue it included a short story, and there were woodcut illustrations.

In 1691 John Dunton, a London bookseller, Richard Sault, a mathematics teacher, and Samuel Wesley, father of the evangelists John and Charles, launched the *Athenian Gazette* (later the *Athenian Mercury*), a single-sheet of questions and answers published on Tuesdays and Saturdays. It covered a wide range of subjects, answering such questions as where fire goes when extinguished, the nature of dryness and moisture, whether it is easier to resist pain or pleasure, and how rats can have foreknowledge of fatal events. 'Which is the best poem ever made?' it asked (Answer: Milton's *Paradise Lost*). 'When had angels their first existence?' (Answer: Who but an angel knows?).

Women's magazines began with a sister paper, *The Ladies' Mercury*, founded by Dunton in 1693, which pioneered advice to the lovelorn. 'Ladies are desired to send in their questions to the Latin Coffee House in Ave Mary Lane', it announced, promising advice about love, dress and marital behaviour to questioners, 'whether virgins, wives or widows'. Adultery and pre-marital sex were among the topics considered.

Soon periodicals began to be designed primarily to amuse rather than to instruct. Edward Ward's *London Spy*, for instance, 16 pages monthly of sketches of London life, was humorous, frequently ribald. However, periodicals in the seventeenth century, like newspapers, tended to be short-lived. They were retarded by a licensing system and pre-publication censorship intended to suppress political opposition and religious dissent, and their numbers rose and fell, though it is estimated that in 1704 the weekly circulation of newspapers and periodicals together was a mere 43,000.

The eighteenth century

In the eighteenth century periodicals became widely read outlets for essayists. In 1709 Richard, later Sir Richard, Steele began *Tatler*, a half sheet published three times a week at a penny. (For another halfpenny a reader could buy a blank sheet on which to write his own message for sending with the periodical to friends.) It had writers of quality – Steele himself, and Joseph Addison, Jonathan Swift and William Congreve. It had style and humour, commenting on every aspect of life, and led to many imitations. Addison and Steele then established the *Spectator*, published every day except Sunday. Its circulation grew to 4000 and it carried a large amount of advertising – for wine, books, patent medicines, perfumes, boot polish, theatres and manor houses. There was also *The Female Tatler*, edited nominally by 'Mrs Crackenthorpe, a Lady that knows everything'. But the Stamp Acts of 1712 and 1725, which imposed taxes on the pages and advertisements of newspapers and periodicals, forced the *Spectator* to double its price and sales slumped to 1600.

The first all-fiction publication, *Records of Love, or Weekly Amusements for the Fair Sex*, began in 1710 with 16 pages of romance for women readers every Saturday, including three-part serials such as 'The Wandering Dancing Master'. The first house magazine – the *British Mercury* – was launched by the Company of London Insurers in the same year and distributed three times weekly to policy holders and subscribers. Children's publications began with *The Lilliputian Magazine, or the Young Gentleman and Lady's Golden Library*, launched in London in 1751 as a threepenny monthly. It was 4 inches by 2½ inches in size and included jokes, riddles and songs.

At the start of the century the word 'magazine' as a synonym for a periodical was still unknown. The first to incorporate the word in its title, and the first general miscellany of the modern type, was printer Edward Cave's *Gentleman's Magazine*, which began in 1731. He used 'magazine' to mean a periodical drawing material from many sources, his 48-page monthly initially being mainly a digest from other publications, though gradually original contributions were introduced. A feature from 1736 was its coverage of Parliamentary debates, of which Cave himself took notes. This was technically an infringement of Parliamentary privilege and after Parliament resolved in 1738 that reporting its proceedings should be a punishable offence, Samuel Johnson, not yet at work on his great dictionary, began a series of thinly disguised reports under the title 'Debates in the Senate of Great Lilliput'.

The *Gentleman's Magazine* led to a score of imitations. In Philadelphia in 1741 Andrew Bradford launched the *American Magazine*, which lasted 3 months, and Benjamin Franklin's *General Magazine* followed, but no American periodical was to achieve a national readership for a century.

Meanwhile, freedom of the press became a major issue as the result of the *North Briton*, a weekly founded by John Wilkes MP in 1762. An article attacking ministers and the king (George III) was declared to be seditious, and an essay on women an obscene libel; he was at various times over a long period expelled from Parliament, fined, jailed and outlawed, but won popular support for a more liberal attitude to publishing.

The nineteenth century

In the nineteenth century came great political reviews. The *Edinburgh Review*, founded by Sydney Smith and Francis Jeffrey in 1802, supported the Whig party, and Sir Walter Scott, William Hazlitt, Thomas Arnold and Thomas Carlyle contributed. *The Quarterly Review*, launched in 1809 by publisher John Murray, supported the Tories; Scott switched his writing to it, and George Canning and Robert Southey were other contributors.

More significantly, magazines, which had been designed originally for coffee shop gossips and had developed into literary publications, began to be published for a wider readership. *Chambers' Journal* and the *Penny Magazine* were started in 1832 and the latter was selling 200,000 copies by the end of the year. The Christmas special number, an annual event in most periodicals today, was introduced with a 16-page supplement in the *Illustrated London News* in 1848, including a verse, 'Under the Holly Bow' (sic) and a drawing, 'Fetching home the Christmas dinner', along with humorous predictions for the coming year and one of the earliest attacks on the commercialization of Christmas.

The first mass-circulation women's publication, *The Englishwoman's Domestic Magazine* of 1852, a twopenny monthly, reached a sale of 50,000 copies. It was started by 21-year-old Samuel Orchard Beeton and included fashion and cookery notes contributed by his future wife, Isabella, author of the famous *Household Management*. It gave away dressmaking patterns and ran the first prize competitions in women's magazines, and a problem page, which featured an eyebrow-raising correspondence on the whipping of girls and the corporal punishment of children. Beeton also edited, monthly from 1855, the first periodical for boys, the *Boy's Own Magazine*. Priced at 2d (1p), it contained adventure stories, biographies of heroes and articles on sport, together with the first prize competitions for children. The winners received silver pencil cases valued at a guinea (£1.05p).

Household Words (1850), which offered 24 pages of poetry, anecdotes and letters for twopence, and its successor *All the Year Round* (1859) were 'conducted' by Charles Dickens. (At this time the word 'editor' meant merely one who prepared a manuscript for the printer, rather than the editorial controller.) *All the Year Round* began with part one of *A Tale of Two Cities*. In America *Harper's Bazaar* began in 1867, followed by *McCall's, Ladies' Home Journal, Good Housekeeping* and *Vogue*. In Britain came *Queen* and *Lady*.

Many professional journals were born, among them the *Lancet* (medical), *Economist* (financial), *Nature* (scientific), *Law Quarterly* (legal) and *Studio* (art). The first parish magazine was published monthly from 1859 by St Michael's, Derby, with stories of missionary life, news of parochial activities, extracts from books and answers to correspondents, while other special interest groups catered for by the end of the nineteenth century included motorists. The first motoring magazine was *La Locomotion Automobile*, a monthly published in Paris in 1894; in Britain the weekly, *Autocar*, began a year later. There were eleven motoring titles by the end of the century, and seventy-four by the outbreak of World War One.

Duties on periodicals and taxes on paper for printing them – long criticised as 'taxes on knowledge' – were repealed in the mid-nineteenth century, and then printing underwent a revolution when hand composition of type was succeeded by the introduction of setting machines. But from the readers' point of view, the biggest development in magazine publishing in the nineteenth century was in the use of photographs. Initially they were used merely as a basis for line drawings, which were converted into engravings or woodcuts, but then the invention of half-tone blocks, in which the light and shade of photographs are reproduced by dots of varying density, made it possible to publish the actual prints. The first magazine to run photographs was *Art Union* in 1846, the pictures being provided by William Henry Fox Talbot, but the credit for being the first genuine illustrated magazine is usually given to the *English Illustrated Magazine* in 1884.

A boom began in magazines as advertising developed to promote the sales of consumer goods. As advertising grew, so did magazines, their readership widened by rising populations, greater literacy, increased leisure time and a redistribution of income. The Education Act of 1870, which made schooling compulsory to the age of 13, combined with cheaper rail travel to create a demand for 'a half-hour read'.

The first periodical in Britain, and probably in the world, to sell a million copies of each issue was *Titbits*, which was founded by George Newnes, a Lancashire printer, in 1881. Its full title was *Titbits From All the Most Interesting Books, Periodicals and Newspapers in the World* and its circulation was built on snippets of the man-bites-dog and elephants-on-roller-skates type, interspersed with human interest stories, stunts and offers. There were competitions for prizes such as a house in Dulwich and the offer of a job, which brought in up to 200 sacks of mail daily. Newnes promised £100 to the next of kin of any reader killed in a railway accident, provided the reader was clutching a copy of *Titbits* as he died. Sir George Newnes, as he became in 1895, said a magazine should give 'wholesome and harmless entertainment to crowds of hard-working people craving for a little fun and amusement'.

It was from Newnes that Alfred Harmsworth got his ideas about popular journalism. Harmsworth, who collected facts like schoolboys collect stamps, was an early contributor to *Titbits* and modelled on it his *Answers to Correspondents* (later known simply as *Answers*), which he started in 1889 when he was only 23. It contained snippets such as 'What the Queen eats' and 'Narrow escapes from burial alive', and also featured competitions. In one of them the magazine asked readers to guess the value of gold and silver in the Bank of England on a particular day for a prize of £1 a week for life, and 700,000 entered. Harmsworth, who became Lord Northcliffe, and his brother Harold (Lord Rothermere) launched many other periodicals, among them *Comic Cuts*, *Home Chat*, *Home Sweet Home*, *Union Jack* and *Half Penny Marvel*, with total sales of more than one and a half million. Countless freelance writers made their first sales to *Titbits* and *Answers*.

The twentieth century

Many innovations were seen in the early part of the twentieth century in America, where the number of magazines had leapt from 700 to more than 3000 between 1865 and 1885. *True Story* was launched in 1919 with the motto, 'Truth is stranger than fiction', and the catchline, 'We offer $1000 for your life romance'. A cover picture of a man and woman looking into each other's eyes was captioned, 'And their love turned to hatred'. The confession magazine was born. All the stories, which had titles such as 'How I learned to hate my parents,' were written in the first person and illustrated with photographs posed by models. All were claimed to have a moral, and contributors were required to sign affidavits that the stories were true. Within a few years circulation had passed 2 million.

In 1924 the same publisher, Bernarr Macfadden, launched *True Detective* and began a vogue for crime story magazines and 'pulps', so called because of the pulp paper on which they were printed. These were all-fiction magazines devoted, according to title, to romance, crime, Westerns, war and science fiction. Movie magazines, which had begun with *Photoplay* in 1911, reached their greatest circulations in the 1920s and 1930s, retailing gossip about the stars at a time when the cinema represented mass entertainment. Their successors in recent years have been the TV magazines, the biggest being America's *TV Guide*, with a sale of 15.8 million, and pop group magazines or 'fanzines'.

The development of 35mm cameras led to *Life* in the United States in 1936 and to *Picture Post* in 1938 in Britain, and photojournalism was established. Paper rationing and other restrictions during the Second World War curbed development of magazines, but then post-war affluence, new consumer products to advertise, and technical developments such as photo-typesetting, improved colour film and web-offset printing made them a growth industry again, though from the mid-1950s with a new and dangerous competitor for advertising in television.

During the 1950s the traditional women's magazines in Britain were joined by newcomers for teenagers, such as *Marilyn*, *Mirabelle*, *Romeo*, *Valentine*, *Roxy* and *Boyfriend*, offering romantic fiction in picture-strip form. In 1952 *Confidential* began a new era of gossip mongering, leading in the 1970s to *People Weekly*, which brought imitators all over the world. Royalty magazines were to follow. Consumerism was launched in 1957 when *Which?* began publishing independent reports on the comparative quality of goods and services, naming names and prices and picking 'best buys'. As the circulation rose to 740,000, *Gardening Which?* and *Holiday Which?* followed, while other publishers brought out *Which Bike?*, *Which Camera?*, *Which Car?*, *Which Computer?*, *Which Video?*, *Which Compact Disc?*, *Which Course?* and similar titles.

Sales of individual publications declined, due to television and to the newspapers' move away from news to provide more features, borrowing from magazines for the design of their feature pages. Colour supplements distributed with newspapers began in Britain in 1962 with *The Sunday Times Magazine*, which was devised to win colour advertising by enlarging the market for the latest consumer products. Its first cover featured photographs by David Bailey of Jean Shrimpton in clothes by Mary Quant. Inside were an article on pop artist Peter Blake, a new James Bond story by Ian Fleming, a recipe for stewed oysters by a then unknown Robert Carrier, cameos of 'People of the Sixties' and a profile of the city of Lincoln. 'This innocent *mélange* gave rise to a new and pejorative term: colour supplement living', says Godfrey Smith, who was the magazine's second editor. 'This was held by those who coined it to exemplify all that was worst about modern Britain: trendiness and gluttony, cynicism and materialism, a kind of glossy heartlessness.' But the magazine succeeded.

Alongside the growth of colour supplements in newspapers in the 1960s there was a boom in part-works – magazine-format encyclopedias of knitting, photography, cookery and modern history, printed in many instalments and, if successful, recycled as soon as they reached an end. Magazines moved into more new areas, such as pop music and puzzles, and began to cater for youth interests and for pressure groups concerned with feminism, gay rights and environmental issues. Music and children's publications were sold with accompanying cassettes, football magazines opened into wall posters, part-works on writers were accompanied by classic novels, and then came an abundance of free magazines.

In the late 1980s a new internationalism came to periodical publishing when the French fashion magazine *Elle* was published in English language versions – not merely translations, but with new contents – in America and in Britain, and *Prima*, a women's magazine with sewing and knitting patterns, launched in France in 1982, was followed by German and British editions in 1986. A similar magazine for women, *Best*, which began in Britain in 1987, was based on *Femme Actuelle* in France and *Mia* in Spain.

Although the magazine share of British advertising expenditure has decreased as television's has risen since 1955, publishers continue to find and to exploit gaps in the market.

Present day

The biggest category of periodicals today comprises trade, technical and professional magazines – nearly 6000 of them in Britain – from the *British Medical Journal* to *Electrical Review*. House journals, published by companies to inform their staffs or to enhance their public image, also fall within this category, and range from prestigious, beautifully designed and printed publications to cheap and amateurish ones. (The worst publish a picture of the chairman on nearly every page, and columns of trivia about employees' off-duty activities.)

The second group is that of the so-called consumer magazines, intended for mass sale, numbering some 2600, with market leaders such as *Country Life*, *Homes and Gardens* and *Tatler*, but dominated numerically by some 100 magazines for women (though most of them, while bought only by women, also have male readers). For years they were mainly devoted to 'the three Rs' – royalty, romance and recipes – with love stories, and features about knitting, dressmaking and caring for husbands and children. They sold 12 million at their peak in the 1950s but were down to half that figure by the 1980s, whereupon they became increasingly concerned with the interests of women outside the home, and also began to deal outspokenly with sexual matters. Britain's big sellers include *Woman's Weekly*, *Woman's Own* and

Woman, but the market has become more specialized, the main classifications being fashion (as in *Vogue*), romantic fiction (*True Romances*), home service (*Good Housekeeping*), young women's interests (*Over 21*), handicrafts (*Pins and Needles*) and general interest (*She*).

Traditionally, there has never been an equivalent sector in publishing for male readers; attempts to produce general publications for them have failed, and 'men's magazines' has become a euphemism for 'girlie' books featuring nudes, cartoons and titillating fiction, though with some articles mainly concerned with sex, cars, wars and male fashions. The most remarkable of them has been America's *Playboy*, which, from a shoestring launch in 1954, grew to give its name to an empire of gambling clubs, hotels, cinemas, model agencies and other offshoots; but by the second half of the 1980s founder Hugh M. Hefner's philosophies seemed dated and retrenchment was taking place. However, there were new attempts to cater for men in the 1980s, among them the fashion-based *Arena* and music-based *Q*.

What men have bought mainly, apart from trade and professional magazines, are those devoted to particular interests such as angling, football, golf and motoring. Among magazines concerned with hobbies and leisure interests the other main concerns have traditionally been photography, gardening, music, the countryside, do-it-yourself and, since the 1960s, pop music, but in recent years there has been great growth in home computer magazines. Within 8 years of the launch of *Personal Computer World* in 1978 there were more than 100 UK computer magazines, half of them concerned with home computers. The first such magazines dealt with computers in general, but they swiftly became more specialized, catering for the users of particular makes. The boom was good for journalists who understand computers; it has been alleged that in the early days all the articles were written by about a dozen of them, using many pseudonyms, and that one writer had some six basic articles on a word processor disc which he could edit swiftly for new markets. However, the number of computer literates grew rapidly.

Children's publications have long consisted mainly of comics, such as *Beano* and *Disney Magazine*, with picture stories and strips (later joined by teenagers' romantic comics) and puzzle books. The latter also have an adult following.

'Journals of opinion', political and literary reviews, such as *The Spectator* and *New Statesman*, tending to be wordy and staid in presentation, have generally been declining both in numbers and circulation. News reviews such as America's *Time*, founded by Briton Haden and Henry R. Luce in 1923, and now selling 4.2 million copies weekly, and *Newsweek* (3.2 million) circulate around the world, but no British news magazine has been successful since *Picture Post* (1938–50), a spectacular flop of the 1970s being Sir James Goldsmith's short-lived *Now!* It is generally held that this is because of the high sales and national distribution of Britain's daily newspapers, compared with the smaller circulation city-based newspapers in other countries, where magazines provide national coverage. Photo-journalism, the picture-led coverage of important events in greater depth than by newspapers, pioneered by *Life* and *Picture Post*, was taken up by Sunday colour supplements in the 1960s and 1970s but has now practically disappeared; it was expensive and readers apparently got enough of foreign wars and disasters on television.

Less easily classified publications include so-called 'alternative', under-ground and cult magazines, which tend to become part of mainstream publishing in time. This was notably the case with *Private Eye*, the satirical fortnightly, which for years following its launch in 1962 seemed immune from libel actions, despite the nature of its stories, because its circulation was small and it was known to have only the slenderest financial resources, though Britain's largest firm of newsagents refused to take the risk of selling it. Eventually it became established, with a healthy sale, high profitability and a considerable influence among journalists and politicians, and was then taken to court and made to pay when it erred.

Listings magazines such as *Time Out* and *City Limits*, setting out 'what's on', gained circulation, as did feminist and gay rights magazines such as *Spare Rib* and *Gay News*. Following on the punk era came 'new wave' or 'street' magazines, with heavy emphasis on fashion and music, and breaking all conventions of design and graphics with eccentric typography. Among a number launched in 1980 were *Blitz*, *i-D* and *The Face*, describing itself grandly as a 'visual-orientated youth culture magazine'.

Distribution

The majority of publications are what are called news trade titles, meaning that they are sold by newsagents, though sales in supermarkets have been increasing at the expense of traditional newsagent–tobacconist shops because of changes in shopping habits and a decline in smoking. However, supermarkets usually offer only big-selling titles, and readers still need other suppliers for minority interest magazines.

There are also subscription journals, mailed to subscribers, and hybrids such as *Time*, which, although also sold on bookstalls, rely heavily on subscriptions, decreasing in price (by as much as 50 per cent compared with the bookstall price) according to the length of time for which the reader contracts. (There are such inducements as digital watches and calculators for introducing new subscribers.)

But the fastest-growing sector of publishing has been that of the give-aways, depending entirely on the advertising they can sell for their revenue.

More than 100 were launched in one year in the mid-1980s, giving Britain more than 450 'freebies'.

Many are the ways in which expensively produced publications are now placed in the hands of readers. Firstly, there are controlled circulation publications, not available to the general public but distributed to 'target' readers by post or other means. Some have very specific markets. For example, *Sports Teacher* is aimed at physical education teachers and coaches in schools and colleges, and 20,000 copies of each issue are distributed through local education authorities to school staff rooms (though it is also possible to take out a personal subscription and have the magazine mailed). The value of controlled circulation publications to advertisers is that they reach a guaranteed number of persons with known purchasing power or influence, and some publishers decline to supply their magazines to applicants who do not meet their specifications regarding wealth, education or status. Other publishers aim more widely. Credit card companies, banks and building societies are among institutions that send magazines to their customers.

Then there are the colour supplements included with newspapers. Fleet Street derided *The Sunday Times Magazine* when it was launched in 1962 but within a year it had added 600,000 to sales of the newspaper, was earning a high revenue for colour advertising pages and had set a trend which others followed, leading climactically to *Sunday*, distributed with the *News of the World* from 1981. Although the majority of its readers are of a lower income group, less attractive to advertisers, it reaches an enormous number of them, nearly 5 million copies being distributed weekly. *Sunday* was started to halt a decline in the parent newspaper's sales, which it did – largely by sensational features about soap opera and pop stars – though at high cost, owing to the size of the print run.

Other magazines are now given away in hotels, at railway stations and on aircraft, and offered for the taking on display bins outside shops. *Airport* distributed at Gatwick and Heathrow, contains articles to interest frequent travellers. *Capital Magazine* is given to homeward-bound commuters at London rail termini. *Girl About Town*, aimed at women of 17 to 34, is given away at railway stations and in the streets. *Symbol* is distributed solely to the owners of Rolls-Royces, Ferraris and Riva boats; *Let's Go Gardening* is available at garden centres; and *Golden Age*, a monthly for the retired, at old people's clubs, libraries and post offices. Further markets and in-expensive methods of distribution are constantly being sought.

Contents

The sharpest division in the content of magazines is between fiction and non-fiction, though fiction, consisting of short stories or serials (often condensed from new novels), is diminishing. (Poetry has almost vanished.) Non-fiction embraces a wide range of material, some of it news (found mainly in the trade press), the rest known simply as 'features'.

Perhaps the most numerous features in all types of magazines, are *interviews*, the mass circulation magazines tending towards film and pop star subjects, while art reviews concentrate on painters, and trade publications on business executives. *Profiles* are usually based on interviews but delve deeper and wider, quoting not only the subject but past and present colleagues and rivals, parents and others. *Multiple interview* features ask a number of, usually well known, people to answer the same questions about, say, their diary-keeping habits or how they spend Saturday evenings or what they carry in the boots of their cars.

Descriptive features may be about places, such as unusual holiday venues, or animals or events. *Investigations* may cover a scandal, or a cause of concern such as drug addiction or dangerous toys. Accounts of *personal experiences* can range from a famous explorer's story of a dangerous expedition to the domestic drama of a mother caring for a handicapped child. *Stunts* set up by magazines can, say, arrange for an actor about to play a statesman in a TV series to visit the House of Commons to meet genuine politicians, or persuade celebrities to dress up as historical characters they would like to have been.

In mass circulation magazines, to provide some continuity and to encourage readers to buy the next issue, there is often a serialization, which may be extracted from a new book, and some regular features such as 'My favourite room,' 'My wedding day' or 'My unfulfilled ambition'. Most such magazines carry one or more regular columns, known as *service features*, covering gardening, motoring, cookery, beauty, fashion, travel, chess, money matters or medical problems, and they may also provide *consumer advice* about the best value in yoghurts, vacuum cleaners, telephone answering machines or lawnmowers.

Other types of feature include gossip columns, reviews, quizzes, picture spreads, children's sections, humour (embracing strips and cartoons), competitions, promotional offers, and readers' letters; the last have the merits of costing nothing, introducing fresh viewpoints, and helping to create a bond with readers. Most magazines are always keen to encourage a family atmosphere.

2 ORGANIZATION AND STAFF

The editor is, of course, the key figure on any publication. It is the editor who gives the magazine its character. It is the editor who is ultimately responsible for the content, appearance and style, and who is the public face of the magazine, going on television and radio to talk about it when it is in the news. The editor is also responsible in law and will have to answer in court if the publication offends.

The editor is in charge of the editorial staff, though normally it is only when a new publication is being launched that editors can choose all the staff. At other times they inherit existing staff and can do little more than bring in one or two key executives or writers to help fashion the publication they want. Even then an editor may not have a free choice: for example, if another publication in a group is being closed, the editor will be under pressure to absorb otherwise redundant employees from it. The new editor of a broadcasting magazine, who hoped to recruit additional writers knowledgeable about television, was obliged to accept staff from a pharmaceutical trade journal that was being closed.

While editors' powers may be wide, and they tend to be in step with their success, they rarely enjoy unfettered freedom. In a publishing group an editor will probably have to answer to an editorial director or publisher with responsibility for a number of publications. In any event there will be someone, possibly a managing director, overseeing not only editorial but advertising and circulation departments, and setting the budget within which the editor must operate, its size depending on the profitability of the publication. Within that budget the editor might have a free hand to determine the amounts spent on writers, artwork, competition prizes and in other areas.

Disagreements between the editor and the advertising department over the division of space between editorial and advertising pages, and the positioning and nature of advertising, will also normally be resolved by higher authority. Of course, an editor with a seat on the board of directors has greater authority than one who has not.

Managing editors and editors-in-chief

The title of editor is an honourable one and simple. Unfortunately, it is now sometimes difficult to know just who is in charge from the masthead of a periodical. One American magazine lists an editor-in-chief and a corporate editor, a managing editor, two executive editors and three assistant managing editors, but no one with the unqualified title of editor. In these circumstances the term managing editor generally equates with editor.

However, managing editor is a post which varies from one publication to another. While on some magazines a managing editor is, effectively, the editor, on others a managing editor is second in command, commonly concerned with production and freeing the editor to concentrate on long-term plans and more creative aspects of the job. In such cases, it is cynically said, when an issue is praiseworthy, the editor gets champagne from the board, but when an issue is poor, late or over budget, the managing editor gets the blame.

In so far as there is any common practice, editor-in-chief usually denotes a senior figure, often a former editor of the periodical, possessed of some authority which may be exercised over several titles, available to the editor for guidance on matters of policy, but not responsible for day-to-day editorial decisions. Editors should, in fact, be allowed to edit without interference and judged on their long-term records; a number of serious errors of judgement (in the eyes of the owners) will, of course, end with a change of editor.

Executives

Staffing levels vary widely, and a typical magazine establishment does not exist. There are big weeklies with 100 editorial staff and magazines produced by one person (though usually with the aid of contributors). There are also publishing groups in which a team of people produces several different titles.

On big magazines the multiplicity of executive titles can be confusing, certainly to the outsider and sometimes even to the staff. The term *deputy editor* is, or should be, clear, describing the person in charge during the editor's absence. If no one is designated deputy editor, an *assistant editor* may be the second in command, but often there are several assistant editors. America's *People Weekly* lists ten, which seems excessive, but it is commonplace to have two, perhaps one with responsibility for the art side of the publication and another for the text. The title is also frequently coupled with another; a chief sub-editor, for example, may be ranked as an assistant editor. This gives higher status, and is a cheaper way of rewarding an executive than paying a salary rise or providing a bigger office. (Incidentally an assistant editor should not be confused with an assistant *to* the editor, who is merely an aide, as the title suggests.)

There may also be *associate editors*. In America, where titles proliferate, *National Enquirer* has six associate editors (in addition to eight assistant editors) while *Publishers Weekly* lists four senior associate editors and four associate editors. The title is almost meaningless to anyone outside the office concerned, frequently indicating only that an executive has had to be slotted between existing strata in the hierarchy.

A big magazine will have a number of executives, all with the word editor in their titles. A *production editor* is responsible for scheduling when different pages go to the printer and for seeing that departments meet those schedules, and works closely with the printers to ensure that they also meet their schedules.

An *art editor* is responsible for the design and appearance of the publication. This is one of the most important jobs on a well illustrated colour magazine and is often dignified by the title of *art director*, though a minor one on a wordy literary review. The art editor may head a team of designers, artists and illustrators. A *picture editor*, sometimes answerable to the art editor, is responsible for commissioning staff and freelance photographers, setting up 'shoots' and obtaining pictures from libraries and agencies with the aid of picture researchers.

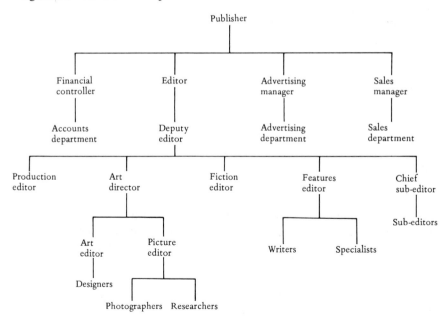

Figure 1 *A typical chain of command on a magazine*

A *features editor*, frequently producing most of the ideas for contents, briefs staff and freelance writers, obtains material from agencies and other sources, and ensures that regular features such as astrology and the various service columns are in the office on time. A *news editor*, sometimes found on trade publications though rarely on general magazines, is responsible for obtaining news, and briefs reporters, while a *chief sub-editor* is in charge of the sub-editors (subs for short), who check facts, correct grammar, trim copy to the required length, write headlines and picture captions, ensure that contents are consistent in spelling and style, and mark up copy for typesetting.

Others who may be designated as editors, though they may not have any staff, are the specialists such as beauty, fashion, travel, motoring, fiction and show business editors. Their importance varies; the *cookery editor* on one publication may have a kitchen in the office building in which to prepare lavish meals for photographic purposes, and an assistant to carry out menial chores; on another the cookery editor's work may merely be providing a weekly recipe. Motoring and aviation magazines often have *technical editors*, usually with engineering degrees or backgrounds in the appropriate industries. Many magazines employ a *books editor* to keep in touch with publishers about forthcoming books of interest, and to read advance proofs with a view to buying extracts or arranging features based on them. There may also be a *promotions organizer*, who arranges 'special offers' of merchandise as a service to readers and a revenue-raiser for the magazine, and sets up competitions, frequently for prizes obtained from manufacturers free or cheaply in return for publicity for their products.

Other staff

Magazines may or may not have staff writers. Because of the expense of employing experts in many fields, most prefer to rely on freelances, some of whom may be under contract. In the absence of any foreign bureaux, some freelance writers are likely to be located abroad in New York and other centres. Photographers may also be staff or freelances. Most are freelances.

There is an increasing use of researchers, sometimes designated *editorial assistants*, who are not full-fledged writers but are used to obtain material for them, to provide dates and statistics and compile simple fact boxes. A magazine may also have *librarians* to file pictures and cuttings, though in a group with a number of publications the library will normally be shared.

On a major magazine there may be a readers' correspondence department to answer letters, make a first selection of those suitable for publication, and advise the editor on reader reaction to features. A magazine may also have its own photographic dark room, but staffing is infinitely variable. Consider the following examples.

A colour magazine distributed with a British Sunday newspaper has an editorial staff of eighteen – an editor, a features editor, a production editor, an art editor with a staff of four, a picture editor with a staff of three, a chief sub (ranking as an assistant editor) and two subs, a researcher, a competitions and promotions organizer and a dark room manager. There are no staff writers or photographers; freelances are used. However, the numbers are regularly reinforced by three or four freelance artists, subs and writers – so called 'casuals' employed by the day or week, which is a common practice on magazines.

A glossy monthly magazine for women has an editor, a deputy editor, a features editor with an assistant, and an art editor with four assistants, including a picture editor. There is a style and fashion editor with two assistants, a health and beauty editor with one assistant, a careers editor with one assistant, literary, design and dance editors, a production editor and a chief sub with four assistants.

Another monthly for women has an editor-in-chief and a deputy editor, an associate editor/art director with two artists and a picture researcher, a production editor, a chief sub and three subs, a poetry and fiction editor, a fashion editor with an assistant, a health and beauty editor, a competitions editor with an assistant, a features assistant and an editorial assistant. A downmarket weekly for women has an editor, a deputy editor, a features editor with a deputy, an art editor with five staff, a picture editor with one assistant, a chief sub-editor with three staff, a production editor, a promotions manager, two staff writers and an editorial assistant. A trade weekly has an editor-in-chief, an editor, a deputy editor who is also features editor, a news editor, a picture editor, a production editor, a chief sub-editor and two subs, and nine reporters and writers.

Though rarely credited, some of the most valuable helpers editorial staff can have are motorcycle messengers, though they are usually hired as required from an agency, rather than on staff. They can be kept busy collecting and returning copy, pictures, artwork, cuttings, press releases and the like, for the postal service can be too slow and unreliable for magazines.

Non-journalistic departments

Of course, an editorial department cannot function in isolation. According to the Periodicals Training Council, journalists represent only 20 to 25 per cent of the total staff of magazines, which also have advertising, sales and accounts departments, the one with which journalists have the most abrasive relationship being advertising. There are few publications which do not carry advertisements, for without the revenue from them the cover price would have to be several times greater; and though readers sometimes complain about the amount of advertising in a magazine, particularly when several advertising spreads are placed consecutively between editorial pages, advertisements can be an attractive feature of a publication.

What journalists like to see, of course, are advertisements featuring good photography and colour for prestige products, such as a desirable car or fashionable clothes. What they do not like to see are crude ads for tawdry products. To be fair, there is no difference of opinion here between journalists and advertising staff, but ad executives have to take what they can get, unless the magazine is highly successful and in a position to be selective.

There is usually friction between editorial and advertising departments, Journalists regard advertising staff as a necessary evil, spoiling the run of the magazine and ruining potentially attractive layouts by their demands for ads to go in specific positions, such as on a right-hand page facing editorial matter. (Higher rates are levied for special positions.) The advertising staff regard themselves as important because, as they like to remind journalists, they bring in money while the editorial department spends it.

Advertising space is sold either to manufacturers of goods or to their advertising agencies. The advertising staff have to know and be able to contact those who make purchasing decisions, and usually they have specific territories to cover. They have to be able to define and describe the market served by the publication, and to demonstrate how their periodical meets the advertiser's needs.

Sales and circulation staff – who tend to be taken for granted by journalists – are responsible for the movement of copies from the printer to their various destinations, and for seeing that the right number of copies are available in every area (in the case of news trade magazines) and that the right readers are being reached (in the case of controlled circulation magazines). Computers are much used.

The term 'circulation department' is outmoded, though, and *marketing* is the vogue word. Titles are marketed, and circulation and distribution departments are increasingly known as 'sales and marketing'. Big publishing houses have their own sales force, while smaller titles usually rely on the services of a distribution firm.

Sales of most magazines are independently audited, so that prospective advertisers can gauge the effectiveness of different titles, and the provision of statistics is one of the responsibilities of the sales department. Sales reps call on trade wholesalers and retail outlets to obtain maximum orders and are normally assigned to specific territories.

The accounts department deals with budgets, financial forecasts and cash flow, and will blow a whistle when an editor is spending too freely. It collects the money from advertising and sales of the magazine, and pays suppliers, of newsprint, stationary, and other goods, and staff and contributors. It also deals with the staff's expenses. In a big group a single department will normally deal with all the different titles.

Other departments found in major publishing houses include public relations (to publicize and promote the publications), syndication (to recoup some of the editorial expenses by selling features and pictures from the magazine elsewhere, usually in other countries) and legal (to handle contracts and lawsuits, and provide advice to the editors on avoiding problems).

Launch of a magazine

New titles are always being launched. Some wither and die; some are enormously successful and give rise to imitations. The key to success, whether of a shoestring magazine or a mass-seller, is the same: identifying a gap in the market and supplying a product that fills it. Some publishers, among them Nick Logan of *The Face*, have done this by backing hunches. Big publishing groups use sophisticated market research; this is concerned with two main factors – the potential readership (its size, age range, and income and educational levels) and the potential advertising support. Some publishing groups have cupboards filled with plans for magazines concerned with a variety of subjects which were considered for publication at some time but eventually shelved. Perhaps one out of ten ideas investigated seriously gets as far as a launch.

If preliminary research suggests a proposed magazine could have a future, the next step is to choose a format. Pages of around A4 size (297×210 mm or 11.69×8.27 in trimmed) are the most favoured, and printing presses are designed to handle this format. An unusual shape makes a magazine easier to distinguish from others on a news stall, but costs more to print, and newsagents are not keen on handling the abnormal. Then comes the choice of paper; a heavyweight, coated paper (say 90 grams per square metre) gives good reproduction of colour pictures and a feeling of quality, but is expensive. A publication with few illustrations or low-income readers can be printed on cheaper, coarser, lightweight stock, perhaps 65 gsm. If distribution is to be by post, a lightweight paper has advantages; the price and weight steps in postage rates may also influence the number of pages. The system of distribution must be settled, along with the method of printing (which will depend largely on the quantity required), the binding (stitching, stapling and glueing), and the arrangements for typesetting and picture reproduction.

Only then can possible expenditure and income be roughly assessed. Some expenditure will consist of 'fixed costs', which, though they may be under- or over-estimated, will not change, no matter how many copies are printed or sold. They include office premises, staff salaries and expenses, the amounts to be spent on articles and artwork, and typesetting. 'Running costs', which vary according to the number of copies published, include printing and binding. All these have to be calculated against the anticipated income for advertising and the proposed cover price. The first will be influenced by the intended circulation and readership, the second by the prices of comparable publications and the affluence of the readers at whom the publication is aimed. If the cover price is set too high, the magazine will not sell; too low, and it may have to be increased within a short time, which will be unpopular with the trade and readers.

Key staff – an editor, an art editor and others – must be chosen, though they may not be contracted beyond producing a dummy at this stage. A title must be chosen, and that can entail a long and wearisome search, with every obvious one turning out to be too similar to a title already in use. The title, when settled, should be registered. (The most extraordinary omission to register a title was that of the BBC, owner of *Radio Times* which, despite launching television in 1936, failed to register *TV Times*, allowing that title to be adopted by a rival programme journal when ITV began in 1955.)

A dummy is then produced. In fact, several dummies will probably be produced, starting with a 'scamp', an artist's rough impression of what the publication will look like, followed by a mock-up incorporating genuine pictures and headlines, though the text may consist of gobbledygook or 'printers' latin' – slabs of type in a foreign language. Magazines have been launched on the basis of gobbledygook dummies, but it is more usual, at least in the case of magazines intended to have a big circulation, to go on to produce a proper dummy, containing specially commissioned features and pictures, because advertisers prefer realism.

Several hundred copies may be printed for distribution to potential advertisers and retailers, which is an expensive exercise. Publishers generally console themselves with the thought that material bought for the dummy will eventually be used in the magazine after the launch, but this is a false hope. It is a maxim of publishing that features used in a dummy never get into the actual magazine, because they will have become outdated or the editor will have lost interest in them.

Office accommodation has to be earmarked for the staff, with space near windows allocated to artists, if possible. The editor will need a private office in order to discuss confidential matters, though ideally it should be big enough for staff meetings. There may be a need for a photographic studio and dark room unless a contract is entered into with a picture agency. Too often overlooked is the need for an interview room where writers can talk to people about whom they are writing; frequently, even on major magazines, writers are reduced, after searching the building vainly for an empty office, to taking an interviewee to a pub or conducting an interview in a big room in which other staff are probably discussing the previous night's television.

Equipment must be ordered: desks, typewriters or word processors, a photocopier capable of enlarging and reducing, light boxes and projectors for the art department, an adequate number of telephones and a fax machine for sending and receiving facsimiles of pages over telephone lines. In the case of a large publishing group some facilities may be shared with other magazines.

Meanwhile a campaign will be mounted to impress the distribution trade and potential advertisers with the opportunities offered by the new publication. Assume it to be a pop magazine aimed at 15 to 24-year-olds; brochures will cite research showing that in one year young people in this category spend £120 million on hi-fi rack systems, £141 million on records and £144 million on cosmetics. They will be shown to be responsible for 36 per cent of cinema attendances, 50 per cent of new current bank accounts and 30 per cent of lager consumption, while 50 per cent of them like to travel abroad, 50 per cent of them enjoy shopping for fashionable clothes and 37 per cent of them try to keep up with technological developments.

If the trade reaction to the dummy is favourable, a launch date will be projected and staff engaged. It is generally sensible to start with the smallest possible number and enlarge as necessary, but it has to be remembered that talented journalists will already have jobs elsewhere and may have to serve out a notice period before they can start work full-time. (It is commonplace for magazines to be launched with some of the key staff still working out their notices with other companies.)

There should be at least one 'dry run', an issue produced in real time to discover unforeseen snags and polish the product. By that time promotion of the new magazine, perhaps with advertising on television, will have been booked. More than £1 million may be budgeted for launching a magazine. The launch date rushes on, after which the magazine succeeds or fails, its fortunes monitored closely by rivals. It is a sad fact that many journalists take pleasure in knocking a new publication and willing it to fail, even when it offers no threat to their own employment and may, indeed, be good for journalism as a whole.

3 INCEPTION AND PLANNING

The first piece of information needed in planning an issue of a magazine is the number of pages, and this will be decided by the publisher. It is governed by economics, the main factor being the advertising department's forecast of the amount of colour and monochrome (black and white) advertising it expects to sell, and that depends on the season of the year and the standing of the magazine. In general, the more advertising available, the bigger an issue can be, though the number of pages in a magazine has normally to be a multiple of four because in its simplest form a magazine is made up of sheets folded in the middle and with two pages printed on each side.

The expected sale of just one additional page of advertising may not justify the cost of enlarging the publication from, say, 48 pages to 52 and including another three pages of editorial. However, other factors may come into the calculations. For instance, a world-beating exclusive feature or set of pictures could boost circulation but would also bring additional costs in paper, production, machine time, distribution and promotion.

Assume the decision is to publish a modest give-away of 48 pages with some pages on which colour can be used and others in monochrome; the number of colour pages scheduled depends on the method of printing, the type of machinery used, and how much the budget allows for printing. Colour is attractive but it increases costs, and so most magazines consist of a mixture of colour and black and white. This is no hardship. Some pictures look better in black and white, and anyway some pages will probably consist entirely of text. The 48 pages may well be divided into 36 in colour and 12 in mono.

The allocation of these pages between editorial and advertising will normally follow a ratio, maybe 70:30 or 60:40 or 50:50 – it varies from one publication to another – but it could be that advertising is allocated 27 pages, of which 24 are colour and 3 are mono. This means editorial has 21 pages (12 colour and 9 mono) and the editor can begin planning the contents.

The conference

The contents of an issue are normally planned at a regular conference, held weekly or monthly according to the type of publication. On a big magazine these conferences will be attended only by heads of departments, who will pass on decisions to members of their staffs affected by them. On a small magazine the staff may need only to pull their chairs closer to confer.

A conference will frequently consider three issues. Since printing schedules customarily call for colour material for an issue to go to the printer before the bulk of black and white material for the previous issue, a meeting may be finalizing plans for one issue, confirming plans for a second and making preliminary plans for a third.

Conferences are rarely popular, for they interrupt routine work, but they are important if everyone is to be informed about plans, and should be held on a regular day and at a regular time; it is more disruptive than need be when conferences are summoned at a moment's notice, or postponed from hour to hour to suit the editor's arrangements. Conferences should not be interrupted by telephone calls, nor should executives come and go to attend to other business. A conference should be concerned strictly with the issue, or issues, of the magazine it has been convened to discuss. A free-ranging discussion of ideas for the future may well come afterwards if the work of the meeting is completed ahead of time, but a routine conference to deal with specific editions should not be allowed to roam over far off future ones, because confusion occurs and the meeting overruns.

One of the first considerations is the material already in the office awaiting an opportunity to be used. There will be features intended for earlier use but squeezed out of the issues for which they were intended by new or more topical ones; there will be others bought from agencies or freelances because they seemed worth having, even though no immediate opportunity for using them was apparent.

A magazine needs some stock of features, if only to have replacements available for features that have to be pulled out, which can happen for many reasons – because they have been overtaken by events (such as the death of the subject) or for legal reasons (the subject may sue) or, in a popular magazine, to obtain a better balance of serious and lightweight features. However, a stockpile should not be allowed to grow too large. Features soon become out of date and the longer they are held, the less inclination there is to use them. Some editors over-commission knowingly, because they like to have a superfluity of features from which to make a selection, but only wealthy magazines can afford to indulge this practice, because commissioned material has to be paid for, whether or not it is used, and even then journalists are never keen to find that they have written for the spike (that is, written a feature which is not published). Added to this, the accountants become unhappy about money spent on unpublished features.

Magazines also receive unsolicited features from aspiring and part-time journalists. Some small, special interest publications welcome and make use of these, but major, high-paying titles rarely do. Some magazines will not even consider material from unknown contributors. *Cosmopolitan*, for example, prints on the contents page of every issue that it, 'cannot consider unsolicited articles, poems and short stories for publication'.

It is not merely that many of the offerings from unknowns are unfit to be published; it is difficult for an outsider, even by studying the magazine, to know the type, style and length of material being sought at any given time by the editor, or what is already planned and in hand. The fact that a magazine has published a feature on a subject does not mean it is in the market for more of the same; the opposite may be the case. Features submitted 'on spec' often bear the marks of having been through many hands, yet a feature written with one magazine in mind is rarely suitable for another without rewriting. However, by persistence, it is possible for an outsider to become an insider. Established freelances are in a different category; they rarely submit material 'on spec' but put forward ideas for features they would like to write or photograph, and their ideas are considered and some of them acted on.

After deciding whether any of the material held may be scheduled for the next issue, the conference turns to ideas for new material. The features editor will have a list, which may have been circulated in advance. The picture editor may also have a list. Both will be concerned principally with what will be topical in the week or month being discussed. This is not merely a matter of being seasonal, though a magazine without topicality can have readers turning to the date on the cover to see if, by chance, they have picked up an old copy. There should always be a reason for slotting a feature. An interview with a motor racing driver with hopes of the world championship might be publishable at any time, but ideally should appear on the eve of a crucial grand prix. Similarly a feature about a popular woman author has more point in a week when she has a new book being published, or an adaptation of one of her stories is about to start on television.

Obtaining topicality

The most valuable sources of ideas for a magazine are therefore lists of coming events. A magazine cannot react to happenings of the day as a newspaper can, because of the production schedule, typically 6 weeks for a colour weekly. For the Christmas issue of a monthly to be on sale in November (which is normal), features commonly have to be written and photographed by mid-October, which means planning and commissioning them in August or September. So, to give an appearance of being up to date, staff need always to be looking some 8 weeks ahead to what will be topical then.

Usually the features editor or the editor will have a large diary, or alternatively a ring binder, sectioned off into weekly or monthly issue numbers. (Incidentally, on a weekly it is quicker and simpler to identify issues by the week numbers found in many diaries and calendars and to refer to, say, week 42, than to try to remember a mid-October sale date.) Information relating to each week or month will be entered in the appropriate sections.

Providing this information is sometimes the work of a small department dignified with a title such as 'Forward Planning'. It may be the task of a researcher, or the features editor may undertake it personally. The list will include any festivals during the period, such as Valentine's Day, Shrove Tuesday, Guy Fawkes Day or Remembrance Sunday. Then are listed any noteworthy anniversaries such as that of a popular car, a television soap opera, a World War battle or a medical breakthrough (depending on the nature of the magazine), along with birthdays of interest: for example, the coming of age of a prince, the 30th birthday of a tennis star, or the 40th of a glamorous actress. (Odd anniversaries such as a 47th or an 89th are best ignored.) Such events as the start of a tour by a pop group, the release of a major film, a theatrical first night, the Cup Final or Cruft's Dog Show are added.

The sources include reference books such as *Whitaker's Almanack*, diaries, dictionaries of dates, leaflets about forthcoming events from tourist boards, and letters and press releases from publicists. Freelance specialists often submit their own lists of coming events in their fields: for example, in television or sport. However, much time has to be spent on the telephone finding out from public relations officers who or what will be in the news in the week concerned.

Another source is newspaper cuttings. It is not likely to be worthwhile for a magazine to follow up the story of a big pools win immediately, for it will be stale by the time the magazine could get a feature into print, but a farsighted features editor might well file it away for a year ahead, when it will be worth finding out how the winner's life has changed. Equally a magazine might go back to persons injured in a terrorist bomb attack on an anniversary of the incident to discover how far they have recovered and are coping.

Armed with these lists, the editor or features editor can work on the most interesting subjects from the magazine's point of view. What remains to be done is to find an original way of presenting a feature on the subject. A prince comes of age, to return to an earlier example, and is about to enter university or the services. One could simply present a pictorial record of his life to date, or get a royal expert to write a profile of the prince at 18, but many other magazines and newspapers will do that. What is needed is a fresh angle, such as getting a youngster a few months older, already a student at the same college, or an officer cadet in the same service, to relate what is in store for him.

If a charismatic actor and actress are about to open in a play, simple profiles of them, or interviews with them, are obvious treatments, but it would be more enterprising to get each one talking about the other. If the headmaster of a public school is about to retire, the straightforward approach would be to have him talking about his work, but a more creative one would be to put together a photograph album of his past pupils and get him to provide the captions in his own words.

Much of the time at conference will be concerned with ways of projecting feature ideas. Sometimes this may have to do with the writing. For example, a feature on weekend breaks in France could be written in franglais, a mixture of colloquial English and French, or one about pantomime might be written in rhyming couplets. Sometimes the projection may concern mainly the art department. For example, a feature about old movies could be illustrated with pictures displayed in strips with sprocket holes along the sides as if from 35 mm film. Sometimes it may combine words and display. For example, an assessment of the performance of government ministers during the year might be presented in the form of school end-of-term reports, with marks and comments such as, 'Has aptitude, but needs to try harder', and the art department might be asked to present the words on 'Westminster School' report forms.

Publicists

Public relations and press officers provide facilities for a large proportion of the features in magazines. They work in most large organizations and companies, from the Arts Council and the Automobile Association, through the BBC, Buckingham Palace, 10 Downing Street and the Church of England to the YWCA and London Zoo. Government departments, airlines, charities and manufacturers of products from adhesives to word processors have them. Even magazines have PROs, to distribute inform- ation about their issues and to field inquiries from other publications. For quick answers to questions about statistics or names and for setting up interviews, PROs can save journalists much time, though they can be obstructive when they see their duty as being to prevent access to certain information or persons. If an airline has a new aircraft of which it is proud, its press officers will be delighted to arrange interviews with some of its pilots; if a new aircraft is giving problems, the press officers will be less accommodating, and a journalist may then find it easier to set up interviews through the press officer of the pilots' union.

In the hope of obtaining publicity for their employers or clients, publicists also approach magazines, which they value for their colour pages and because many reach a more specific market than newspapers. Sometimes they offer to supply free features, which should be treated with caution, because while there can be nothing against accepting a motoring organization's offer of tips for winter driving, a free feature from a tourist board about holidays in the country it promotes is unlikely to be objective. Publicists are generally employed to present their principals and products in the best possible light, and they will not dwell on aspects that mar the image they wish to create.

Communications from publicists arrive at magazines by every post. Many of them are time-wasting. It is by no means uncommon for a magazine concerned with sport to receive press releases about new industrial plant or for a magazine about life in Sussex to receive hand-outs about happenings in Wales. In 1986 the editor of *Electrical Times* claimed in a letter to *UK Press Gazette* that about 60 per cent of the mail he received from PROs was 'instantly binnable', and that in one month 252 companies had sent information wildly irrelevant to his readership.

Again, much of the information will be unusable because of the time factor. Magazines with a 6-week 'lead time' or production schedule regularly receive news about events taking place within a fortnight. Invitations to press conferences, champagne receptions and lavish lunches to launch new products and campaigns are timed for the benefit of newspapers, and while they may be pleasant, are rarely of value to magazines because what is announced will be out of date or stale by the time a feature can be published. Some enlightened press officers realize this and hold confidential briefings for magazines 5 weeks or so before those for newspapers.

There is still a drawback: that everyone present can acquire the same information. If a magazine journalist has an original idea for a feature, it is a mistake to disclose it during a conference and make a present of it to every other journalist there. The best scheme is to wait until the business of the conference ends and then try and speak privately to the person with whom one needs to talk. Unfortunately, other journalists are likely to have the same plan; when questions are invited at the close of the conference all will sit mute, and then converge on one person the moment drinks are offered. In those circumstances the most sensible plan is merely to introduce oneself and arrange to make contact with an idea a day or two later.

However, press officers also telephone magazines with useful proposals. A television company with a new series about the United States may suggest that a magazine runs a tie-up competition with prizes of trips to America, which the TV company has arranged to get free from an airline and an hotel.

Another may offer facilities to visit a factory to meet workers who have formed a cooperative to run it. There are snags, though. The first question to be asked is who else is being offered the same facility, for no magazine wishes to find almost identical features in others in the same week. However, a deal works two ways. A magazine should be prepared to give an assurance that, barring the unforeseeable, a feature which it is given exclusively will appear, for if the magazine is not going to run it, the press officer needs to know in time to offer it elsewhere.

Even if a magazine cannot obtain an interview exclusively, it should stipulate that the facility will not be offered to direct competitors. If this is not possible, one way to beat rivals is to schedule the feature a week early. If a new TV series is due to start on a Wednesday, the obvious time for a Sunday magazine to cover it is on the preceding Sunday. However, *Radio Times* and *TV Times* will carry coverage in issues on sale by the previous Monday, so the editor may bring the feature forward to the Sunday before that. Unfortunately, this can lead to publications vying to get ahead of each other, and features appearing so early that readers will have forgotten them by the time the series is screened, while from the press officer's point of view the campaign's impact is dissipated.

Journalists and publicists have much in common, for many publicists, and certainly the best ones, have been journalists, and understand that a free lunch does not guarantee a feature, let alone a favourable one. But relations are not always smooth. Journalists regard publicists as about as honest as used-car salesmen, and publicists see journalists as ingrates, always ready to bite the hand that poured them free drinks. But in today's media world they need each other.

Finding ideas

A magazine can never have too many ideas for features, and they can never come from too many sources. One person's ideas tend to have a similarity, reflecting personal interests. To the extent that these are the editor's, this can help to give the magazine a distinctive personality, but there comes a time when fresh ideas from people with totally different interests are needed to provide variety.

On some publications staff are regularly asked to put forward ideas for features. Arguably this should not be necessary; if any members of the staff have ideas they should put them forward unbidden. In practice, only a few do so. One person nurses a grievance at not having been thanked or given full credit for an idea which was adopted in the past. Some take the view that ideas are the features editor's job, not theirs. Others are just too busy to bother, yet when instructed to do so, they deliver.

Some ideas are predictable and can be discarded immediately. In general magazines there are such hackneyed regulars as 'How rich is the Queen?', 'We find the country's most eligible bachelor', and 'How women are moving into traditional male areas, such as fishing, darts and snooker'. Trade magazines have their outworn equivalents, but there will always be some which bear consideration, or will, at least, suggest to the features editor a usable variant.

Here are some examples put forward by the staff of a Sunday colour supplement, when asked for ideas. Some of the best were, inevitably, the most topical, linked to events long since forgotten, and will not bear repeating now, but they give an idea of the sort of features suggested:

- *Prince Charles goes to Chicago* to open a British promotion. Let us profile the city that Britons identify with gangsters of the 1920s, and fake up pictures of Charles in Al Capone outfit with fedora and tommy gun, Di as gangster's moll.
- *Fish 'n' chips*, the national dish. We compare quantity and quality in North and South.
- *Of relative importance . . .* a star's sister writes about the problems of being overshadowed by her famous sibling. Accompanying piece draws comparisons with other practically unknown relations of the famous.
- *Miss United Kingdom.* Just how do beauty contest judges go about their work? Do men judge on busts and legs, women on smiles and carriage, or possibly vice versa? We get experienced judges to tell us their personal checklists.
- *The real differences between men and women.* A big survey that covers everything, ranging over height, weight, health, longevity, attitudes to sex, food, sport, TV, gossip, insomnia . . .
- *Heroin babies.* Emotive interviews with heroin addict mothers racked with guilt about their babies born addicted.
- *Living off the fat of the land.* Or the diet charlatans. We find fat volunteers to test hypnosis, diet powders and pills, acupuncture, psychotherapy and gyms. With a doctor's verdict on each, plus the doctor's safe diet.
- *Boxercise your weight away.* We adapt exercises used by boxers, such as skipping, shadow boxing and weight training to body shaping for women, with picture of girl in short shorts and boxing gloves.
- *What it would cost to get a whole new body.* Detailed drawing showing all the bits that can now be transplanted, replaced or radically changed.
- *I wish I'd never said that . . .* Celebrities' quotes and how they bounce back to embarrass them years later.
- *Revenge is sweet.* Various ways people have devised to get their own back on those who have crossed them.

In lists which made a bulky file there were also many ideas for celebrity series such as, 'My hero', 'My first job', 'If I had a year off', and 'I'd just like to thank . . .'

Think tanks

Another idea-raising operation is to hold a 'think tank', at which the staff are assembled to discuss ideas. It is surprising how a tentative, only half thought out idea from one person can be seized on and developed by another. Think tanks are even less popular than requests for lists of ideas, and it is a problem to set a time for them, as writers will always have, or claim to have, interviews to carry out or overdue features to write, and subs will always be trying to get an overdue page to the printer. One solution is to meet during a lunch hour, with the firm providing food and wine.

While think tanks may include only executives and department heads, they can sometimes be enlarged profitably to include everyone on the staff. An apparently none-too-bright messenger may be discovered to be an expert on racing pigeons or some other esoteric subject, and while he may have nothing to contribute on anything else, one good idea will justify his presence. Think tanks can be particularly valuable when the editor is faced with the problem of finding a new formula for a Christmas number or an issue coinciding with the opening of an Olympic Games or World Cup.

One editor, deciding to link her magazine with a drive to raise money for a charity, held a think tank at which ideas for possible stunts were solicited. These were some put forward:

- *A sponsored bike-in.* Simultaneous bike riding throughout the country, like Sport Aid's Run the World. A major event in Hyde Park with celebrities leading the way, while at centres all over the country ordinary people are sponsored to ride a specific number of miles. Magazine T-shirts to be available.
- *A greyhound called Sweet Charity.* Readers send £1 and their names go in a draw. The winner gets a year during which the dog runs in his colours and he keeps the winnings. A dog food company meets training costs.
- *What I'd give to see . . .* A (a boxing champion) in the nude, B (a macho actor) in a frilly dress, C (a TV woman presenter) being hit by a custard pie. Find willing celebrities and fix a price to show it in the magazine, totalling readers' pledges until enough is raised.
- *A countrywide treasure hunt on one day*, all clues in rhyme. Entry forms for a fee beforehand. Answers to be found in one issue of the magazine after a bit of searching.

Essential ingredients

Editors have, or should have, a clear idea of the ingredients intended to be the staples of their magazines, working by hunch or personal inclination, or on market research and preferences expressed in letters from readers. Some ingredients will appear in every issue. For example, in a magazine for car owners the editor might decree that in addition to regular service features such as road tests, a financial column about buying and selling, hire purchasing and leasing cars, a motorist and the law column, and tabulated performance and price charts of all current models, every issue must contain one feature to interest sports enthusiasts (for example, an interview with a Formula One team chief about the new season's cars), something for those concerned with the motor industry (such as a profile of the new head of design at a car company), something for those who use their cars for tourism (a report on a tour of North Africa in a small car towing a caravan), and something for the home mechanic (an article on fitting a car radio).

On a general magazine the editor might have a longer list of ingredients not necessarily to be included in every issue but perhaps within every three issues. The list might include food and drink (for example, an interview with a woman wine taster), health (learning to live with a new hip), sport (a woman trainer with a horse in the Grand National), the outdoors (a shepherd and his dogs), money (a best-selling novelist and her earnings), show business (a film star profile), a campaign (on behalf of children with a crippling illness), and royalty (who is popular and who is not).

The list need not be written down provided everyone knows what is wanted, though the features editor will find it helpful to write out a checklist of the category headings in case the magazine has acquired a stockpile of show-business interviews but has no medical or open-air stories beyond those for the immediate issues. The features editor can then give priority to redressing this balance.

The list also makes it easier to preserve a balance between heavy and light subjects in an issue. Often it becomes apparent at a late stage that an issue is all froth and little substance, whereupon the editor will need to pull out one of the lighter weight pieces to substitute something more substantial. Equally, an issue may seem worthy but dull, and a heavyweight feature may have to be sacrificed for, perhaps, some show-business sparkle.

It also helps for everyone to know the editor's aversions. At least one British women's magazine has a rule barring any mention of sport or sports personalities on the debatable grounds that sport bores the majority of women.

Commissioning

Following the conference, a list of the proposed contents of the issue will be drawn up and circulated to department heads (some of whom usually leave meetings with differing views of what has been decided). It will list the proposed subject of the cover, which on a popular magazine might be the Princess of Wales, and then the intended features, with the number of pages that each seems worth. For example, in a sample issue:

Di's clothes: 3 pages, early in book, colour.
New faces in soap opera: 2 pages colour.
Test pilot: single page mono.
Young musicians: half page mono.
Cartoon cats: half page mono.
Safari book extract: 4 pages mono, back of book.

These lists should never be left littering desks where they may be seen by anyone. Many visitors to editorial offices, such as freelances and publicists, go into other magazine offices, and a 'leak' can be serious. Journalists like to know what their rivals are doing but they do not want their rivals to know what they are doing, for publishing is a competitive business.

After the conference, the commissioning of necessary work begins. The features editor will contact writers – staff or freelance – briefing them on what is required and the deadline. Whenever that may be in reality, the features editor will probably advance it a day or two when talking to writers, having learned from experience that by so doing the copy may actually be ready by the time it is needed.

The features editor will, as far as possible, try to match the right writers to features – 'horses for courses' as the saying has it. A mature male writer is likely to establish a better relationship with a war veteran than a trendy girl, while the latter should be more in tune with a pop group, though this is not always the case. One writer may be good at hard-hitting investigations, and another at narrating moving stories of illness and hardship, known on women's magazines by the acronym 'TOT' for Triumph Over Tragedy. One writer can dig out all the facts but presents them baldly; another writes colourfully but may be inclined to skimp research. A National Union of Journalists' directory lists freelance writers and their specialities, but editors prefer to use writers who have worked for them before, not necessarily because they are friends, though they may be, but because the editors know their strengths and weaknesses, their speed and reliability.

The brief should be specific as to length, treatment and when needed, and if dealing with a freelance, the editor or features editor should confirm arrangements in writing to protect both parties. Editors often change their minds about the projection of a feature at a later date, with the result that an aggrieved writer, who carried out the original instructions faithfully, has to undertake a rewrite. Equally a writer may misunderstand, forget or depart from the brief and deliver a feature on unwanted lines. There can also be differences of opinion on the deadline agreed, and about the ownership of copyright in the feature, such as whether the writer is selling only the first rights to publish, or all rights, in which case the magazine might syndicate it (sell it elsewhere) later.

There are many good reasons why a brief should be set down in writing, though this is far from universal practice. The best system is one where the commissioning editor fills out a briefing document. On it appears an instruction such as, 'Research and write 1,500 words on the different ways in which characters have been written out of TV soap operas'. The number of the issue for which the feature is intended, the deadline, fee, and expenses authorized are also set out, and the document bears a standard printed statement about rights required. For example, 'In consideration of the fee, the copyright in this material is assigned to the publishers'.

Both commissioning editor and writer sign the top copy of the document, which the writer retains. A carbon copy is filed by the features department and another is sent to the accounts department for payment so that the writer has no need to submit an invoice.

While the features editor is commissioning words, the picture editor will be commissioning pictures by staff or freelance photographers, again briefing them on exactly what is required – for instance, an action shot of a personality on his farm in muddy boots – and telling them who the writer is in each case so that writer and photographer can liaise. If necessary, the picture editor will also assign a researcher to get archive shots from a library or agency.

The art editor will commission any artists' illustrations that may be required. Short stories are normally illustrated by artists, and it might have been decided that a feature about laughable mishaps on a camping holiday could best be accompanied by cartoons. A profile of the prime minister, or another cabinet minister who has been much photographed, might be illustrated for a change with a caricature. A story about a woman politician who says her secret ambition is to play a principal boy in pantomime might be accompanied by an artist's impression of her as Dick Whittington. Artists will be given rough sizes to work to, for artwork is normally drawn at one and a half times or twice the size at which it will be published. Reduction makes the lines appear more solid. All the requirements for the issue are eventually in hand.

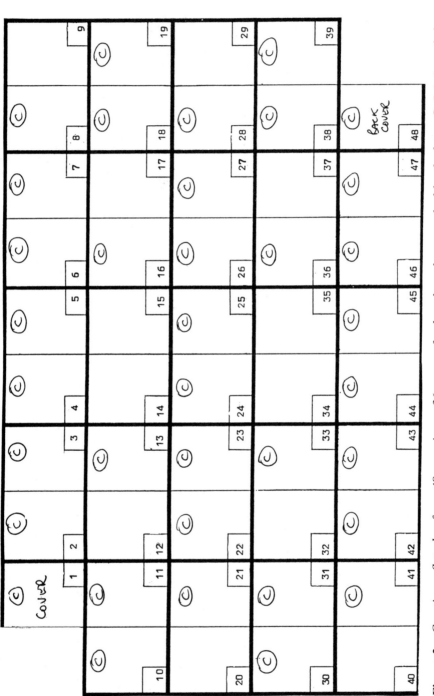

Figure 2 *Creating a flat plan for a 48-page issue; 36 pages of colour have been marked by the letter C. It is intended to allocate a total of 27½ pages for advertisements, 24 of them in colour, and 20½ pages for editorial, 12 in colour*

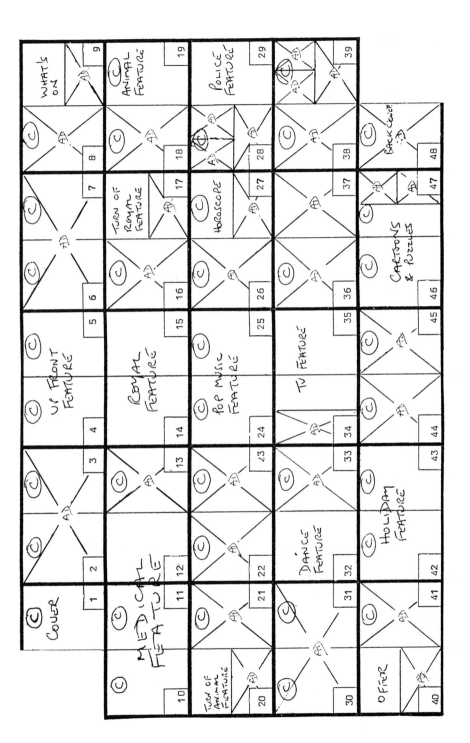

Figure 3 *Completed flat plan indicating the positions of features and advertisements. A good flat plan is essential for an attractive magazine*

Flat plans

Someone now has the task of marrying the requirements of the editorial and advertising departments within the pages of the issue, and this usually falls to the production editor. It is complex. Certain editorial features will have fixed positions to give a sense of continuity and familiarity, and should be where regular readers expect to find them. The list of contents, for example, may belong on page 3, and a gossip column or a spread of pictures on pages 4 and 5, while a 'long read', perhaps an extract from a book, is customarily placed towards the back of the magazine. In a popular publication the last editorial page facing the inside back cover may be the regular spot for horoscopes and the 'next month's issue' blurb.

On top of this, the editor has laid down which features should occupy colour pages, and the production editor has to accommodate them. It is important to avoid placing all the good things at the front of the book and all boring or disappointing pieces and 'turns' at the back.

The advertising department will also have specific requirements. Rates charged for advertisement pages vary, with colour naturally costing more than mono, while for both colour and mono special positions in the magazine command higher rates. Some of these positions, which are self-explanatory, are inside front cover, outside back cover, facing editorial, right-hand page facing editorial, half-page under editorial, first spread (two facing pages) in magazine, and spread with editorial preceding and following. Advertisements for which special positions are not required are sold ROM (run of magazine) and can be slotted wherever convenient, although there may still be complications. A client whose advertisement includes a coupon will not want it backing the coupon of another advertiser because readers will only be able to complete and send off one of the two. A cigarette company will not want its advertisement adjoining that of a rival brand and it would be unacceptable to have an advertisement for a slimming course facing one for a convenience food.

These problems are compounded when the editorial matter is taken into account. Food manufacturers will not want their ads facing pictures of starving children in Africa, the cigarette advertisement cannot be scheduled alongside a story about research into lung cancer, nor a holiday firm's advertisement against the story of a couple's fight for compensation after a disastrous holiday. The production editor has to pick a path through a maze, a path made more difficult by the fact that there will be only certain pages on which colour is available.

This is determined by 'impositions' provided by the printer, relating to the arrangement of colour and mono pages as they will go on the machine in order to be in sequence after folding. A magazine is printed in 'sections' of 4, 8 or 16 pages, so a 48-page issue can be 12 × 4 pages, 6 × 8 pages or 3 × 16 pages. The imposition is governed by the number of plates or cylinders used and the method of dealing with the second side of the paper, which may be printed simultaneously or by a second pass through the machine, according to the system of printing. The imposition decided on may offer the 36 pages of colour on pages 1 (the cover), 2 and 3, 4 and 5, 6 and 7, 8, 10 and 11, 14 and 15, 18 and 19, 21, 22 and 23, 24 and 25, 26 and 27, 28, 31, 34 and 35, 38 and 39, 41, 42 and 43, 44 and 45, 46 and 47, and 48 (the back cover).

With the list of the editor's requirements – the features to go in colour and mono, the number of words intended and the positions desired for them – on one side, and a list of advertisements, with the positions for which they have been sold, on the other, the production editor works out the possibilities on a flat plan. This is a large sheet of paper on which the pages of the magazine are represented diagrammatically by printed rectangles. Working on a 48-page issue, for example, the production editor takes a sheet marked with 48 numbered rectangles. The first rectangle, marked 1, represents the front cover; the last, marked 48, the back cover. The spreads, which are facing pages such as 2 and 3, 4 and 5, 6 and 7, are enclosed by thicker rules.

The production editor indicates colour pages, either with coloured ink or by circling the page numbers, then begins marking in what is to go on each page. There can be immediate snags, such as accommodating a mono advertisement which has been sold for a right-hand page when the editor wants a feature to start on a right-hand page in mono and turn to a spread in colour; or giving the editor three consecutive pages for a feature when an advertisement sold as a half page under editorial matter has still to be placed. Sometimes the production editor has to ask the advertising department to persuade a client to accept a different position at a lower rate, or the editor to accept turning the end of a feature to a page at the back rather than on to a consecutive page.

It may be necessary to try alternative impositions. There will be a choice of several. The production editor will work in pencil because there will be much erasing as different ideas fall and new instructions are delivered. For example, advertising manages to sell another colour ad to a valued client and seeks an extra colour page. The editor has a change of mind and wants to put a proposed colour feature in mono and a proposed mono feature in colour. There is an advertisement which the production editor thinks unsuitable for the type of readership and recommends the editor should veto. Shuttling between editor and ad manager, the production editor will eventually achieve the best plan possible to provide an issue that will be attractive to readers, give a good display to editorial features and satisfy advertisers and the editor.

The schedule

Before circulating copies of the flat plan to department heads, the production editor adds at the bottom the dates on which pages, consisting of copy, pictures and layouts, have to be delivered to the printer. These dates are extracted from a long-term master schedule agreed by the production editor and the printer.

On a major weekly perhaps half the total number of colour pages will be due with the printer a week after distribution of the flat plan, and this might be 38 days – calendar days rather than working days – before the issue is to go on sale in newsagents' shops. That day will be designated Day 38. The remainder of the colour may be due 5 days later – on Day 33. Possibly the first half of the mono pages will be due on Day 31 and the remainder on Day 27. (Though it is no concern of the editorial department, advertisements will have been sent in similar batches between days 40 and 30.)

While the later pages are being sent away (and usually outer sections are last, carrying the latest copy, such as news and classified advertisements), proofs of the earlier ones will be coming back from the printers for amendment and correction. Half of them may have to be dealt with and passed for press on Day 25 and the rest on Day 23. This will complete the editorial department's work on the issue, though, during the fortnight it has taken, the cycle will have begun again on another issue. The first issue will then be completely in the hands of the printer. On Day 18 the machines will start running off copies of the magazine and by Day 2 all the copies should have been distributed to newsagents – but this is leaping ahead.

Such long production cycles, making topicality difficult to achieve, are a cause of concern to magazine journalists, but they are commonplace. News reviews achieve swift coverage of events in colour as a matter of course, but at the cost of huge staffs and expensive printing and distribution arrangements, which is one reason there are so few of them. For general magazines to include colour of a national occasion or a major sporting event before it has passed into history means making special arrangements for editorial and production work, which would not be possible or profitable on a regular basis. However, so-called 'new technology' speeds production. For example, direct input of copy by writers and editing on screen by sub-editors, followed by typesetting by computer, cuts out the need for secondary keyboarding by compositors and correction of proofs and is one reason why computerized production is going to grow.

4 FINDING THE WORDS

Writers and photographers are the front-line troops of a magazine. They travel and meet people, whereas most other staff are office-bound. There is, inevitably, a wide difference between the lives of those on a small trade publication and those on a big general magazine. Some will move in a close-knit community near to home, others will travel the world, with handsome expense accounts, in search of stories. (It is sensible to keep passports and vaccinations up to date, and credit cards to hand.) What writers have in common is an interest in people, a curiosity about what is going on in their particular field and in the world in general, and an ability to discover facts and to tell a story entertainingly.

These attributes they share with newspaper reporters, which many of them once were. But the most important ability of the reporter is to get a story and turn it into words quickly and accurately; most of a reporter's stories will be a matter of mere hundreds of words often dictated over a telephone from scrappy notes. For the reporter to be a stylish writer is a bonus. The feature writer works under less pressure of time, but must be a talented writer, and able to cope with features running into thousands of words.

Interview features

What makes a good feature? Ideally it should have some news content. A feature about Hannibal's crossing of the Alps might be readable but it would be hard to justify running it in a magazine today unless there had been some discovery, or there was to be a new film following his route. A feature should make readers think, because of the views expressed by persons quoted or by the writer, and it should be well written. A feature in a downmarket publication has to be punchy and entertaining or challenging, but while polysyllabic and abstruse words may be barred, it should also be stylish and grammatical. All this applies whether the feature is an interview, a profile, a gossip paragraph, a stunt or even a quiz.

There are two main categories of features – the quick and the in-depth. Competent writers, asked for quick features on the use of firearms by British police, a boom in cycling or an actress in a soap opera, will produce them swiftly after looking at cuttings and making a few telephone calls – to police spokesmen in the first case, to trade organizations, manufacturers and retailers in the second, to the television company publicist and, if possible in the time, to the star in the third. At the other end of the scale is the in-depth feature. The writer of the police feature would visit instructors and pupils at weapon training, talk to chief constables and possibly the Home Secretary, and might visit New York and perhaps some Continental capitals to draw comparisons. The writer of the cycling feature might find half a dozen assorted regular cyclists, such as a judge, a model, a tycoon, a vicar, a professional bike racer and a factory worker, and compare their usage of their machines, the models and mileages. The writer of the soap opera feature would interview the actress at length, preferably at home with her family, and also visit the set to watch her at work and to talk to the producer, writers and other members of the cast about her.

The in-depth feature is obviously the more rewarding to work on. Much depends on the economics of the magazine, the space to be allotted and the projection of the feature. In some small-budget magazines many features are hashed together from telephone interviews and cuttings; other publications give writers time and facilities to produce something worthwhile. But most features depend on, or at least contain interviews, though some are simply to obtain information or quotes, and others are meant to reveal a person's character, life and opinions.

In the first category come multiple interview features in which a magazine may present its pick of promising new artists, designers, writers or politicians, or in which celebrities are asked to give their views on topics which can range from love at first sight to euthanasia. For one such feature celebrities were asked to name their favourite hymns. A woman MP, unable to think of a hymn, said, 'Just pick a nice one for me, dear', and an Air Chief Marshal refused to disclose his favourite unless his opposite numbers, an Admiral of the Fleet and a Field Marshal, were also willing to do so. The magazine's request for their favourite hymns was therefore placed at the top of the agenda for a meeting of the Joint Chiefs of Staff, who eventually decided to keep the information secret.

Of course, not every feature contains interviews. Specialist writers (and their specialities range from wine to veteran cars, and from birds to royalty) can write on their own subjects without needing to quote authorities, because they are themselves experts and entitled to air their own opinions. However, they may use quotes from others to introduce different views.

Certainly they will interview many experts in the course of their work, accumulating knowledge even if they have no immediate use for it.

Setting up interviews

In some offices the features editor or an aide will set up major interviews, and writer and photographer have only to keep the date. In most offices this cosseting is accorded only to busy, sought after freelances; generally writers and photographers are told what is wanted and left to organise the feature themselves.

The first problem can be making contact with the person to be interviewed, not always easy in the cases of a cabinet minister, a tycoon or a criminal. If the writer has had dealings with the person in the past, it may be possible to get in touch directly. More often, an interview will be arranged through a press officer or other contact. But where the persons are out of the public eye, it can be a problem even to find them. Locating a former bandleader for a 'Where are they now?' feature about once-famous personalities entailed asking many musicians, agents, record companies and union officials before he was traced to a modest bed-sitter where he lived alone in reduced circumstances. All writers need to keep contacts books in which to list the office and home telephone numbers of all notable people and helpful agents, publicists and others with whom they have been in touch. To neglect this can cause one hours of unnecessary work, for the same names will crop up again, however unlikely it may seem originally.

The point has already been made that while any conversation in which questions are put and answers obtained can be termed an interview, there is a difference between the interview which is merely part of a quest for information or a quote and that which is intended to reveal something of a person. The first kind is carried out by writers every day, mostly over the telephone, which is why the cultivation of a pleasant telephone manner is important. The writer should sound friendly but not oily, persistent but not brusque or bullying. The manner should suggest that the interviewer knows what he or she is about and is not time-wasting. Such interviews may also be carried out face to face, but the venue, whether in an office or at home, is not important.

The revealing interview, however, is more satisfactorily carried out face to face, and the meeting place can make a great difference to the feature. For example, a police officer works with, or on behalf of, handicapped refugee children. For the purposes of a feature he should obviously be photographed among such children; this will also help the writer more than seeing him at home.

Despite the number of interviews conducted over lunch (often because the subject expects to be entertained in return for helping, or is only available at lunchtime), restaurants are best avoided. It is difficult to make notes while eating, and a tape recorder on the table, apart from attracting the attention of other diners, will pick up an extraordinary amount of cutlery rattling and plate clashing and a background hubbub of conversation and music. The human ear is selective and filters out background noise when one is listening attentively to another person. The tape recorder does not, and a tape made in a restaurant can be difficult to transcribe. Much the same applies to public houses. Old-fashioned clubs for men should also be avoided, for it is part of their tradition that members do not conduct business in the club. Production of notebooks and documents is frowned upon and a tape recorder is totally unacceptable.

The best place for an interview is most often the subject's home, which will reflect the owner's style of living; the garden, books, pictures and possessions will also provide talking points. Alternatively, places of work can provide some colour for a feature if they are interesting, as farms, factories, hospitals and ships can be, but offices tend to be impersonal, and while a dressing room in a theatre when an actor is in a long run counts almost as a second home, a dressing room in a television centre is used by different people in different productions every day and is usually as bare and functional as a motel room. However, an unpromising venue can sometimes work to a writer's advantage: an interview in a limousine speeding along a motorway to an airport, for example, may not be the ideal choice but it can provide some colour for the feature.

Incidentally, interviews are usually best conducted in some privacy. Most people are inhibited about talking about themselves in front of an audience, whether eavesdroppers at a nearby table in a restaurant or even a spouse or colleague.

A basic question is whether writer and photographer should travel to a job together. There are occasions when this is sensible. When working on a feature about novice parachutists making their first descents or about young entertainers competing in a talent contest, for instance, it is helpful to operate as a team, drawing each other's attention to interesting people and ensuring that the photographer gets pictures of everyone the writer has talked to, and that the writer talks to all those the photographer has shot.

On straightforward interviews, however, even though the person being interviewed may suggest dealing with both at the same time, the interests of writer and photographer tend to conflict, for few people can pose for pictures and deal with searching questions simultaneously. The writer will want to sit down with the subject and talk, while the photographer will want the subject in different locations, poses and maybe clothes. Perhaps the journalists have been allotted an hour. If the writer monopolizes the subject, the most the photographer may be able to get are some static 'mug shots,' while if the photographer takes precedence, the writer will be unable to get the celebrity's full attention; so it is often better to make separate dates. Unfortunately, the photographer, following in the wake of the writer, may then pose the subject beside an intriguing painting which the writer did not even notice, or the writer, following the photographer, may discover that the interviewee has a hobby which would yield good pictures, but about which the photographer had not heard.

Research

Before embarking on an interview, a writer should research the subject in the office library. When a former international film actor, about to return to the screen in a minor television role, was interviewed by a group of journalists, the opening question was: 'What was your first big film role?' The question was not only time-wasting but rather insulting, showing that the writer had not taken the trouble to carry out even 5 minutes' preliminary research.

A magazine office should have available, either on the editorial floor or in a reference library (and preferably both), the most useful standard reference books. A basic collection might include the following:

- *Concise Oxford Dictionary*, *Oxford Dictionary for Writers and Editors* or *Chambers' Twentieth Century* (though feature writers and subs will find it saves time to have their own *Oxford Paperback Dictionary* or *Penguin English Dictionary* in their desks).
- A reputable and up-to-date encyclopedia, *Pears Cyclopaedia*, *Guinness Book of Records*, *Whitaker's Almanack*. *Who's Who*, *International Who's Who*, *Chambers' Biographical Dictionary*, *Kelly's Handbook to the Titled, Landed and Official Classes*, *Who's Who in Television*, *Vacher's Parliamentary Companion*.
- The *Times Concise Atlas of the World*, *The Illustrated Road Atlas of the British Isles*.
- *The Oxford Dictionary of Quotations*, the *Penguin Dictionary of Quotations* and the *Penguin Dictionary of Modern Quotations*.
- *The Encyclopaedia of Dates and Events* or *Chambers' Dictionary of Dates*.
- *Brewer's Dictionary of Phrase and Fable*.
- *Willing's Press Guide* or *Benn's Media Directory*.
- *Roget's Thesaurus*, and *Fowler's Modern English Usage* or *Sir Ernest Gowers' Complete Plain Words*.
- A street directory, a guide to hotels and restaurants, air and train timetables and a complete set of telephone directories.

What others will be required depends on the publication. A television-oriented magazine will need *Spotlight* (the directory of actors and actresses), *Halliwell's Film Guide*, *Halliwell's Filmgoer's Companion and Halliwell's Television Companion*, guides to pop records and groups, *Rothmans Football Yearbook*, *Wisden Cricketers' Almanack* and other sports reference works, but may be able to manage happily without *Baily's Hunting Directory* or *Brown's Nautical Almanack*. A women's magazine can probably do without *Jane's Fighting Ships* or *Ruff's Guide* to the *Turf* but will almost certainly need *Black's Medical Dictionary*.

The feature writer will often require books not to be found in the office – for example, a biography of a person to be profiled, a history of World War Two or a book on stately homes – and membership of the nearest public library to home or office is desirable. Even better in London is membership of the London Library, which has a remarkable collection of books on open shelves, though there is an annual membership fee.

Cuttings

However, in all magazine offices the most valuable and most frequently consulted sources of reference are newspaper cuttings. These can be more up to date than annual reference books – a person's marriage may have ended in divorce since even a current reference book went to press – and they contain more colourful details than reference books. They should, of course, be used only for reference and not copied word for word. Facts and figures are not copyright, but the form in which a writer sets out and interprets them is, and lifting without permission or acknowledgement constitutes plagiarism.

But cuttings are invaluable for checking what has been written recently about a personality before deciding whether to set up an interview, and also before going to carry one out. If an office does not maintain its own collection, and to do so requires several staff to cut and file material, it will be necessary to arrange to use the facilities of a newspaper office, or to pay a fee to borrow cuttings as and when required from an agency.

The traditional cuttings library consists of folders arranged alphabetically under subjects, the majority about personalities, some of whom will have been written about so much that simple chronological filing is inadequate and it becomes necessary to create additional files divided into such categories as 'Property and possessions', 'Health and accidents', 'Articles by', and so on. Libraries will also have cuttings on topics such as violence at football matches, and drug abuse and addiction, usually found as sub-divisions of major sections: for example, 'Sport, Association football, United Kingdom, Hooliganism' and 'Health, Illnesses, Drugs'.

Some libraries cut only newspapers, which can mean having to read many short, sometimes conflicting stories, written in haste and sometimes inaccurrate. When researching the background of a personality, writers will find lengthy profiles from magazines more helpful.

However, the resources of libraries are limited, not only by the number of staff but by space. Pressure on space has caused many to reduce cuttings photographically and store them on postcard-sized sheets of film known as microfiche. One microfiche can store sixty A4 pages and a filing cabinet can hold as many cuttings on microfiche as a whole room of originals. A viewing machine (a 'reader') is necessary, and should have the capability to print out a full-sized copy of any cutting at the push of a button. In addition to such machines in the library of a publishing house, there may be others on the editorial floor, but staff should never be permitted to remove microfiche from the library, because the temporary loss of even one can cause problems. Microfiche are easily duplicated within seconds on machines which should also be found in libraries. Unfortunately, it takes longer to scan a microfiche than to riffle through a folder of actual cuttings, and sometimes it can be difficult to get a legible print-out; but space considerations mean that the use of microfiche will continue to grow, until superseded by computerized files viewed on a computer screen.

The major problem with cuttings is accuracy. No matter what the source, they should be used only as an aid and never relied upon without an independent check. Occasionally libraries muddle cuttings referring to two different people of the same name. Even if a story were correct when published, it may be no longer true. A recent cutting may say that a couple have been reunited after a separation; they may well have parted again since. A story may also be inaccurate as the result of a misunderstanding, or even a fabrication. Knowledge of a publication in which a story appears, and the writer whose byline is on it, gives experienced journalists some ideas as to which stories are likely to be accurate and which should be regarded with suspicion.

To find the same information in two separate publications does not guarantee the facts are right. They may be by the same writer under different names, or the second writer may have lifted from the first. If three or four sources give the same information, the probability that it is right is increased, but there is no substitute for personal checking, by telephoning sources and getting first-hand or official information. It is not always possible to check satisfactorily, even such apparently innocuous matters as the age of an elderly man if he declines to cooperate, but writers have to try, because it is no defence to a complaint to say, 'I took it from a cutting'.

Unfortunately, when an error gets into a newspaper or magazine story, it can go on being repeated for years. A talented but diminutive actor has complained frequently at being described as 5ft 3in. tall, claiming to be 5ft

5in. Apart from the irritation this causes him, he could be discounted from consideration for certain roles, but writers continue to consult cuttings and describe him as 5ft 3in. Repeating other mistakes from cuttings can have more serious consequences: for example, describing a man as having been convicted of a crime, when he was acquitted.

All errors in published statements that are notified to an office should be drawn to the attention of the librarian so that a warning can be filed. When the cuttings are kept in original form, this is simple, and it should be standard practice to paste red warning stickers on the cutting and on the cover of the file, drawing attention to the error so that it is not repeated. It is harder to attract attention on microfiche but not impossible. Details in established reference books are much less likely to be wrong, but they can err. An actor may be described as having made his debut in 1967 when the year should read 1976. The book should be annotated for the benefit of colleagues when such mistakes are discovered.

Errors in magazines are even more embarrassing than errors in newspapers. A newspaper can run a correction next day, but a magazine may not be able to publish one until months later, and a mistake in the date of a coming event will probably be impossible to refer to until after the event has taken place, when an apology may be merited but correction is pointless.

Interviewing

After researching, the interviewer should formulate some questions before talking to the subject. Inexperienced interviewers should write them down in a logical order for use as a prompt in case they forget a vital one, or dry up during the conversation. For this purpose a page in a notebook or a sheet of paper which can be referred to when necessary is preferable to a clipboard, which tends to encourage the user to race from question to question, trying to put all of them, when it might be more rewarding to pursue the answer to an early question further. An interviewer should be prepared to be flexible if an answer leads in a unexpected but interesting direction.

Unless one is merely checking facts, questions inviting 'yes' or 'no' answers are to be avoided. Questions should be phrased so that they call for longer responses. To suggest to the subject, 'You must have been pleased?' invites the simple answer, 'Yes'; but asking 'How did you feel?' may produce a more quotable reply.

There are professional interviewees who have been interrogated by journalists so many times that they have met all the likely questions, and will start answering one with a pat response before the interviewer has finished putting it. It can be worth trying to catch them off balance with a surprising question in order to provoke some new response, though a novice is unlikely to succeed. A good example of this technique was seen in a television interview with a racing driver where the interviewer began by asking if the driver believed in God. This question led on to his religious beliefs and to his attitude when he knew he was driving beyond the limits of safety and courting death.

However, the everyday television interview is not the best model for a magazine journalist. It may last only a minute or even 30 seconds on the screen and the interviewer has to be careful not to appear to be biased either towards or against the subject (unless playing the devil's advocate and putting points that opponents would raise). The interviewer must pare the questions to the bone and put them baldly, but the interviewee will have been warned in advance of the necessity for this, and not to be offended by it. Magazine journalists with more time available, and no viewers watching to criticize their technique, have no need for brusqueness. The aim is to get the subject to talk freely, to expand, and writers will get better results by being encouraging and appearing friendly, even if they do not feel it.

The writer can afford to open with an easy lob to get the subject talking and warmed up, leaving any awkward questions until later. Questions that are likely to be unwelcome, such as, 'How much money are you expecting to make out of this?' or 'Doesn't this amount to sharp practice?' may best be left until later, so that the conversation can be pleasant and productive up to that point. Ask such questions at the beginning and the subject may well be on the defensive or hostile all the way – if indeed the interview goes any further. On the other hand, leaving a vital question too late can be a mistake; an interview may be terminated prematurely by the subject being called away.

Interviewees frequently ask for information to be 'off the record'. If the writer agrees, this promise should, of course, be respected, but agreement should not be given without consideration. The first point to be established is whether the subject means, 'This is not to be used', or 'You can use this but don't quote me as the source'. If the latter is the case, it may be that the information is worth having on those terms. This depends on the source and whether it will be possible to persuade someone else to talk on the record. If the request is not to publish the information at all, it is normally better to say, 'If you don't want it used, don't tell me, because I may already know what you are going to say, or I may be told it later – without any strings attached – by someone else'.

Sometimes a person talks freely and only then adds, 'That's off the record, of course'. There can be no 'of course' about it. If the information could not be published for legal reasons, or is of no interest, there is no problem, but if the writer wants to use it, it is necessary to point out that the interviewee should have made the stipulation first. Always, when faced with requests not to publish something, journalists should be careful not to make promises on behalf of the editor or the magazine. They can promise to put the request to the editor (and do so) but they are not entitled to speak for the editor or tie the editor's hands.

Subjects of interviews also frequently ask to see the feature before publication – 'Just to make sure the facts are right'. It is hard to object to this in principle because it is in everyone's interest to make sure facts are correct, but the trouble is that the interviewee usually wants to go further – to soften words said about a rival or a former marriage partner, to withdraw this, change that, and polish something else – and what started out as a prickly, bitchy, amusing interview can end as simply boring. Interviewees may even want to change physical descriptions of themselves: a knight objected strongly to being described as 'dapper', because he was 5ft 8in. tall, he said.

So journalists will normally resist such requests. However, some celebrities insist on the right to approve the copy as a condition of giving an interview, and if a magazine wants the interview, it has no option but to agree. From the writer's point of view it is reassuring to know that the copy has been read and signed as approved, and that therefore there should not be any complaints, at least from that source, after publication.

Recording an interview

Notebooks used when interviewing should be unobtrusive. A large pad or clipboard is intimidating, suggesting the taking of an official statement. A small one has the merit of being pocketable, but to go to the extreme of using the back of an envelope suggests that one is treating the interview altogether too casually and may be careless with facts.

However, the use of shorthand has declined, though it is still a useful skill to have and students on magazine courses are expected to master Teeline. Many writers now carry tape recorders, which, apart from making sure that every word is recorded accurately, free the user from having to concentrate on getting words down on paper. This enables a writer to pay full attention to the subject, consider how the interview is shaping, and frame the next question in the light of what is being said.

Another advantage is that one is safeguarded against acccusations of misquoting. The public relations chief of a major organization once telephoned a writer and thanked him for providing a proof of an interview with his chairman (who also happened to be a director of the magazine company) but said the man had been misquoted on one point. When reminded that the interview had been tape recorded, he changed gear smoothly and immediately, saying, 'I'm sorry, I will rephrase that. The Chairman regrets that he gave you a misleading answer to one question and would be grateful if you would allow him to amend it'.

Many professional interviewees prefer an interviewer to use a tape recorder, feeling more confident that they will be reported accurately. On the other hand, some are intimidated by a tape recorder, and while these are mainly those unaccustomed to being interviewed, they are not confined to them. A former British ambassador insisted on a writer telling him the questions he proposed to ask before he would allow the recorder to be switched on, despite an assurance that no one other than the writer was ever going to hear the tape. The Director General of a large organization went further, demanding a promise that no one else would hear the tape and that it would be wiped immediately after being transcribed (after all of which, what he had to say was hardly worth publishing).

The best type of recorder for the journalist is a small battery-operated cassette machine with a built-in microphone. Placed in the centre of a desk or table, these machines are sensitive enough to record a round-table conference. The cassettes available for them have various running times, the most suitable being the C90, which allows 45 minutes recording on each side. For long interviews there are C120 cassettes giving an hour on each side, but the tape is thinner and less reliable, and in practice a C90 is usually adequate.

These recorders are ideal for lengthy interviews and meetings where journalists are sure of their welcome, but for shorter interviews, occasions where the writer wishes to be as unobtrusive as possible, and when moving from person to person at a reception or luncheon, there are smaller micro-cassette recorders (often used as dictation machines) which slip easily into a pocket. Though the quality of recording is poorer than a C90's, they are useful aids, and voice-activated models will automatically halt recording during a pause in conversation, which saves tape and time on transcription if there has been a long silence while perhaps the interviewee is trying to locate a document to show the writer. Micro-cassettes will record for an hour (30 minutes per side) in normal mode, but can be played at slow speed to double this time, with some loss of quality. Both types of recorder can be attached to telephones by rubber suckers to record important conversations.

Writers make it easier for interviewees if they familiarize themselves with the machines they are using, because it makes the subject nervous if the interviewer keeps fiddling with it or looking at it to check that the spools are turning. The equipment should always be checked before an interview. One journalist had a long meeting with the late Peter Sellers during which Sellers told funny stories in a variety of voices, but when the tape was played back, it was unintelligible because tape speed had been fluctuating grotesquely. The interview was salvaged only by getting a sound engineer to hand-crank and re-record the tape several times.

It is polite to switch off the machine ostentatiously when the interviewee takes a telephone call or someone comes into the room to deliver a message. It also saves time winding on tape when transcribing. Do not be in too much haste to stow away the recorder at the end of an interview, for often the interviewee will add something significant while relaxing and preparing to show one out.

If transcription is to be done in the office, earphones are essential to avoid annoying colleagues. To save batteries it is worth having an adapter so that the recorder can be connected to the mains; alternatively, of course, compact cassettes can be played back on a radio recorder or hi-fi cassette deck at home.

Ghosting

A celebrity byline gives a magazine the attractions of a big name and added authority. A champion ice skater's views on the hours of practice necessary will be more to the point than those of a sports writer, and a former prime minister's insight into 10 Downing Street as a home and office will be more interesting than that of a political correspondent; but even gifted writers can have inhibitions about writing magazine articles. A distinguished playwright found that the writing of a feature about his creation of a particular play defeated him, and had to ask the magazine which had commissioned it to send a writer to interview him instead. For even when celebrities are literate and capable of writing articles, they may not be able to produce them in the time available, or may find it difficult to write in the style of the magazine. After agreeing to deliver an article on, say, 'The person from whom I learned most', celebrities are likely to produce pages of waffle, with few specific examples of what they learned.

More often, a celebrity is incapable of writing a readable feature, and of course there is no reason why a footballer whose talent is for scoring goals should be expected to be able to write like a journalist. The answer is a ghosted feature, the celebrity providing his or her thoughts for a writer to stitch together. Some become masters of this technique. A former motor racing driver, asked for 1500 words on a motoring topic, would say briskly, 'Got a tape recorder? Then I'll come into your office at 3 pm and dictate'. He would arrive on the hour and, addressing himself to the tape recorder, would speak rapidly for some time, before announcing, 'I think you'll find that is about 1500 words'. He would be right to within a few words. He would then ask if there was anything he had omitted, or any point on which he should elaborate. The writer might invite him to say something on a particular topic, he would dictate an add with equal rapidity and then depart, pausing only to ask for his cheque. His words needed little work on them beyond perhaps rearranging the sequence of some paragraphs, the deletion of colloquialisms and the checking of dates and facts. (Celebrities are as likely as anyone else to be vague about dates, places and names, and the fact that, for instance, a politician took part in an historic debate in the House of Commons does not mean that he will recall correctly the year of it, or the name of the speaker he followed.)

There is nothing wrong with this combination of a celebrity's expertise and a writer's skill. Unfortunately, when contracted for a series, celebrities are frequently reluctant to keep their side of the deal. Some are like the naturalist commissioned to write a weekly column for a children's comic, who delivered the first article on time but nothing more. After several telephone calls failed to spur him into activity, a writer had to be sent to his house under orders not to return without at least two overdue pieces.

Many ghosts have experienced having to do about 90 per cent of the work on a regular column because a celebrity has become impossible to contact. Another racing driver, whose name appeared on a weekly motoring column, was pleasant to meet but it was almost impossible to arrange meetings after the initial one, and difficult even to contact him on the telephone; so the ghost had frequently to write what he thought the man would say on a topic and hope that he would give approval and make any amendments in time for publication.

Sometimes a celebrity may be bylined as 'talking to', or 'in conversation with' a named journalist. This is a practice which should be more widespread. It is honest, and gives credit where due. Ghostwriting is largely unrewarding. Certainly the celebrity will get a much bigger fee than the writer for less actual work, but this is understandable because, apart from specialized knowledge, the celebrity possesses a famous name and the name has to be bought. A Labour MP, who had an article about a murder case involving a constituent ghosted for him, and subsequently sent to the writer's home address a cheque with a note saying, 'You did most of the work, you should share in my fee', was a rare species.

There is a skill in ghostwriting. There are magazines in which every celebrity writes in the same manner, which is the same way that all the articles in the magazine are written. This slickness is a mistake. Even the most obtuse reader will suspect that the bylined author did not write the words. The skill in ghostwriting is to produce words that read as if the celebrity has written them, but this is not always easy, for the true voice of the celebrity may not match the public idea. There are particular problems with comedians. Editors expect them to sound as they do on television or radio, but rarely is this the case. The jokes of the public performance can be those of scriptwriters; offstage the comic may be more thoughtful and intelligent than might be expected, but not funny. Provide a verbatim transcript of what the comic said and the editor will complain, 'It doesn't sound like him'. Normally the writer has to throw in a few lines or catchphrases from the comic's public performances to achieve the flavour expected.

For ghosted pieces a tape recorder is invaluable, for even copious notes can fail to capture the rhythms and idiosyncracies of a person's speech. The racing driver's confession, 'I made a porridge of it on the first bend', is more colourful than if the words are reduced to a bald, 'I spun at the first bend'. Sometimes, however, a first-person piece is not a good idea. A test pilot was so concerned that colleagues would accuse him of line-shooting that he played down dramas in his career until he made test flying sound as exciting as accountancy. The answer was to over-dramatize everything he said, and present him with a draft for his corrections. He would read it, wincing, and complain, 'A bit exciting, this', as he reached for a pen, but that way enough survived to be readable. His was a story that would have been better told in the third person, when a writer would have been able to spotlight his courage and skill in a way in which obviously he could not do himself.

A celebrity bylining a feature is, of course, entitled like any other writer to approve it in its final form before publication if changes have been made. Staff writers may be rewritten totally by sub-editors who think the writer has missed the point, or who have to tailor the copy to cover pictures the writer never saw, or to match a headline or introduction thought up belatedly by the editor. Staff writers can always fight their corner about this treatment and, if dissatisfied, demand the removal of their bylines, but such liberties should not be taken with outsiders' copy.

5 WRITING THE WORDS

Most journalists begin by writing features longhand and typing them later. With experience it becomes natural to work directly on to a typewriter or word processor and eventually it can become difficult to write by hand anything longer than a letter. Some writers – to be envied – can type just one draft and follow it with a polished fair copy. Others find it necessary to write and rewrite again and again before they are satisfied. This is nothing to be ashamed of. Many of the best writers in magazine journalism agonize over every feature.

Within the limits of the publication for which a journalist is writing, style should be what comes naturally. A tendency to flippancy may have to be played down when writing for a serious-minded publication, or a magisterial style lightened for a popular one, but it is a mistake to try to adopt a totally alien style; it will be hard to sustain and will probably jar on readers. It would be better to seek work on a periodical that appreciates the writers's natural style.

A feature should have a design: a beginning, a middle and an ending. It can be helpful to jot down the main points of a feature, in any sequence, as they occur to one, and then arrange them in a logical running order. The introduction should grab readers immediately and make them want to read on. To adopt simple chronology beginning, for example, with where the subject was born and raised, is rarely the best plan, for it suggests a history book or an encyclopedia. In a feature it is more usual to begin with the person or institution today, what they are doing, or about to do, or have just done. After this the writer can go back to the subject's early years and progress chronologically from this point. Ending can be difficult, but a feature should not just die away. A common practice is to revert to the starting point, and leave a person reiterating plans for the future, or to pay off with a good quote, again preferably forward-looking.

Opening words

The hardest part of writing a feature is beginning it. Newspaper reporters are taught that they should tell the story – what is news – in the first paragraph. This can also be done in a feature – for example, 'Mary Jones will be 100 years old this week' – but there is no rule. This information can conveniently be carried in the form of a **standfirst**, an introductory paragraph in bold or italic type before the feature. In fact the feature may not contain any news. The writer need have no inhibitions. The purpose of the opening words is simply to hook the readers. Here, from an unsigned profile of Princess Michael of Kent in *You Magazine*, is an introduction which really does that:

> The Prince was supervising the barbecue, patiently brushing the chicken with herbs, prodding at the sausages, taking charge of the whole slow process. It was too slow for the Princess. She fretted and fumed and finally grabbed half a pound of butter, ripped its wrappings off and flung it on to the barbecue – which then went up in flames. The chicken was burnt. Half the guests' eyelashes were burnt. The Princess looked contrite. 'Cross Michael. Must slap Marie-Christine,' she cooed in a baby voice, taking his hand and slapping her wrist with it.

Compare that with this intro:

> Symbol and abstraction have increasingly become motivating forces in American policy – a curious development for so practical and direct a people. Americans have always attributed a large moral significance to the nation's policies, but the present situation differs in a fundamental way from those of the past.

Admittedly, this is from an upmarket American magazine, and introducing a discussion of political issues, but there is no need for it to be so uninviting. The article could just as well open with a revealing anecdote, as the Princess Michael feature did. Here is another, less than riveting introduction, this one under the headline, 'Ceramics for Collectors', in an airline giveaway:

> Clay has a history of human use almost as old as recorded history. The sun-dried clay brick and adobe are among the oldest of building materials. In Jericho, the world's oldest city, sun-dried clay brick has been dated back to at least 8000 BC.

It seems hardly likely to capture the interest of in-flight passengers awaiting the arrival of the drinks cart. One might equally begin a feature on polo by explaining that it is a ball game played on horseback using mallets with handles 52 inches long, and that it originated in Persia about 525 BC; but Val Hennessy, writing in *You Magazine* about a visit to a match, had other ideas:

For upper-class women there is no greater aphrodisiac than the aroma of a polo player. That intoxicating mingle of leather boots, crushed grass, horse sweat and expensive bodysplash has weakened the knees of many an aspiring husband-hunter. This I learn from Lucinda Hughes (not her real name) who is sipping champagne and swivelling her shrewd eyes about in the Dunhill marquee at Smith's Lawn, Windsor, where the air is heady with flower scents, cigar smoke and the rustle of silk frocks.

That will not be to everyone's taste, but it is intriguing. However, probably the commonest way of opening a feature is to indicate why the subject is interesting. Here are some examples from an assorted batch of magazines:

Back home in Pakistan, squash champion Jahangir Khan is a god. He is bigger than any rock star, mobbed in the street, the first of his country's sportsmen to be pictured on postage stamps.

When Peter Boardman was born, his father, Stuart, of How Hill Farm, Lugham, Great Yarmouth, decided to put down a holly orchard instead of a cellar of wine. Now, 52 years later, Peter owns the only commercial holly farm in Britain,

At one time Helen Brown fancied being an ambulance driver. That way she could combine her love of the outdoor with her desire to help others. Waiting to reach 21 was, however, rather tiresome. So, instead, she became a shepherd. The job has its similarities; suicide is a favourite pastime among sheep.

If an intro comes readily to mind, the rest of the feature will usually flow from it. If an intro does not emerge, it is not worth waiting for inspiration. The best plan is to start setting down on paper all that one has to say in the feature, in any sequence, and an intro will usually emerge from somewhere, to be lifted to the start. The intro might be a description of a scene:

A man crouches uncomfortably in the doorway of an aeroplane flying 2500 feet above the ground. He's wearing what looks like an oversized rucksack on his back and a mournful expression on his face. You can tell from the way he's twitching that he's not too happy about what he's just been told to do, which is jump.

Bulging port and starboard nets come swinging heavily inboard together, gushing gallons of water. Winches bang to a stop. Ducking smartly out from under, two of the crew pull the net-release ropes and the deck is awash in a profusion of fish. The men stomp over the fish in their haste to clear the nets, to get them back into the water, to start earning again.

Some news magazines favour a style that consists of piling up small details – for example, this intro from *Time*:

It was precisely 9am when the second Baron Denham arrived at the peers' entrance to the Palace of Westminster. After striding through the Gothic arch, he hung his topcoat on a brass hook marked with his name. Adjacent hooks were reserved for the Prince of Wales, the Duke of Edinburgh and the Duke of Wellington. Clutching a red and gold dispatch box, Denham passed through a labyrinth of corridors festooned with such paintings as *King John Assenting to Magna Carta* . . . By 9.05am Denham had reached his office to begin his duties as the government's chief whip in the House of Lords.

On interview features a common type of intro is to describe the circumstances of the meeting:

A fire crackles comfortingly in the grate. Bob Geldof leans back into the corner of the sofa and smiles a deep, languorous smile. Slow and sexy. Hooded eyes and one-day stubble are a fatal combination. From the handsome tapestry slippers to the soft black sweater, Bob Geldof is looking distinctly savoury, but is quick to deny it.

A variation is to begin with a quote from the subject, though this is barred by some magazines in which the practice is to start with an oversized capital letter, because a quotation mark does not sit happily in front of it. Another objection to opening with a quote is that it can be meaningless until readers know who said it. For example, 'The world will end in five years time', is a sensational quote if it comes from a scientist of world renown, but a joke if it comes from an astrologer. Even so, an opening quote is frequently used. For example:

'I do wish you would dispel the idea that I'm a fast-living, international jetsetter', says Peter de Savary. 'I live very quietly.' He is saying this in the Great Hall of his recently-bought £7 million stately home, Littlecote, near

Hungerford, having arrived by helicopter from a weekend's sailing in Cornwall.

'I'm in the spy business these days,' drawls the elegant white-haired lady in the large tinted glasses. She gives a slight smile, and her upper-class New England drawl lulls you into accepting that it is the most natural occurrence in the world that an 83-year-old, dressed in Yves St Laurent, and sitting on the ninth floor of Washington's Watergate, should be enmeshed in the US secret service network.

Features may also open with the writer relating a personal anecdote, which may be told humorously, as in this example from *Punch*:

I was proceeding in a northerly direction through green traffic lights when I noticed that the vehicle had begun to travel sideways instead of forwards, and there was a lot of glass about. The chap who careered through at red and wrote my car off hadn't been drinking, but it's just the sort of daft thing that a tanked-up party-leaver would do . . .

Intros should normally be crisp, the sentences short. There are journalists who maintain that no sentences should contain more than fifteen words and no paragraph more than five sentences at any time, but such rules are too arbitrary and restrictive. Just to prove there are no rigid rules, here is a quirky intro from an article by Pat Jordan in the American men's magazine *GQ*. It should not, however, be taken as a model to copy.

When I finally got my 1976 Alfa Romeo GTV sorted out – that is, after I had its body purged of rust and repainted Alfa red, its clutch and suspension and engine rebuilt (more than once), after I found a mechanic who knew not only who Edoardo Weber was but also how to tune his *carburatore*, and after, blessing of all blessings, I found a gas station only 30 minutes from my door that dispensed 102 octane racing fuel (for *only* $3 a gallon), which would free me from changing fouled spark plugs every Saturday morning to the taunts of my neighbor, 'Hi, Pat! Changin' the plugs again, eh?' – in short, after five years of frustration and $13,000 of expenses, not to mention the cost of the car, which was $5500, used, in 1981, the inevitable happened. I chanced to park it, during spring break, on the street alongside my apartment in Fort Lauderdale, where, at three o'clock on a warm Florida morning, it was irrevocably damaged by a gray Chrysler Le Baron driven by an 18-year-old boy who insisted to the arresting officers that he had had only 'nine or twelve beers' at the Candy Store while engrossed in its midnight Wet Nightie Contest, and who, it was later discovered, was one of 11 children of a recently widowed mother with no car insurance.

Specialist vocabularies

Words should be appropriate to the readership of the magazine. This is not merely a matter of avoiding polysyllabic words when writing for a mass market or a juvenile one; it also means using the correct technical terms when writing for knowledgeable readers, and substituting more homely ones when writing for a wider readership. For example, here is the start of a report on a new camera in *Camera Weekly*:

> A full feature model with choice of programs, auto and manual exposure. Programs, exposure modes selected by slider switch using large LCD panel on top of pentaprism housing. Prism cover also houses pop-up flashgun, which has integral AF spotbeam illuminator, making SFX self-contained for shooting in all lighting conditions.

Regular readers of the magazine and other camera enthusiasts will have no difficulty in understanding that, and would in fact probably be irritated by the spelling out of abbreviations such as LCD, AF and SFX, and explanations of such components as a pentaprism. But a survey of state-of-the-art cameras in a general magazine, which might well be given a place in early summer, would need to be written in words capable of being understood by occasional snapshotters. Here are two more examples:

> Those takeovers were topped in the chutzpah stakes by Blue Arrow's $1.2 billion hostile bid for Manpower, the world's biggest employment agency. Not only did this represent an astonishing step for a company that only three years earlier had joined London's Unlisted Securities Market capitalised at just over £3 million, it also necessitated the UK's largest ever rights issue. The funding mechanism illustrated the advantages that UK raiders have over US groups.

> The Giants' front line is good, not great. The secondary is average. The linebackers control the tempo. They're big enough to take on an offensive guard or tackle, and nifty enough to clamp on wide receivers in the short zones.

The first paragraph is from a business magazine, the second from an American sports magazine. Again the words are right for their readership, but would be wrong in magazines for the general public.

Clichés, circumlocutions and tautology

No journalist should need warning against writing *avoid like the plague, well and truly, fresh as paint, alive and well* and *sickening thud*, but equally outworn are *hitting the headlines, cut-throat competition, conspicuous by their absence, bitterly disappointed* and *immaculately dressed*. Clichés of more recent time include *wide-ranging discussions, sweeping changes, mounting pressures, radical alternatives* and *chilling scenarios*. Blondes are too frequently described as buxom, brides as blushing, babies as bouncing or bonny, authors as best-selling, semi-detached bungalows as neat, mercies as tender, danger as serious and records as all-time. Nurses are angels and teenage mothers are gymslip mums.

The phrase *the best thing since sliced bread* was once amusing but it too has become hackneyed. A challenging exercise for any writer is to devise replacement phrases for *having all the charm of a cement mixer, as rare as rocking horse manure, needed like a fish needs a bicycle, somewhat to the right of Genghis Khan*, and *doing for peace what Herod did for post-natal welfare*. It is generally a mistake to settle for the first adjective or simile that comes to mind, for that is likely to result in a cliché. Good writers mint new phrases.

Writers should bar:

- **Circumlocutions** – roundabout ways of saying something, using several words where one would suffice. For example, *cups that cheer but not inebriate* (tea) and *the long arm of the law* (police).
- **Tautology** – saying the same thing twice in different words, as in a *new innovation, one after the other in succession, a pair of twins, rising up, protruding out, together with, true facts, razed to the ground, grateful thanks*, and *mixing together*.
- **Coy euphemisms**, such as *the smallest room in the house* and *powdering one's nose*. Journalists should not be over-genteel and should write about *women* rather than *ladies* (unless for effect, as in *little old lady* or *a gracious lady*).
- **Mixed metaphors**, such as *the ship of state is travelling a rocky road*, or *one smells a rat darkening the sky*. A less obvious example is that targets are meant to be hit, not beaten or passed.
- **Unnecessary words**. *The question as to whether* means no more than *whether*, and *he is a man who* can be cut back to *he*. *Owing to the fact that* should be changed to *because*, and *in spite of the fact that* to *although*. The following are better replaced by the words in brackets: *as of this moment* (now), *at an early date* (soon), *during the course of* (while), *effect a saving* (save), *filled to capacity* (full), *leaves much to be desired* (is unsatisfactory). Pare sentences whenever possible. The qualifiers *rather* and *very* can usually be omitted without affecting meaning.

Writers should also be sparing in the use of:

- **Words rarely used** (except by journalists), such as *pulchritudinous* and *curvaceous*, *bid* and *probe*, and **vogue words** such as *meaningful* and *hopefully*. The following words are also better replaced by those in brackets: *residence* (home), *terminate* (end), *purchase* (buy), *ameliorate* (make better), *observed* (saw), and *donation* (gift).
- **Foreign expressions**, such as *de rigueur* and *demi-monde*, which suggest snobbery, and **dialect** – unless the writer has a gift for reproducing it – for it is hard to capture in print a rustic or Geordie accent without seeming either snobbish or patronizing.
- **Colloquialisms**, such as *don't* and *isn't*, *didn't* and *haven't*, which are acceptable when quoting someone, or when setting out a list of *Don'ts* but should not normally be used in copy. It is acceptable to quote a person as saying, 'Mummy and Daddy have been marvellous', if that was what was said, but *mums and dads*, *kids*, *aunty* and *hubby* should generally be avoided. Outworn slang expressions, such as *with it*, *super*, *smashing*, and *flavour of the month*, make a writer sound old, and the use of quotation marks, as in *the 'in' thing*, worsens errors by drawing attention to them.
- **Exclamation marks**, known to journalists as 'screamers'. Their real place is after exclamations or commands, such as 'Good grief!' or 'Halt!', and not after any mildly surprising statement.
- **Negative expressions** when it is possible to use positive ones. *Frequently* and *near to* are more direct than *not infrequently* and *not unadjacent to*.
- **Overstatement**, such as *superstar* and *megastar* for mere top of the bill acts, and *the most desirable man in the world* for a reasonably presentable person. Not every accident deserves the label *horror tragedy*, nor is every urgent errand a *dramatic life and death dash*. *Top*, as in *top architect*, *top store* and *top model*, is also overworked.

Common errors

Increasingly common in print are *it's* for *its* (and vice versa). The first is a contraction of *it is* or *it has*. The second is a possessive pronoun meaning *of* or *belonging to*. So, *it's* wagging *its* tail.

Sentences should not be fragmented, despite the delight of advertising copywriters in such paragraphs as *It's a brand new product. A major step forward. A breakthrough in the communications field. And it's British.* This should not happen on editorial pages; the points should be replaced by commas and lower case used for the words that follow.

Related words should not be separated, resulting in sentences like *Being old and rusty I was able to buy the car cheaply*, when what is meant is *I was able to buy the car cheaply because it was old and rusty*.

Also increasingly common is the misuse of words. *To aggravate* means to make worse; *to irritate* means to annoy or chafe. *Uninterested* means not interested in, or uncaring; *disinterested* means impartial. *To imply* is to indicate; *to infer* is to deduce. *Alternate* means first one, then the other in turn; *alternative* relates to a choice. *Alright* is wrong; *all right* is correct. *Rising to a crescendo* is wrong because *crescendo* means becoming louder, a gradual increase in loudness, not a climax. *Almost unique* is wrong; the word means without like or equal, so there can be no degrees of uniqueness. *Compare to* points to a resemblance; *compare with* points out differences: for example, *he compared his love to a rose* and *life is easy now compared with life in grandfather's day*. It should be *fewer* when a number is concerned, *less* when referring to quantities, so *fewer cars* and *fewer accidents* but *less trouble*, *less money*. *Amid*, *among* and *while* should be used rather than *amidst*, *amongst* and *whilst*.

Meanings change. It is useless now to argue that *furore* used to mean a wild burst of enthusiasm and acclamation, since it is now more often used to mean a roar of anger or a storm of controversy, but journalists should not take it on themselves to push the boundaries further; err on the side of conservatism and, when unsure, check in a dictionary. All journalists can profit from studying one of the many paperbacks on English usage and re-reading it from time to time.

Presentation of copy

Most offices expect copy to be typed on A4 paper, unless word processors or direct input have been introduced. More follows on those subjects, but assuming typescript to be required, only one side of the paper should be used, and copy should be typed with double line spacing to leave room for corrections and insertions. That much is common on practically every magazine. After that, preferences differ. Some magazines provide printed top sheets on which writers are required to set out their names, the date, the issue number and the subject of the feature. More often writers type these details at the top of the first sheet, name and date generally going on the left, the title of the publication and issue number or date in the centre, and a one- or two-word catchline to identify the feature, followed by the number of the folio (or typed page) on the right.

A feature on cars in a general magazine might be catchlined simply 'Cars'; however, in a motoring magazine, where every article concerns cars, something more specific is needed, such as 'Ferrari' or 'Tyres' or 'Indy' (for 'Indianapolis' – it saves time and labour to use a short catchline rather than a long one). Similarly in a Christmas issue of a magazine, where most features will concern some aspect of the festival, the word 'Christmas' is not helpful;

Henry Lewis   Mag Magazine No. 41   Windsor 1

The ex-King's voice was harsh and tragic as he broadcast to the
nation from Windsor Castle. "You all know the reasons which have
impelled me to renounce the throne. I want you to understand that
in making up my mind I did not forget the country or the Empire...
But you must believe me when I tell you that I have found it
impossible to carry the heavy burden of responsibility and to
discharge my duties as King as I would wish to do without the help
and support of the woman I love."

    It was December 11, 1936. The man who that morning had been
King Edward VIII, was now again Prince Edward and about to become
the Duke of Windsor, was saying a moving farewell to his people-
most of whom had known nothing until eight days earlier of the
crisis that had come to the Monarchy and the Government.

    It had been only on December 3 that British newspapers had
revealed the story of the King's desire to marry American divorcee
Wallis Simpson. Before that date there had not even been a hint of
the romance. The shock to the public was overwhelming.

    Yet newspapers had known about the King's friendship with Mrs
Simpson for years, as had leaders in society, politics and the
Church. In America and on the Continent it had been the subject
of scurrilous press stories, and months earlier the New York Journal
had told its readers in a headline: "King will wed Wally."

                                                        mf

Figure 4   *Copy typed on paper ruled to ensure 66 characters per line*

the catchline should be 'Pud', 'Carols', 'Tree' or another more specific indicator of the subject matter.

Avoid joke catchlines. It may be amusing to catchline a piece about a pompous politician with the word 'Bore' but it will not be funny if the subject sees it or gets to hear about it, or if somehow it gets into print – which has been known to happen. It is not necessary for the writer to devise a headline, and in fact it is impractical before the art department has produced a layout because the writer will not know how many words will be required to fit it. However, the suggestion of an apt headline may be appreciated, even though it may require amendment to make it fit.

The writer should leave generous margins at top, bottom and both sides of the paper, for instructions by executives and for editing markings by subs. Some magazines require writers to type an ordained number of characters (such as 60) to each line, which makes it easier for designers and subs to calculate how many printed lines the copy will fill in the magazine. (This is, of course, only enforced on staff writers, though freelance contributors' copy may be retyped on such paper by staff in the office.)

On some publications this is made simpler by providing copy paper printed with two vertical rules between which copy must be typed. In one office these are $4\frac{1}{2}$ inches apart, allowing for lines of 54 typed characters when using a machine with Elite type (12 characters to an inch). Each typed line then equals two printed lines in the magazine, given its normal column width and size of body type, though a sloppy typist can, of course, defeat the system by deletions and corrections.

However, correction fluid and photocopying machines have made life easier for writers who are maladroit typists. It was once commonplace to have to type with as many as half a dozen sheets of carbon (to provide copies for editor, deputy editor, features editor, art editor, picture editor and chief sub) and a mistake or an omission discovered half way down a page meant ripping them all out, assembling another batch of paper and carbons and starting over again. Today the writer usually needs to produce only one copy, can make amendments with the aid of correction fluid, and then run off on a copying machine as many clean versions as are needed.

At the foot of the first page (and subsequent ones) writers type 'mf' to indicate more follows. Omit this and a final page which becomes detached may be lost and never appear in print. If it will be some time before the final page becomes available, writers type 'mfl' for 'more follows later'. Incidentally, sub-editors prefer a folio not to end in mid-sentence. At the top of the second sheet and subsequent ones the writer's name and the catchline appear again, and at the foot of the last page the writer types 'end'. Pages should then be clipped or stapled together – never pinned, for the reason that caused newspaper owner Lord Beaverbrook to send a plaintive cable to the secretary of one of his editors, 'Tell Blank not to use pins. I have pricked my finger'.

Word processing

Increasingly, offices and freelances are replacing typewriters with word processors. A writer may regard a word processor merely as a super typewriter, which indeed it is, having a conventional QWERTY keyboard, plus extra keys for additional functions; but the words typed appear on a monitor screen, where they can be checked and amended before being printed out by a linked machine. A word processor – essentially a programmed microcomputer – provides a set number of characters on every line and automatically moves to the next line when necessary without the need to use a carriage return. It will print a set number of lines to a page, making word calculation easy (though some machines count words automatically). It will provide italics and bold type in a number of sizes. It will delete unwanted text without trace.

It can do much more. If one realizes a vital fact has been omitted, the text can be 'scrolled' back to the appropriate place, the cursor (a small pointer of light) positioned where the insertion is to be made, and the new material typed in. The machine will rearrange lines automatically to accommodate it. Blocks of type can be moved around and text inserted at will. A writer can type in research from one source, add information from a second, third and fourth and, if competently done, the result will be clean and free from corrections. The machine can number pages and automatically add the writer's name and the catchline at the top of every page, and 'mf' at the foot. A 'search and exchange' facility enables the computer to seek out a name or phrase and change it wherever it occurs (useful if one has misspelt Dixon as Dickson). An increasing number of programs include electronic dictionaries which will check spellings, and query dubious ones, and style monitors which will draw attention to long sentences, obscure words and over-use of personal pronouns.

When the writer is satisfied, the computer will instruct the printer to print out the copy, commonly by means of a *daisy wheel* (a disc with letters embossed at the end of each 'petal') or *dot matrix*, which used tiny needles to create letter shapes on the page. Daisy wheels are now obsolescent, and are being replaced by non-impact printers such as *ink-jets*, which shoot droplets of ink on to the paper from a cartridge, and *lasers*, which work like copying machines.

What is typed can be stored on a disc and recalled at any time for further changes and another print-out. A single floppy disc can hold all the words of a book, while more expensive hard discs will hold even more. Discs must, however, be treated with care. They can be damaged by spilt coffee or burning cigarettes, so should always be kept in a cabinet when not in use and never left littering a desk.

Much more paper is used with a word processor than with a typewriter because it is so easy to run off another copy. With a typewriter a journalist may think of a point which might have been included in a feature but, after several hours at the typewriter, be reluctant to retype or cut-and-paste any more. With a word processor the task is easy, and a machine can change a writer's methods of working. Most writers claim that their productivity is increased, though the effects on writing style are argued about; some claim that ease of use induces verbosity, while others find that the ability to edit and re-edit results in terseness.

When linked to a telephone line by means of an electronic circuit called a *modem*, a word-processing computer has another valuable use to a journalist. It can be used to call up databases (computerized libraries) such as that of the British Library for research material. Databases now offer files of information ranging from government statistics and company reports to recipes and biographies, which can be viewed on the writer's desktop screen and stored as required.

A computer with a modem can also access the Internet, the global electronic bulletin board that is effectively a new publishing medium of awesome potential, with thousands of companies, institutions and individuals offering material. A subscription to one of the many Internet access providers enables one to trawl the contents and also to book hotels and flights, and correspond by electronic mail with other computer users worldwide at merely local telephone rates.

Direct input

From the point of view of publishing companies, word processors are part of a revolution which has already begun, in which features are entered by their writers into an office computer for subbing and laying out on VDU (visual display unit) screens. Double keystroking (typing by writers and then typesetting by compositors) is eliminated, for the computer can handle the setting. Direct input, as it is known, began in magazines in Britain in 1986 after its introduction in newspapers, though some publications introduced it only for staff journalists and employed print union members to keyboard contributed and advertising copy.

The financial savings on magazines are less spectacular than on newspapers because, unlike newspapers, which normally have their own printing machines and staff on the premises, magazines are generally printed elsewhere under contract, and this dependence on contract printing will govern the use of direct input. However, there are savings in terms of later deadlines and a better product.

The Economist (circulation 244,000) introduced direct input in 1987 and, after a couple of issues had been produced with the new technology, the then editor Rupert Pennant-Rea told *UK Press Gazette*:

In terms of involvement with the journalists, having direct control has made much more of a difference. You never get the feeling now that your story is going off into a vacuum . . . The costs are coming down. It is really a matter of whether the companies concerned want to make that leap. In our business we cannot afford not to be up with our competitors in technological as well as journalistic terms.

Probably the time will come when 'hard copy' contributions typed on paper will be unwelcome, and even freelances will be required to submit features on floppy discs or keyboard them into an office computer from a work station or portable terminal. Modems have already made it practicable for freelances to deliver their copy electronically without going near a magazine's office, and the practice will grow as portable computers increase in number and decrease in price, and greater compatibility is established between the products of different manufacturers.

The word processor is a tool of the present which has a bigger role to play on periodicals in the future, so it is worth the effort of learning to use one. Self-tuition is possible but not easy, and a journalist offered an opportunity to go on a word-processing course should leap at the chance to acquire the skill. Some journalists are still concerned about possible dangers to health in spending long hours in front of a monitor screen, though many early fears have now faded and the hazards seem mainly such mundane, though unpleasant, ones as eystrain, headache and backache, all of which should be avoidable by correct lighting, seating and posture, by switching the point of focus of one's eyes from time to time and taking reasonably frequent breaks.

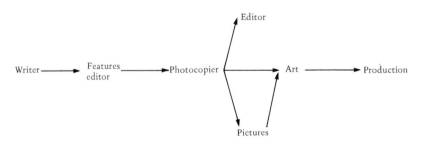

Figure 5 *The route of a writer's copy from typewriter to production*

However produced and delivered – on a typewriter or a word processor, by human messenger or electronically – the words go from a writer to the features editor, who may call for amendments or additions if they do not meet the brief. When the features editor is satisfied, the feature will be photocopied and copies distributed to the editor, art editor, picture editor, chief sub and other executives, or the text will be made available on screen to those requiring access to it.

6 PICTURES

On some magazines, particularly literary reviews, pictures are used mainly to relieve large slabs of text, but on mass circulation magazines they can rate more importantly than words, and there is little likelihood of a feature, no matter how well written, being used unless exciting pictures are obtainable. In some cases, if a magazine is offered dramatic pictures, a feature may be written to accompany them. Writers are naturally reluctant to recognize this, but on many magazines words accompany pictures rather than the other way about.

Picture research

The work of a picture desk divides into two main categories. Firstly there is research, i.e. locating and obtaining existing pictures of subjects which can range from a film still to a brass rubbing, or from an obscure vegetable to a Russian missile. Given a feature, a picture researcher prepares a list of possible pictures to be sought. Popular sources are film, television and record companies, motor manufacturers, tourist boards, the armed services and other organizations, whose pictures usually have the merit of being supplied free in the interests of publicity. (A fee may, however, be asked when a magazine is seeking an historic picture of an artist, programme or product which the company no longer has any interest in publicizing.)

Pictures may also be sought from photographers likely to have covered a subject, and from personal photograph albums. If, for example, a magazine is seeking pictures of someone as a child, it will usually be necessary to contact that person directly. Unfortunately, people have curious ideas of how they look, and how they want to be seen; actresses, in particular, will plead with a magazine not to use a technically excellent studio portrait of themselves, claiming they look awful and promising to send a much better one – which, as often as not, turns out to be a typical family snap of mediocre quality. A television newscaster telephoned a magazine in a rage after publication of a photograph of himself with his baby son, for which he had posed, claiming it must have been deliberately and maliciously selected from those available because he looked stupid and the child looked an idiot – yet everyone on the magazine genuinely thought the picture delightful.

Mostly, however, pictures are obtained from agencies and libraries, the former being mainly concerned with selling new pictures, and the latter with selling from stock built up over years, though the two are much alike to deal with. Agencies range from general ones, with as many as 10 million pictures on file, to small firms specializing in particular subjects as varied as racehorses, fungi, the Bible lands and historic cars. Some of their pictures are the work of staff photographers, others of freelances whose work the agencies sell in return for a commission, usually in the region of 50 per cent.

A selection of pictures of a given subject can be delivered swiftly to a magazine by motorcycle messenger, but some big libraries have now invested in digital archiving on optical or hard discs, together with systems allowing remote accessing. By use of a password a magazine's picture desk can pull low resolution images on to its computer screen and make its selection, then draw down reproduction quality images. However, it will take many years to transfer all a library's historic stock to digital storage.

Picture researchers will negotiate fees if dealing with an unfamiliar source and settle any copyright problems if borrowing pictures from someone who may own the print but not the copyright. If photographs have to be credited in the magazine with the name of the photographer or agency, researchers will note the names for passing to the subs. For self-protection, picture desks should log all pictures in and out of offices. Too often some are mislaid, which can happen easily when desks are deep in 35 mm transparencies, individually small yet often valued at hundreds of pounds each. This is why magazines commonly insure against loss of transparencies. A photographer who was fortunate enough to have a whole parcel lost by a publisher received compensation sufficiently handsome for him to buy a villa beside the Mediterranean.

Photographers

Picture desks also commission new pictures from staff and freelance photographers, and, in the case of freelances, should issue briefing documents similar to those given writers. Photographers are normally paid a fee representing a day or half day's work, however many pictures are shot, rather than per picture. Fashionable studio photographers, however, name their own, considerable, fees.

While most newspaper photographers shoot mainly in black and white, most magazine photographers shoot mainly in colour. On occasions when it has been decided that a magazine feature will be in monochrome, a photographer will usually shoot black and white, but even then may take some colour as well, or instead. For there may be a late change of mind in favour of using colour, or a need may be foreseen for colour of the person or place in a future issue, and colour pictures can always be converted to mono (though with some loss of quality), whereas the reverse is impossible. The availability of colour pictures also makes a more saleable package for syndication, and sales of pictures to foreign magazines may more than cover the costs of obtaining them.

Another difference between newspaper and magazine photographers is that the former, unlike the latter, are mainly shooting events as they happen, often of people unwilling to cooperate, and the important thing is to get a picture, for there may be no other chance. Composition and quality are secondary considerations. The feature photographer is more likely to be taking pictures by invitation, able to pose the subject and shoot at leisure, and the resulting pictures should be of a standard, both artistically and technically, to justify the better paper and printing of a magazine.

Generally, the news photographer is concerned with getting one striking shot, for newspapers rarely use more than one of a subject. A magazine photographer will aim to bring back a series of at least four different shots, since that number is commonly used to illustrate a feature. For a story on a television actor, for example, a magazine photographer might picture him finishing a meal at home with his wife and children, driving his car through the gates of the television studios, being made up, changing into costume, listening to instructions from a floor manager in the studio, eating in the canteen with other members of the cast, and, with feet up, resting in his dressing room.

When newspaper and magazine photographers meet at photocalls – the equivalent for photographers of press conferences for writers – the former will be looking for a single gimmicky picture while the latter will be seeking more conventional shots, but a greater number and variety of them. Fashions change but in recent years there has been a move away from close-up portraits and a vogue for wide-angle shots of people. An industrialist, for example, rather than being photographed at his desk (pen in hand or telephone to ear) is photographed in front of one of his company's properties or in one of its showrooms or stores with its products piled high behind him and stretching into the distance.

Subjects, whether people or trees or windmills, should not normally be posed in the centre of the frame; a better composition is obtained by positioning them a third of the way into it. Similarly, in shots showing a horizon, it should not normally divide the picture into equal horizontal halves; it should be placed about a third of the way down the frame. In photography this is known as the 'rule of thirds' and is a basic principle of composition.

Studio sessions

Staff photographers and general freelances can be expected to take competent pictures of any subject, and usually enjoy the variety of work. However, for some pictures, magazines will often engage specialist photographers who work in their own or hired studios. A typical studio is a large, bare room painted matt white, with a solid vibration-free floor, wide doors to allow the entry of 'props', and plenty of electricity sockets. Windows are of little importance, since studio photographers normally rely on controlled electric lighting. There are reflector boards for casting light back into shadows, stepladders for providing high viewpoints, and large rolls of paper in a variety of colours and backgrounds.

For a scientific or technical journal a commission might be for pictures of a small object – a component or an insect. This calls for skill in close-up work, and critical measurement of distance and focus. The photography of food is another specialist field, when the call can be for the mouth-watering colour of a particular dish to fill a whole page. Cutlery, wine glasses and possibly a dining table may be borrowed from a store in return for an acknowledgement in the magazine. The cookery editor or home economist will cook the food on the premises, or bring it part-prepared to the studio, and primp every lettuce leaf and arrange every parsley sprig to look delicious. In fact the food is probably inedible. Usually it is undercooked (vegetables often being merely dunked in hot water). Sausages may be painted with liquid paraffin to make them glisten, the peeled fruit with lemon juice to prevent them turning brown. Ice cream may be less deliquescent whipped potato mash, and cream may be shaving foam from an aerosol. Tissues or crumpled foil may pad out or prop up the food, and steam apparently rising from a dish may come from a kettle of boiling water.

However, food photography is a minor operation compared with fashion shoots, for which models are engaged at hourly rates fixed by their agencies. The fashion editor will choose them from 'composites' – sheets of small pictures showing each model in different poses and costumes. There are models in all age ranges, from schoolgirl to stereotype grandmother. Some are glamorous, some homely, others bizarre. Their best features, and the main reasons for their employment, may be their lips, their teeth, their hands or their legs. Models should always be required to sign a release form, assigning copyright in the pictures to the magazine, for the ownership of copyright in pictures can be a matter of dispute and, additionally, it is possible that the model may, in later years, become famous, giving the pictures greater value.

■■ MAGAZINE ■■

Model Form

In consideration of your agreeing to pay me my fee for posing for photograph(s) taken or to be taken by you, I hereby acknowledge and agree:

1   that the entire copyright (which includes all rights of reproduction) in the photograph(s) belongs to you.

2   that you and/or your licensees or assignees are entitled to make whatever use of the photograph(s) and all reproductions thereof, either wholly or in part, in any manner or form whatsoever and in any medium and either separately or in conjunction with other photograph(s), part or parts of photograph(s), drawings or other forms of illustration you or they decide.

* I am over 21 years of age.
* I am not over 21 years of age but by parent/guardian has agreed to my undertaking this work and to the use of this/these photograph(s) as mentioned herein. I have read and fully understand the terms of this contract. I authorize you to pay my fee for posing viz. £   p

* to my agent/ ....

* to me ....

Signed .... Date of sitting(s) ....

* Delete whichever does **not** apply.

Magazine ....

Figure 6   *Model release form*

A designer may be employed to create and furnish a setting, hiring or borrowing materials and props to create the impression of a bar, an office or a space capsule as required. On the day there will be the photographer, with possibly an assistant to load films, check light readings and distances and move lights, the models with attendant beautician and hairdresser, the fashion editor, mouth full of pins, nipping and tucking the clothes at the back, publicists representing the makers of the garments and the store that is selling them, all with ideas on how they should be displayed. On these occasions photographers customarily shoot Polaroid instant pictures to check lighting and arrangement before taking the transparencies to be used in the magazine.

Equipment

For the type of studio sessions mentioned above, photographers use large format cameras taking sheet film of 5 × 4 in or even 10 × 8 in for optimum quality; however, staff and general purpose photographers require more portable cameras. Though 35 mm is now universally acceptable, a larger film format is still preferred, particularly for magazine covers, because the quality derived from 6 × 6 cm ($2\frac{1}{4}$ in square) negatives is proportionately better. However, the 35 mm single lens reflex camera, with its vast selection of interchangeable lenses, is more versatile. Generally, photographers tend to shoot $2\frac{1}{4}$ in square during a posed session where time is available, and use 35 mm for action shots, e.g. at sports events and work under pressure.

So photographers tend to travel (by car, whenever possible, because of the amount of equipment) with a rollfilm camera, frequently a Hasselblad, and interchangeable backs for loading with colour and mono, plus perhaps three 35 mm Nikon bodies with a selection of wide-angle and telephoto lenses for different kinds of work at different ranges. Preferences vary, but one respected feature photographer carries a 28 mm f2 wide-angle lens, an 85 mm f2 medium telephoto, a 75 mm to 150 mm f4 zoom lens, and a 300 mm f4.5 telephoto with a 2× converter which can give it roughly the capability (though not the quality) of a 600 mm lens. Photographers may also carry a couple of electronic flash guns, an exposure meter, filters for colour correction and special effects, studio lights, a tripod and sometimes a stepladder for gaining height, plus many rolls and cassettes of film.

A photographer may use between 6 and 18 films in a day. From a major shoot one may return to the office having exposed 10 rolls of 120 film (12 pictures per roll) or half a dozen cassettes of 35 mm film (up to 36 shots per cassette). It is a curious psychological fact that a picture editor may be happy with 3 rolls of 120 film, but if offered a cassette of 35 mm film containing the same number of pictures, is likely to suggest that the photographer has not really done a comprehensive job.

Colour is always shot on reversal film, producing transparencies which give more detail than prints from colour negative film. To provide for considerable enlargement without graininess the rule is to use the slowest possible film that lighting conditions allow. In practice, photographers may carry quantities of 64 ISO Ektachrome for good light conditions and 200 or 400 ISO Ektachrome for poor. While the same considerations apply with monochrome, and photographers who like to capture beautiful cloud formations also prefer medium speed, fine-grain films, staff photographers generally standardize on 400 ISO film such as Tri-X, which has good latitude, is reasonably fast and capable of being uprated where necessary in low-light conditions.

All the photographer's gear, apart from the tripod, lights and stepladder, is normally carried in a strong metal case fitted with foam inserts cut out to cushion the equipment. This luggage has to be pared down when flying abroad, probably to the 35 mm equipment, though the photographer may carry perhaps 90 films (40 mono and 50 colour) divided between two speed ratings. With personal baggage as well, the company of a writer is welcome then to help carry and guard it. The prudent photographer also carries abroad a list of the equipment, including camera and lens numbers, and a letter on headed notepaper from the editor which can be shown to Customs officers certifying that the equipment is the property of the office, was legitimately bought in Britain, and will be returning to it.

Working abroad in an exotic country is obviously more exciting than working near the office, but photographers can never be completely happy until the results are seen, and that usually means after returning to the office, for few would risk an unknown processor. The main hazards are inadvertently using the wrong film, sticking camera shutters, flash guns that fail to synchronize with shutters, condensation, salt water and, of course, theft of the equipment.

Processing

Photographic darkrooms should be sited where they are free from vibration by machinery or road traffic, and from dust and extremes of temperature. Surfaces should be impervious to chemicals, and electric wiring must be safe in view of the amount of running water. Big publishing houses have their own darkrooms capable of dealing with colour and mono films. Smaller offices usually deal only with mono, and send colour away to a processing house, while some magazines contract out all their work.

Photographers rarely process the films they take; this is usually done by darkroom staff, whose other work frequently includes enlarging and reducing headlines and artwork. The darkroom will normally handle simple retouching of mono pictures, hand-spotting negatives or prints, and there may also be occasions when the darkroom is required to produce manipulated printing or such special effects as grain, solarization, bleach-outs and bas relief. Unofficially, in summer, darkrooms may also cope with processing and enlarging the holiday snaps of members of the staff.

Colour is normally returned to the picture desk after processing in strips of several frames in transparent sleeves. They will be examined on a light box, with a magnifying glass, to check on details and quality. Over-exposure of colour film results in weak colours, under-exposure in dark ones, which is worse, because printing results in some loss of brightness. Such pictures, and those with colour casts or confusing colour – for example, a woman's dress clashing with background – will be discarded. Selected frames will be clipped from the strips and either mounted or placed in individual transparent envelopes. They are never sandwiched in glass as some amateurs like to do; glass is easily broken and may damage the transparency.

Mono pictures are proofed, same size, on sheets. The picture editor or researcher will indicate on the proof with a chinagraph crayon which frames are required to be enlarged, and these will normally be printed to 10 × 8 in or 12 × 10 in size, though, if only 'thumbnail' size heads are required (possibly of authors to accompany bylines), they may be printed smaller. For best reproduction, prints should not need to be enlarged by the printer; normally they will be reduced, but should not be of a size to require reducing more than seven times.

They will be printed on glossy untextured paper, but unglazed, for the best reproduction. They should then be captioned. Caption information is the responsibility of the photographer. If shooting a person with a pet animal, the photographer should always record its name, because it can take much time and effort to discover such simple information later; though if a writer is present he or she may be persuaded to take notes to save the photographer having to stop shooting to make them.

At this stage it is sufficient to list the captions on a sheet of paper, when they need only say, beneath the photographer's name and date, something like this:

> *Competition winner Mary Smith in Paris*
> Film A: frames 1 to 5: leaving Charles de Gaulle airport
> 6/9: checking in at Hotel Georges V
> 10/15: at Eiffel Tower

and so on. A selection of the best pictures will then be offered to the art department and the remainder filed.

Filing pictures

Filing of black and white prints and negatives is simple. They are normally kept in folders or envelopes, alphabetically arranged under names and subjects. The prints should be captioned on their backs with the photographer's name, the date shot or filed, and basic information relating to the picture. These captions can be written with pen or pencil but care has to be taken that no impression is made on the surface, and that ink does not smudge prints, so it is better to write the captions on adhesive labels or on strips of paper which can be attached with adhesive tape or a smear of rubber solution.

Colour transparencies present more problems. If mounted, there is room for basic information on the card mounts, but more often they are in strips in transparent sleeves and it is necessary to write captions on sheets of paper to file with them. Too often this is not done, or done in only the sketchiest way. Everyone who has shot holiday snaps will know the problems that can occur later. Ten years on there is doubt about the location, the people, the year. So it is with magazine pictures. In a group of half a dozen people, let alone a sporting eleven, some will be instantly recognizable, others will not. The only answer is to file the information at the time, indexed by the frame numbers on the films.

Problems of filing become more acute the longer a magazine exists. Some picture libraries have adopted microfiche for storing black and white pictures. Up to eight pictures may be reduced on one microfiche and when a picture is requested, it is enlarged from the microfiche. In other systems pictures are digitized and stored on magnetic discs from which they can be called to a monitor screen for examination, after which selected pictures are printed. Indexing, alphabetically or numerically, is increasingly computerized; movements of the pictures, for sale or between departments, can also be logged on computer discs.

7 PRESENTATION

Words, pictures and other illustrations come together in the art department, which is responsible to the editor for the appearance of the magazine, and hence for the display of features. Artists working in it need a flair for design backed by some knowledge of typography and photography. Words and pictures for a feature are given to one of them, selected by the art editor, together with a copy of the flat plan showing the pages, or space on a page, the feature is to occupy and, possibly, instructions about the treatment.

Word counting

On some small magazines, copy is sent as a matter of course to be set in a standard size of type and column width, and the set material is returned in the form of galley proofs. In such cases a designer has only to measure the text with a ruler to see how much space it is necessary to allocate to it. However, this allows little flexibility or flair in design, and on bigger magazines, unless they are computerized, a designer starts with the writer's typescript and the first job is to count the words in it to calculate how much space they need.

If a feature is short, an artist may count every word; with a longer one an easier course is to count the number of words on a full page of typescript and multiply by the number of pages, making allowances for short or over-long ones. Another method is to take perhaps fifty full lines and find the average number of words per line, then count the number of lines on several full pages to find the average number of lines per page. Multiplying the two gives the average number of words per page, which is finally multiplied by the number of pages.

This is where typescripts with lines of a consistent width and number on each page make life easier. When some lines are much longer than others, it can be helpful to rule a vertical line in pencil where the majority end, average those to the left of it and count the odd words to the right separately. All this work is, however, unnecessary if a magazine has introduced direct input by writers into a computer, because the computer will provide an immediate and accurate word count.

The next task is to determine how much space the words require. A designer will know already the number of words per column inch in a printed issue of the magazine, using its normal body type and column width, but if he or she wants to use a different type or column width, the figure can be worked out by calculating the number of words per inch in a piece set in that type and width. Small examples of settings in various widths may be found in specimen books supplied by printers, and typesetters can always be asked to provide samples.

Typefaces

The space to be allocated for copy clearly depends on typeface and size. There are thousands of different typefaces, modern and old-fashioned, ornate and austere. There are serif types with cross strokes at the end of limbs (such as Plantin, Century and Times), and sans serif types without them (such as Gill, Helvetica and Univers) See Figures 7 and 8. Sans serif faces are more modern but rarely as easy to read (though they score by being legible in the small sizes needed for charts and tables). The majority of magazines use mainly serif type, though they may use sans serif for contrast in subheadings and columns such as readers' letters.

42pt

abcdefgh12340
ABCDEFABCD
ABCdefghij12340

Figure 7   *Example of serif typeface: Plantin*

42pt

abcdefgh12340
ABCDEFGHIJ
ABCdefghij12340

Figure 8 *Example of sans serif typeface: Univers*

A family of type comprises all the upper and lower case characters and punctuation marks in that typeface in all the different sizes available, in different weights (from extra light and light through medium to *bold* and *extra bold*), proportions (from condensed to expanded or extended), angles (upright Roman and forward sloping *italic*) and also in combinations such as *heavy italic* and light extra condensed. Within a family a complete set of characters in one weight and style is called a fount (pronounced *font*).

First considerations in choosing a type are technical. While some are suitable for all kinds of paper, others look best on particular surfaces; the same type can look very different on coated (shiny) paper and uncoated paper. Typefaces with greatly contrasting thick and thin strokes are generally better on uncoated paper. Garamond, for example, looks well on uncoated but can appear spidery on coated paper.

The method of printing is also a factor. Some faces designed for obsolescent letterpress (relief) printing lose appeal when used for modern lithography, in which there is no significant difference in height between printing and non-printing areas of the plates. (The systems are explained in Chapter 10.)

Then come artistic considerations. Some typefaces have individual letters, accents or fractions that are unpleasing. Some have only a limited number of founts available. Typefaces of the same name are not necessarily exactly the same in photocomposition as in hot metal setting, and in digital typesetting can vary further. To avoid an anarchic visual appearance it is wise to avoid employing too many different typefaces. One family alone, such as Plantin, will provide within it Roman, *italic* and **bold** and an adequate range of sizes.

ABCDEFGHIJKLMNOPQR

ABCDEFGHIJKLMNO

ABCDEFGHIJKLM

ABCDEFGHIJKLM

ABCDEFGHIJK

ABCDEFGHIJKLMN

ABCDEFGHIJK

ABCDEFGHIJKLMNOPQRST

ABCDEFGHIJKLMNOPQ

Figure 9 *Fancy typefaces – Futura Black, Dynamo Shadow, Gallila, Broadway, Candice In-line, Old English, Palace Script, Flash Bold and Futura Demi-bold*

Figure 10 (opposite) *Some of the varieties of style available in just one family of type: Univers. From top to bottom they are Light, Light italic, Medium expanded, Medium, Medium italic, Medium condensed, Medium condensed italic, Bold expanded, Bold, Bold italic, Bold condensed, Bold condensed italic, Extra bold condensed, Extra bold, Extra bold italic, Extra bold expanded*

ABCDEFGHIJabcdefghijklm

ABCDEFGHIJabcdefghijklm

ABCDEFGHIJabcdefghi

ABCDEFGHIJabcdefghijklm

ABCDEFGHIJabcdefghijklm

ABCDEFGHIJabcdefghijklmnopqrstuvwx

ABCDEFGHIJabcdefghijklmnopqrstuvwx

ABCDEFGHIJabcdefg

ABCDEFGHIJabcdefghijk

ABCDEFGHIJabcdefghijk

ABCDEFGHIJabcdefghijklmnopqrstu

ABCDEFGHIJabcdefghijklmnopqrstu

ABCDEFGHIJabcdefg

ABCDEFGHIJabcdefghijk

ABCDEFGHIJabcdefghijk

ABCDEFGHIJabcdef

Type sizes

Type is measured effectively from the top of the highest ascenders (the parts reaching above the body on letters such as b and d) to the bottom of the lowest descenders (the tails of p and q) and the sizes are traditionally expressed in points, a system devised in France in the eighteenth century. In the version standard in Britain and the United States a point equals 0.01383in. (0.351mm) but for practical purposes there are 72 points to an inch, so the depth of any type is roughly its point size divided into 72. Therefore 36-point type is half an inch deep and 12-point is a sixth of an inch.

Figure 11 *Dotted lines show the 'x' height of the letters in relation to the ascenders and descenders. The type is Franklin Gothic lower case*

However, the size of characters can appear to vary within this. When one looks at the x-height, which is the height of lower case letters without ascenders or descenders (such as x and o), 8-point Century looks larger than 8-point Plantin, and that is appreciably larger than 8-point Perpetua, the ascenders and descenders being proportionately smaller. Rockwell and Helvetica are other so-called 'large-appearing' typefaces; Bembo and Garamond are 'small-appearing' faces.

On an established magazine, of course, a standard body type will have been settled (though it may be changed every few years to freshen the look of the publication). It may be available in sizes from 6-point to 120-point. The sizes most used by magazines for body matter (the text of articles and stories) are 8, 9, 10, 11 and 12-point, with 6 and 7-point for competition rules, tables and the like, and 14, 18, 24, 36, 42, 48 and occasionally 60-point for headings and display. With computerized setting such sizes are usually formatted into the computer, although an infinite variety of point sizes can be called up to get a headline to fit. Unconventional sizes are not, however, encouraged, and are banned by some publications to avoid an undisciplined appearance.

Some printers and veteran journalists still use names for the different sizes: Nonpareil (traditionally pronounced 'non-prul,' and written *nonp*) for 6-pt, Minion (*min*) for 7-pt, Brevier (pronounced 'brev-eer' and written *brev*) for 8-pt, Bourgeois (pronounced 'burjoyce' and written *bour*) for 9-pt, Long primer (pronounced 'primmer' and written *lp*) for 10-pt and Pica (pronounced 'piker') for 12-pt. There is no merit in listing them further since Pica is the only name commonly met today.

9pt
abcdefghijklmnopqrstuvwxyz1234567890£.,-()[]

10pt
abcdefghijklmnopqrstuvwxyz1234567890£.,

11pt
abcdefghijklmnopqrstuvwxyz1234567890

12pt
abcdefghijklmnopqrstuvwxy12345

13pt
abcdefghijklmnopqrstuvwxyz1234

14pt
abcdefghijklmnopqrstuv12345

16pt
abcdefghijklmnopqrstuvwxyz

18pt
abcdefghijklmno1234567890£.,:,''

20pt
abcdefghijklmnopqr12345670

22pt
abcdefghijklmnopqrs12340

24pt
abcdefghijklmnopqrstuv

28pt
abcdefghij12345678

30pt
abcdefghijklm12340

36pt
abcdefghijk12340

Figure 12   *Sizes of type: Times Roman in a range of sizes from 9-pt to 36-pt*

A widely acceptable face and size in magazines is 9-point Plantin, but many designers do not like the rather dense effect of a column of type 'set solid' and prefer extra white space between lines. Therefore, rather than using the type 'solid', they will choose to have 9-point type body on 10-point, known as '9 on 10' and written *9/10-pt*. For still more space they might have 9 on 11 (*9/11-pt*). This is known as 'leading' (pronounced *ledding*) from the practice of inserting blank slugs of lead between lines in hot metal typesetting. Line spacing can be formatted to suit style in photocomposition, which adapts easily to house practice. Sans serif typefaces and those with large x-heights benefit particularly from leading, as do wide lines, but too much leading or line space looks worse than none.

Measuring the number of lines in a column is simple because rulers in editorial offices are marked not only in inches or centimetres but in lines of type, with 5 and 10-point on one edge, 6 and 12-point on another, and there are also plastic measures or type gauges calibrated in a much wider range of settings.

One complication of the points system is that France and some other countries use a different version – the Didot point – which is slightly bigger at 0.1776in. (4.51104mm), so that there are $67\frac{1}{2}$ Didot points to an inch rather than 72. And a third form of measurement has now emerged. This is a metric system known as 'cap height', because it measures the height of capital letters in millimetres. In this system the space between lines is called 'line feed', and is also measured in millimetres. Metric measurement is growing, due to the rapid advance of computerized printing, although most systems still measure in points.

Column widths

The space to be occupied depends also on the width of the columns and the traditional measurement used by printers and journalists is the *em*. Strictly, this is the square of any typesize, so there can be 6-pt ems measuring 6 points by 6 points, and 10-pt ems measuring 10 points by 10 points. In practice, when talking about an em, journalists and printers mean a 12-pt em, sometimes known as a pica, which is the width of a 12-point, or pica, letter 'm'; though all that is necessary to remember is that it is one-sixth of an inch. So a width a lay person would call 2 inches is known to printers as 12 ems, and 3 inches is 18 ems.

Some typographers claim that for the easiest reading a line should be about one and a half alphabets. As an alphabet consists of 26 letters, this means 39 characters to a line. It is not necessary to accept this slavishly, but certainly the wider a column, the larger the type and the greater the leading needed for easy reading, and the longer paragraphs should be made.

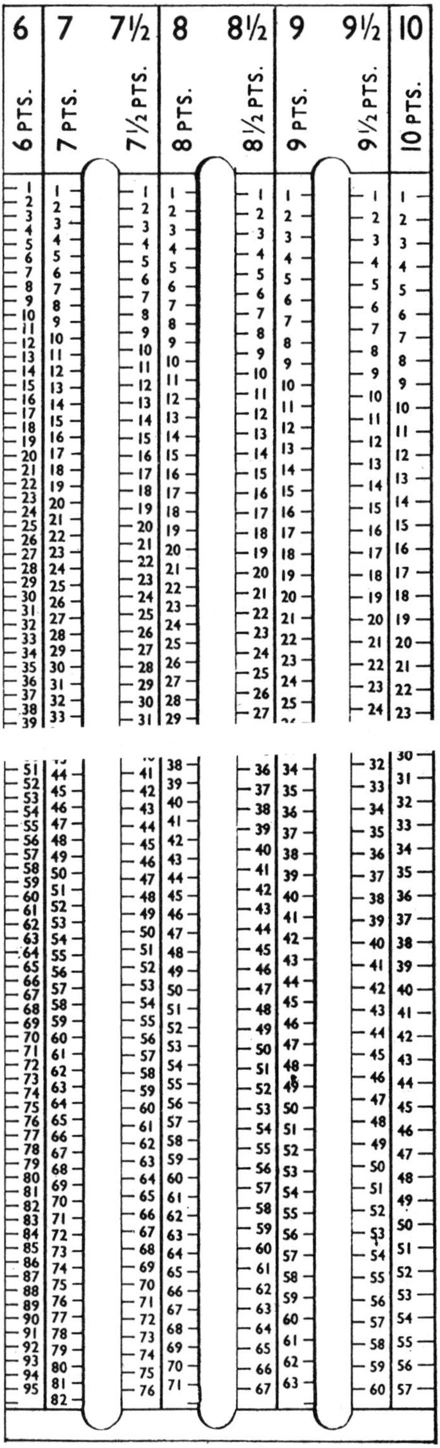

Figure 13   *A type gauge*

Most magazines have columns of 9 to 18 ems because narrower measures can result in too many broken words at the ends of lines and patterns of white space known as 'rivers', while anything wider can be difficult to follow. Many publications use different measures for variety: for example, three columns to a page for general features, two columns for book serializations and short stories, four columns for readers' letters and news.

Half an em is known as an *en* (which some veterans call a nut). This is variable like the em, a 6-pt en being 3 points wide, a 10-point en being five points wide, but again the word en without qualification means a 12-pt en, and is therefore a twelfth of an inch. It is written as a half em, e.g. *11½ ems*. Its other use is that, as an en is the average width of a normal lower case letter, typesetters traditionally quote for contracts at so many pounds per thousand ens.

There is no difficulty about working in ems: 12-point graduations on office rulers correspond to ems (and 6-point to ens).

However, setting widths in computerized systems are usually formatted in picas and points, due to an American preference for these terms over ems and ens. A pica is, as has been said already, simply another name for a 12-pt em, so the main difference is that a setting width of 11½ ems would become 11 picas and 6 points, expressed as *11p6*. This system is a little more precise than that of ems and ens: for example, a measurement might be given as *10p9*, meaning 10 picas and 9 points. Where setting widths are frequently used, they can be formatted on to one key, which saves time in keyboarding setting instructions.

For measurements other than those for typesetting, e.g. picture widths, art departments now tend to use centimetres and millimetres when designing pages.

Justified, unjustified

A further consideration after type size and column width is the way in which text should be arranged in a column. The commonest is 'justified', which means that lines start flush with the left-hand margin and end flush with the right-hand margin (as in this book), words being spaced or broken and hyphenated at the end of lines to make them fit. Spacing between words obviously varies.

Sometimes, however, for contrast, features such as the readers' letters page are set *unjustified*, and some magazines are set entirely in this style. Unjustified lines are usually *ranged left*, which means they start flush with the left-hand margin and are ragged at the right, like a typescript, though it is also possible to have them *ranged right*, in which case the ragged edge will be to the left; this is mainly used when a caption is placed to the left of a picture

Among the brightest
stars of the candidates
for the White House are
the husband-and-wife
team Bob and Liddy
Dole. The problem is,
the pundits can't work
out which one is doing
the running

No longer do they rule
the roost, wear black and
expect to be waited on.
Today's grandmothers
are an independent lot
while still cherishing a
special relationship with
their children's offspring

Despite the horrified
squeaks of protest when
they get sent down, the
ex-public school upper
classes take to life
behind bars so
remarkably well, some
of them are almost sorry

Figure 14
*Unjustified type,
ranged left,
ranged right and
centred*

in order that the lines butt against the edge of the picture, though this is harder for the eye to scan. In unjustified setting words are not broken at the right-hand edge, and the word spacing is standard.

Two other styles are *centred*, in which lines are ragged on both edges, and *asymmetrical*, in which lines are of different lengths arranged according to the designer's whim. But these styles are used only for display purposes, such as standfirsts introducing features.

Picture selection and retouching

Having assessed roughly the space needed for the words, an artist turns to the illustrations, colour transparencies and black and white prints. He or she normally spreads out colour on a light box, though for important pictures transparencies may be put in a slide projector.

An artist looks first for a key picture. It could be a portrait or an action shot, but it should have impact and set the scene for the feature. For instance, if a feature is about an opera singer's gross bulk, a head and shoulders portrait is inadequate; the picture should show him full length and looking bloated, or seated and eating. Features about sporting champions should show them in action rather than in repose. A feature about a haunted castle or a fast car needs a picture that conveys the mood. Unfortunately, the most dramatic picture may show movement or be less than sharp, and the best picture technically may be static and the least interesting, and often a compromise has to be accepted.

The key picture will be given the biggest space on the page. Others will complement it, for it is rarely a good idea to print all pictures the same size; the result tends to look like a snapshot album, and no one picture has any impact. In mono, if the key picture is to be reproduced at the same size as the print, subsidiary pictures might be reduced to half size. With colour, a key transparency might be enlarged three times and the others only twice.

Sometimes, when a picture has a fussy or muddled background, the central figure may be isolated to increase impact. Although known as 'cut-outs', the pictures need not be actually scissored. It is only necessary for an artist to outline the figure with a thick line of process white ink to separate it from the background. On other occasions an artist may touch out a confusing background, such as a telegraph pole that appears to be growing out of someone's head, with an aerosol spray or brush of neutral grey.

Black specks on a mono picture can be lifted with the point of a scalpel, and white spots filled in with a dot of black watercolour. A scratch mark, particularly if it falls on a person's face, may similarly be retouched. This work is normally done in the darkroom, which may also be asked on occasion to combine two prints.

**FRISKY
BUSINESS**

SHALL WE PRANCE?

enters a room without his constant companion; humour.

Indeed, Gaultier sees little distinction between fashion and the somewhat rarefied artform of classical dance, 'It is, after all, just another form of expression.'

Furthermore, Gaultier was 'very excited' at the prospect of working with someone as 'energetic and revolutionary' as Chopinot. The feeling was a mutual one.

Gaultier met Chopinot, who'd moved expressly from Lyons to Paris to set up her own company, after she'd tried, unsuccessfully, for three months to 'get an appointment with Thierry Mugler'.

'But,' she says, 'I realised that even if the elusive appointment materialised, I'd probably have no rapport with

someone so unapproachable and cut off from reality.'

A friend suggested that Chopinot contact Gaultier, then a newcomer on the international fashion circuit, who prided himself on being accessible (an attitude copped from British 'street fashion' – JPG is an ardent Anglophile) even if his prices were not. After one telephone call, Chopinot had an appointment and their rapport was instant.

'The moment I walked into the room and met Jean Paul, I knew I had found a friend and, more importantly at the time, a designer for my ballet.'

Gaultier's ignorance of dance design proved to be a

18

Figure 15 *Example of a cut-out from* Elle

Figure 16   *Improving pictures by altering backgrounds*

With colour these are skilled jobs that can only be done in specialist art houses with the expensive equipment and expert staff required. There the first job is always to duplicate and enlarge a transparency to 10 × 8 in so that it is big enough to work on. Retouching is always done on a 'dupe', never on the original. Specialist colour houses are adept at removing crow's-feet and wrinkles, opening eyes, lightening and brightening, removing local colour casts (tinges of alien colour perhaps reflected from a wall or car) and fading down to allow overprinting of type. A girl in a bikini photographed in a studio can be given a new background of sparkling sea, while a sailing boat seen leaving an unphotogenic harbour can be relocated off a coral island.

Such trickery, which is accomplished by masking out girl and boat and overprinting, is simpler with black and white pictures and can usually be handled in an office darkroom. However, while such practices are acceptable in order to improve innocuous illustrations, they should not be used freely. There is no harm in photographing an actor in a Father Christmas outfit in a studio and then superimposing him on a snowscape, nor need there be too much concern about an obvious and light-hearted spoof, such as creating a montage depicting a Chancellor of the Exchequer as a bishop or a policeman – provided he has a sense of humour – but attempting to pass off a faked picture as genuine is unethical.

Sizing pictures

The mathematical way to find out how deep a picture will be if enlarged or reduced to a certain width is to multiply the required width by the actual depth and divide by the actual width. A simple example is a print 8 in wide and 10 in deep (a common size), which is to be reduced to 4 in wide. The sum is therefore $4 \times 10 \div 8 = 5$ in., and this is obviously correct because the picture is being halved in size, but it does not matter if two different units of measurement, such as inches and ems, are mixed. The depth will be in the same units as the required width. So, if working in ems and reducing the picture to 24 ems wide, the sum is $24 \times 10 \div 8 = 30$ ems.

To discover how wide a picture will be if enlarged or reduced to a certain depth, multiply required depth by actual width and divide by actual depth. Assume the same 10in. × 8in. print is to be reduced to 100mm deep. Then multiply 100 by eight and divide by 10, and the answer is 80mm.

The practical, as opposed to mathematical, way of working (which has more uses) is by scaling the picture with a diagonal line. With a black and white print this is easy. A Chinagraph grease pencil is sometimes used on the surface of the print, but this is not good practice. It is better to place the picture face down on a light box; it is then possible to work on the back of the print. Better still is to use an overlay of tracing paper and even then markings should be made with minimum pressure. (A felt tip pen is suitable).

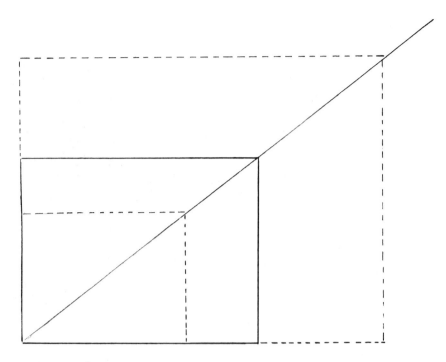

Figure 17 *Sizing a picture. In the sketch broken lines indicate a possible reduction and enlargement*

If a straight reduction of the entire picture is required, select the critical dimension required, either width or depth. Assume a print 10 in wide and 8 in deep is to be reduced to 30 ems wide. Using a ruler, draw a diagonal from the bottom left of the picture to the top right. Measure 30 ems from the left edge of the picture to cut the diagonal and draw another line down from that point to the bottom of the picture. The two lines show the reduced area of the picture, which will, of course, be 24 ems deep. The instruction can be written on the overlay: 'Reduce to 24 ems deep × 30 ems wide'. (It is customary to give depth first, width second.)

To enlarge a picture, place a larger sheet of tracing paper over the print, draw the diagonal and extend it until it reaches the desired width (or height).

It is clearly impossible to work this way on a 35 mm transparency, because it is too small. One answer is to Sellotape a transparency (in a protective sleeve) to copy paper and make the marks on the paper, but this is inaccurate. Normal procedure is to have a rough black and white enlargement made from the transparency in the darkroom and to work on that; alternatively, there are desktop devices which will produce an instant Polaroid enlargement print from a transparency.

Figure 18   *Overall areas of photographs and drawings always reduce or enlarge along their diagonals*

Figure 19 *A straight reproduction of the whole of a photograph, an illustration of the same size achieved by enlarging a portion of the original, and a different format achieved by cropping*

Picture cropping

In practice, the whole of a picture is rarely used. A print 10 in deep by 8 in wide may include an uninteresting expanse of sky and a 2 in strip could be trimmed off the top of the picture without loss. In that case, after positioning the overlay, a horizontal line is ruled 2 in below the top edge, reducing the picture area to 8 in square, and the scaling process is carried out on that area.

For real impact, however, it is often better to crop a picture drastically. Pictures tend to have more impact the further they are removed from a square format, so a picture may be cropped to tall and thin, or wide and shallow; the method of scaling remains the same. A picture may also be cut at an angle, or tilted. A featureless patch of foreground or shadow may be 'pierced' with a panel cut out to carry the caption or 'notched' with a three-sided slot to accommodate one end of a headline – a useful device for linking a headline and text. Corners may be rounded with the aid of a mask; in a story about television, for example, it is appropriate to round corners to suggest a television screen.

Because it may be expensive to call for a considerable number of enlargements or reductions on a page – a printing contract usually stipulates a maximum number of 'proportions' per page, or an average over all pages – black and white pictures may be printed in the office darkroom to the actual dimensions required so that they can all be sent for reproduction S/S (same size). Alternatively a number may be schemed to have the same amount of reduction, perhaps half or one-third print size, and may be mounted on a board as they will appear on the page; this way all the pictures will be reduced in one operation under the process camera and the sizing controls need not be altered, and the work is charged as a single reduction. However, this means accepting a compromise exposure, averaging the pictures, so they need to be of much the same degree of tone and contrast.

Design

With words counted and pictures selected, an artist can begin the work of design, which is done on a layout sheet, sometimes known as a grid (see Figure 20). This is rather larger than a spread (two facing pages) in the magazine, with generous margins for instructions, so that everything can be shown at the actual size it will occupy. Printed rules, usually pale blue so that they will not show up when photographed or photocopied, indicate actual page areas before and after trimming at the bindery, the type area within the trimmed pages, and columns and margins. Columns are ruled in the magazine's normal format, maybe five of 9 ems each per page.

On some magazines the same layout sheets provide a choice between, say, three columns of 15 ems (shown by unbroken rules) and four columns of 11 ems (shown by dotted lines), though this can be confusing. Other magazines provide different layout sheets for different formats, and usually they are provided in two weights – flimsy paper to allow tracing of pictures and headings, and thin card on to which proofs can be pasted.

Down the sides of the layout sheet are marked either lines of the standard type – there might be 78 of 9-point – or units of 5 mm, from 0 to perhaps 275 mm. Some layout sheets are also ruled in horizontal lines, dividing the pages into rectangles. Pictures are meant to be cropped to meet those lines, and type to begin or end on them, which gives a more disciplined effect. But trends are against too much discipline.

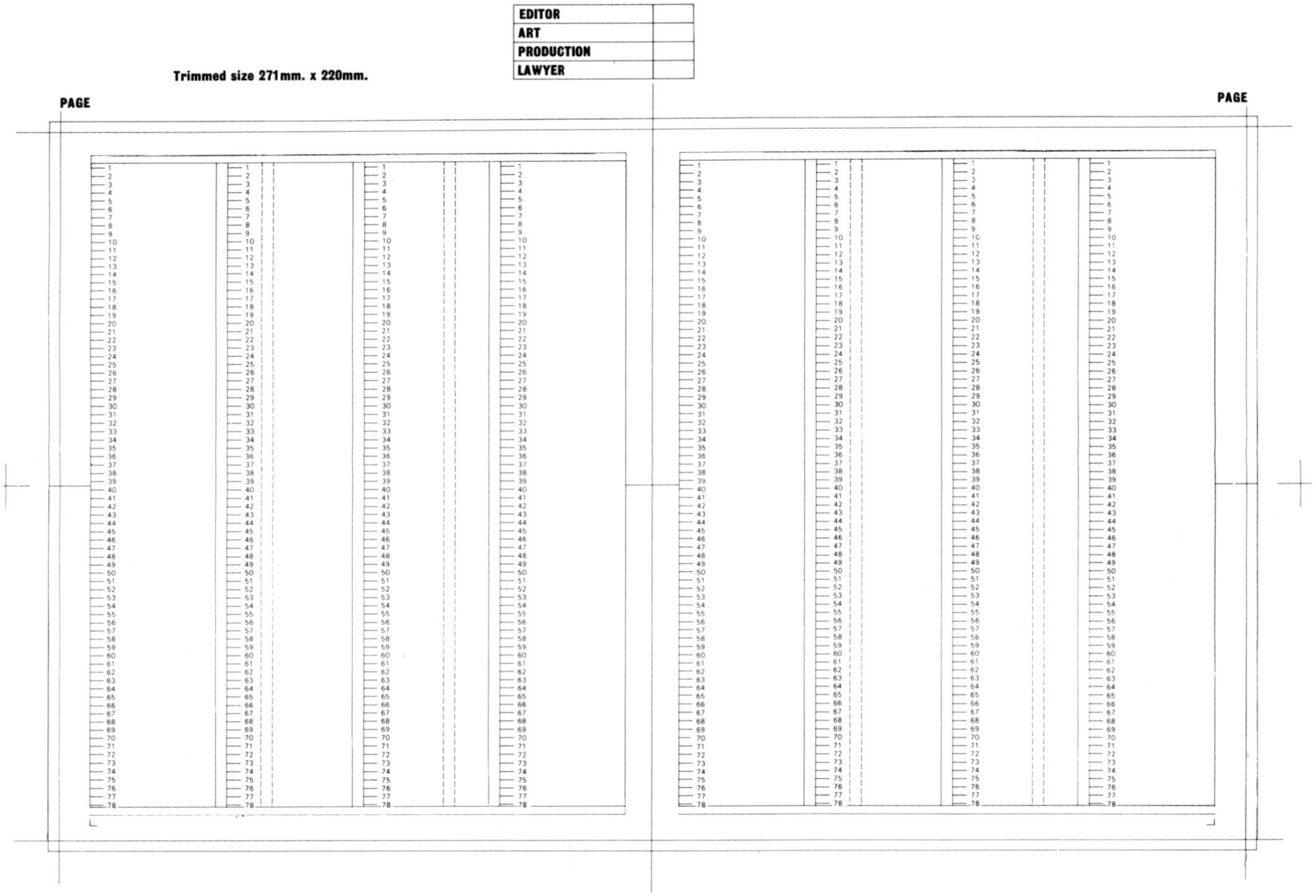

Trimmed size 271mm. x 220mm.

EDITOR	
ART	
PRODUCTION	
LAWYER	

PAGE

PAGE

Figure 20 *Example of a layout sheet*

ON WITH THE DANCE

Having recovered from her ignominious dismissal from TV-am, Angela Rippon's putting her best foot forward in 1988 as the new presenter of BBC1's *Come Dancing*

Mention *Come Dancing* to all but the programme's most dedicated followers and certain images will waltz before their eyes. Several million miles of billowing tulle to begin with. Closely followed by Latin American frills that enter the ballroom a yard or more ahead of the wearer of the garment. And then those chilling fixed grins: too-white teeth surrounded by tired, waxen skin. It's all somewhere between those ancient Anna Neagle and Michael Wilding movies and *Nightmare On Elm Street*.

This may not be exactly what flickered through Angela Rippon's mind when she was first asked

REPORT BY BILL HAGERTY
PICTURES BY JOHN ROGERS

Figure 21 *A spread from* You Magazine/Mail on Sunday *with two bled-off pictures. The one on the left has been bled-off on two edges of the page, the one on the right on three edges. The central gutter is the white margin between the two facing pages*

to present a new series of the programme, but she admits to remembering it was somewhat . . . well . . . old-fashioned. 'I hadn't watched *Come Dancing* in a long time,' she says, 'and there was this image of ladies with gownless evening straps or looking like sequinned barrage balloons. But I was sent a couple of recent tapes and they were astonishing.

'The dancers are all so *young* – nearly all under 25 – and their energy and showmanship is amazing. The Latin American section now is the sort of thing you would expect to see at a cabaret and in the Offbeat section they are coming out with things you saw in movies like *Saturday Night Fever* and *Flashdance* and *Seven Brides For Seven Brothers*. It really is a revelation.'

It is, too. And so, come to that, is Ms Rippon. Stomping back and forth across the ballroom floor at the Guildhall, Southampton, where *Come Dancing* is being recorded for transmission by BBC1 early next year, she is patently having a jolly good time. She laughs a lot and has the demeanour of someone whose life, if not exactly a bowl of cherries, is bearing fruit nicely.

'Well, I am very lucky,' she says, pausing in her cavernous Guildhall dressing-room. 'I've had the opportunity to do such a variety of work and now, after 21 years in television, I have gone back to doing all the things I was doing before I read the national news as well as other programmes of the type I made at that time, like *The Antiques Roadshow*. All that came to an end when I went to work for TV-am. That was when I thought, "Where do I go from here?"'

It is a little less than five years since Ms Rippon, as one of the Famous Five, helped launch the ITV breakfast-time station. She was sacked after two months, an experience which, she now reveals, came close to wrecking her career.

'That was a bad time for me because nobody would give me a job. I was unemployable. There must have been other reasons, but I was suing TV-am – a case I won – and I assume people did not want to be associated with someone involved in a court case with an ITV company. I don't really know. Anyway, nobody would employ me, apart from Capital Radio in London and Channel 4. Capital was absolutely marvellous and Jeremy Isaacs was the only controller in any ITV company who would actually give me some time. But it was a bad patch and the reason why I went to work in America. The offer of a job in Boston was just right. It allowed me to prove to myself that I could still do it.'

After a year in the United States she bounced back to Britain and plunged into a new work pattern which led to *Masterteam*, two 'outdoor' series for BBC Bristol and periods standing in for Jimmy Young on his Radio 2 show, a happy chore she will be repeating at Christmas and New Year. And now *Come Dancing*, the longest-running musical television series in the world.

As *CD*'s presenter she follows the urbane David Jacobs, whose smooth manner suited the show but who never got to wear any nice frocks. The hanging-rail in Ms Rippon's dressing-room bears evidence that she has been busy shopping for the gowns she will wear, a different one for each of the five heats and two more for the semi-final and final. 'Basically,' says Angela, 'I ▷

She might have wide-ranging tastes as these two outfits show, but Angela Rippon's clothes 'have to fit the mood of the programme and I have to feel comfortable in them'

111

On the layout sheet the artist begins roughing out the design, trying to reflect the nature of the feature. A story about gangsters or war needs tough, stark treatment, a touching love story a daintier approach. Because a page can have colour does not mean that every picture, headline and panel must be in colour, unless a garish appearance is sought. A mixture of colour and black and white is often more effective. Sometimes the use of both colour and mono actually helps a story. For example, in a profile of a veteran television actor it is appropriate to show his current work in colour, and pictures of him from the 1950s (before viewers saw television in colour) in black and white, even thought colour stills may have been shot at the time. There are many other occasions when it is helpful to use colour for modern pictures and mono for flashbacks.

If a feature opens with a spread (two facing pages), the artist may scheme the headline to run right across the page, but this requires caution. There are no problems when the pages constitute a natural spread, as in the centre of a small magazine, and can be treated as one page (though it is necessary to be sure that staples will not spoil the appearance of a picture, protruding through perhaps an eye or a nose). On a split spread it may be asking too much of the folding to expect the headline to be level, and half a character may be concealed in the central gutter. Similarly, the left and right halves of a portrait placed across two pages may not quite align.

Bleed offs

The key picture may be schemed to go top right, the headline top left, a picture linking the two pages. Where possible, if the printing contract permits, the artist will bleed a picture, which means taking it right off the page, across the margin, because bleeding increases the area of the picture, and gives it more impact. A picture can be bled off top, bottom, outside edge and into the central gutter of the page – all four for maximum effect – but a bleed must extend at least 3mm beyond the trim line to allow for trimming at the bindery. It is therefore dangerous to bleed a picture which has any vital detail near an edge to be trimmed.

A big picture should not normally be placed at the bottom of a page, where it looks as if it might fall out, particularly if bled. Nor should it go across the middle of a page with text continuing from above to below it; the eye tends to move on to the next column rather than looking beneath the picture. (However, the space below such a picture can be used very successfully for a box or separate piece of copy.) Big pictures should normally go at the top of a page, where type holds them up.

Figures 22 and 23   *Portraits should look into pages rather than out of them*

Picture balance

Portraits of people should have them looking into a page rather than out of it, which will lead readers' eyes off the page; and cars should be travelling into a page, not out of it. Therefore an artist may need to ask the picture desk if there is a shot of the subject facing the other way. Sometimes a picture may be reversed, but this can be dangerous if done unthinkingly. Someone is standing in front of a shop sign, a poster or a clock which appears to be seen in a mirror. Retired admirals have come near to having heart attacks when magazines have shown naval officers on parade with medals on the wrong side of their chests and swords in their left hands, owing to inadvertent reversal.

A quick calculation then to see if copy and pictures are likely to fit is necessary. It may be possible to increase or reduce the proposed size of the pictures or a headline, but an artist must bear in mind the house style, which may rule on the amount of white space around a headline. An artist will not normally be too inhibited by trying to accommodate every last word of a feature, unless told that the words are sacrosanct – for example, the work of an eminent or difficult writer. On popular, display-conscious magazines it is considered not worth spoiling a good layout for the sake of a few lines of copy, which subs can easily cut; but on others, such as scientific journals, words are regarded as more important.

Headings

Some magazines, such as news reviews, have a standard style and position for headlines, and the artist has only to indicate this on the layout. On other magazines there is more freedom, and an artist can use his imagination as regards positioning and size. Headings may be centred, ranged left or right, or staggered. With headings of several lines, the length of the lines should usually be varied, e.g. long, short, long, short. It looks better if the first line is longer than the second.

The editor may already have indicated the required headline on the copy, for it is often helpful to settle the selling point or treatment of a feature early on. For example, the chosen headline may be the single word RAPE!, to be displayed as boldly as the width of the pages allows, with an introductory strapline above it, explaining the reason for the feature. The artist will choose appropriate headline type to hit readers between the eyes. On the other hand, a headline on a feature about autograph-collecting might be in a cursive script like copperplate handwriting, on a royal wedding in an elegant italic, on a secretary in Typewriter type, or on a Gothic horror story in drawn letters dripping blood.

ADGE

ABCDIKLMNOP

ABCERSTUWZ

ABHIJMS

ABDCFI

ATMO

Figure 24 *Some headline types: Plantin Titling, Gloria Condensed Titling, Condensed Titling, Gill Bold Condensed Titling, Wondersans Outline Titling and Gill Extra Heavy Titling*

Money loses
its voice

Cunard's
novice sailor

Figure 25 *Conventional wisdom is that, in a two-deck heading, it looks better if the top deck is longer than the lower one*

Headlines once tended to be in capitals but it has become accepted that everyday upper and lower case is easier to read. Some magazines maintain a strange style in which every word other than short prepositions and conjunctions is decorated with an initial capital. This makes for a Curious and Unattractive Spotty Effect: for instance, this headline from America's *National Enquirer* on a widower raising five babies:

> I Could Tear My Hair Out
> When They All Cry at Once
> – But Their Smiles Make
> My Life Worth Living

For headlines a word count is not accurate enough; a character count is required. This means counting every character and space, though with large type a simple character count is not accurate enough either, because, unlike typewritten characters, printed ones are not all given the same space. *M* and *W* are thick and *I* and *J* are thin. As a rule of thumb, capital *M* and *W* are counted as two units each, *I* and punctuation marks and spaces as half units, and other capital letters as one and a half units. Lower case *m* and *w* are one and a half units, *f, i, j, l, t* and interword spaces are all half units, and all other lower case letters are single units. For greater accuracy, letters can be traced from a type book.

In a computerized office, however, a proposed headline can be viewed on screen in the desired size. Computers have also solved the size limitations which were imposed by hot metal type. It used to be the case that a range might offer 36-point, which would make an intended headline too short to fill the space, and 42-point, which would make it too long. What was required was perhaps 40-point, which might not exist in the printer's stock.

Figure 26 *An unconventional style of heading on a short story (top), and an appropriate one on a feature about handwriting (bottom) in* Over 21

One answer was to set in 42-point and reduce the result photographically to fit. (Better reproduction is obtained by reducing rather than enlarging.) However, with computerized setting it is only necessary to specify the required width and the computer will produce type to fit exactly, perhaps $41\frac{1}{2}$-point, which never existed in metal type, though if this capability is exercised too freely a magazine will have too many variations of type size and look undisciplined.

Alternatively, an artist may choose to use Letraset rub-down adhesive letters, available in a wide range of standard styles; or, for a special effect, have the headline hand-lettered.

Frequently, on a routine feature, no headline has been written and it will be left to the sub-editors to write it. Then the artist will simply scheme some gobbledygook in a space of suitable size, based on the magazine's normal headline type.

Boxes and panels

An artist may build in one or more boxes, a useful device for breaking up a

FILM TEST

WORTH THE WAITING: GOLD 400

On sale on Monday, Kodak's Gold 400 at last gives the range a high speed option. How good is it?

Kodak's much-delayed Gold 400 colour print film finally hits a shop near you next Monday. First announced at the Photokina show in Germany this time last year, the film has almost been available a couple of times since then, but various factors have held up its launch. Now this film, made and packed in the UK — so who says we haven't got a photographic industry? — is about to take its place in the high-speed shapshot film battle, just in time for the shortening days of autumn and winter.

The importance of ISO 400 films shouldn't be underestimated, even in these days of superfast film like Kodak's own VR1000, Fuji's Super HR 1600 and even Konica's new SR-V3200. After all, for millions of owners of snapshot cameras, the low-light shooting choice is simple — put away the camera or use an ISO 400 film. That's because plenty of snapshot compacts have just two film speed settings — ISO 100 and 400. So the implication is that you use ISO 100 in good light, switching to ISO 400 when lighting levels drop or the weather gets worse.

VIVID BUT CONTROLLED

Surprising, then, that Kodak have taken so long adding an ISO 400 film to their Kodacolor Gold range. The faster product has been on the cards ever since the company first rolled out Gold 100, but somehow things haven't gone too smoothly, and the debut has been repeatedly delayed.

So now it's here, how good is it? Good, is the simple answer — the film will more than stand up to the challenge of Fuji's Super HR 400 print material, which must be the nearest rival to Kodak's debutant. In situations from bright sunlight to after-dark pictures of neon lights, the film turned in results which had colours at once vivid and controlled. What's more, there was none of the granularity we encountered with Konica's 3200 film, for

example, just good solid black where there should have been blacks, and detail in the shadows where that was appropriate.

In fact, looking at the prints through a magnifying glass showed the grain was extremely restrained, true to Kodak's claim of improved sharpness and reduced grain. This bodes well for enlargements made from Gold 400 negatives. The secret behind this improvement lies in the tabular-grain (T-grain) technology introduced in Kodak's VR1000 film, and later adapted to Gold 100 and 200, which have been on sale for some time.

Colours are punchy in Gold 400 shots, if not as brilliant as those from Fuji, for example. But then the colour handling is a matter of taste — if you like your colours larger than life, go for the Fuji, if you want them a little more natural pick Kodacolor Gold. How does Gold 400 compare with Gold 100? Well, the colours aren't quite as 'jump-out-of-the-print' on the faster material, but there seems to be little extra grain as a trade-off for the added sensitivity.

Kodak say of Gold 400 that it gives improved colour reproduc-

tion over rival products in the green, blue, yellow and red areas of the spectrum. That's interesting — a major Fuji strength has always been its ability to reproduce greens accurately.

One very impressive aspect of the performance of the new Kodak film is its handling of mixed lighting. We shot a whole lot of portraits around the **CW** offices, which have a particularly nasty mix of lighting. Apart from the big windows, there's fluorescent background lighting with a little tungsten, in the form of spotlights, mixed in. Not the best of conditions under which to shoot flattering pictures, but Gold 400 coped well, whether trying to handle daylight or artificial lighting.

NATURAL SKINTONES

The negatives were good enough to let the minilab we use produce fairly natural-looking skintones. True, the tungsten-lit shots were a little warm, and the fluorescent-lit pictures slightly cool, but neither would be noticeable unless you knew what you were looking for. In other words, Gold 400 passed all the snapshot tests with flying, and pretty

natural-looking colours.

While snapshooters will be delighted with Gold 400, the enthusiast is going to be pretty pleased, too — it's amazing how much more usable the ISO 400 sensitivity can make your camera when you need to shoot action in failing light. And if you've an interest in nature or macro work in the great outdoors, the natural colours of this film will be just fine.

Indoors? Well, we've already shown how good the film is with low indoor lighting levels — you need only look at the portrait shot on the page opposite to see that. Now admittedly we were using a Minolta 7000 with an autofocus 100mm f2 lens on it, but the fact that we were getting an exposure of 1/100sec at f2.8 suggests this kind of shot will be possible with much more modest gear.

Prices? This film will be available in 35mm only at first, at £2.29 for a 12-shot roll, £3.15 for a 24-shotter, and £3.99 for a 36-frame cassette.

Worth the wait for Gold 400? You bet! This is a film that's going to win a lot of friends through the gloomy days of autumn and winter ahead! ∎

HOW THE OTHER ISO 400 PRINT FILMS COMPARE

At the beginning of August, we published a test of all the then-available ISO 400 colour print films, and featured in that test a preview of Gold 400. At the time, test samples of Kodak's new films weren't available, so now we've taken another look at that test, and compared those films with Gold 400.

The most noticeable aspect of Kodak's new film is its almost total lack of

grain, which attracted plenty of comment in the CW office.

● Agfa XR/XRS 400: Hobby and pro film respectively, very good on natural colours such as greens.

● Boots 400: Good grain, but reds, greens a little muted.

● Fuji Super HR 400: Nearest on performance to Kodak, fine grain, strong greens and bright colours.

● Konica SR 400: Colours a little subdued, but fine

grain — look out for the new SR-V400 on its way.

● Ilfocolor HR 400: Good colours, good shadow detail, but the film is let down a little by noticeable grain structure.

● Scotch HR 400: Unobtrusive grain, reds and greens muted but blues, in particular, very strong.

● Tudor XL 400: Good, natural colours — a little grainy, and shadow detail rendition could be better.

Page 68 CAMERA WEEKLY October 3 1987

Figure 27   *Use of a box: a page from* Camera Weekly *about a new film, with comparable films listed in a tinted box*

page. A feature about a racehorse trainer, for example, may incorporate a list of the trainer's successes, which can be better set out in a table in a fact

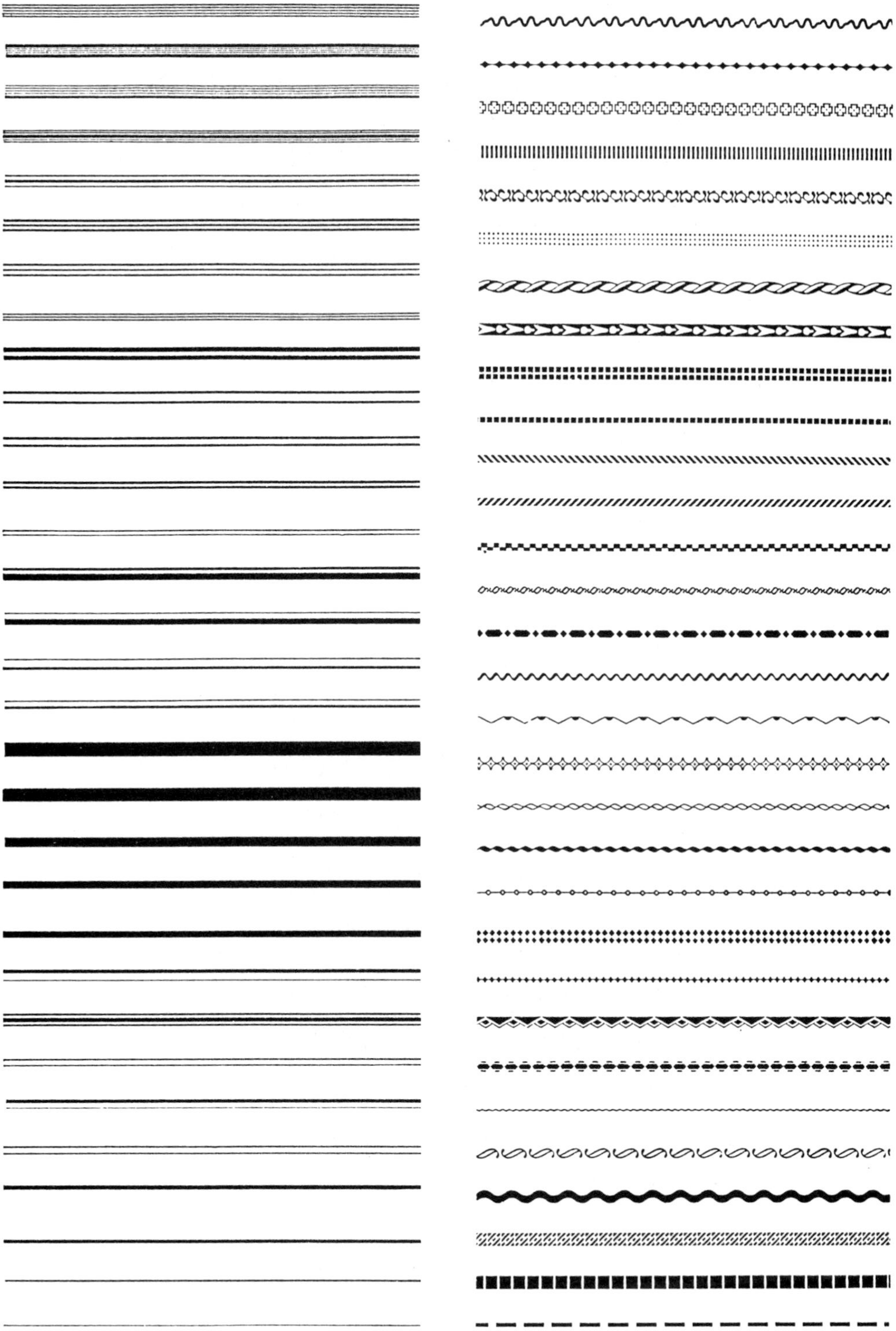

Figure 28 *Examples of rules*

Figure 29 *Examples of ornate borders*

box or a linked panel known as a sidebar. This can add to the visual attractiveness of the page and also make the main feature easier to read. A feature about a wedding in a soap opera might incorporate a list of previous marriages and divorces in the soap, and one about a new fighter aircraft a history of its predecessors; these may be separated similarly. The designer may enclose a box with fancy rules or place it on a tone panel, provided by a mechanical tint – a film of dots available in a range of densities increasing in 10 per cent steps.

To brighten the display an artist may decide that every paragraph will start with a small open or closed circle or square, or call for 'hanging indents', which is the reverse of the usual practice of indenting the first line of every paragraph. Instead, the first lines of paragraphs are set 'full out', so that they run the full width of the column, and all the following lines are indented.

Another possibility is to 'reverse out' type to appear as white on black, though this is not as legible in small sizes as black on white. Type should be large enough to prevent filling in by ink, so light types, particularly serif

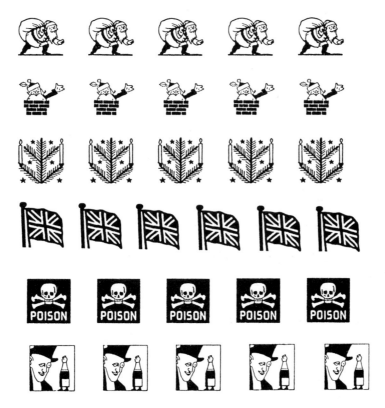

Figure 30 *Conventional typebreakers held in stock by many printers*

types, should be avoided; for clarity a bold sans serif type of 12-point size is best. A strapline (an introductory headline above the main one) may also be reversed out white on black, or overprinted on a mechanical tint. On a colour page the possibilities are many. After black on white the most legible colours for type panels are black on yellow, followed by green on white, blue on white and red on white. The worst are red on yellow, green on red, and red on green.

Typebreakers

There are several ways of breaking up long slabs of text. One is to use subheadings – known as crossheads if they are centred in the column, sideheads if ranged to one side. Except in a trade publication or an instructional work, where they may relate to steps in a procedure, such as *Stripping*, *Priming*, *Undercoating*, they normally have no function other than breaking up the text or filling out space. Usually they consist of single words, *Regrets*, *Remorse*, *Forgiveness* or a few words such as *Happy days*, *End of a dream*, *My shame*, taken from the text.

They can be set in capitals or italics or in a contrasting face, such as a sans serif when the body type is seriffed; they can be underscored, boxed, overprinted on a tone panel, or reversed out white on a black panel. Normally the first line after a crosshead will be set 'full out' without any indent.

On occasions some magazines use a small piece of artwork such as a holly leaf in a Christian issue, wedding bells in a story about a marriage, or clown masks in a circus story – printers can often provide such embellishments from stock – but this is an old-fashioned device. Many magazines create a line space and begin the next section with an oversize capital letter descending perhaps four or five lines (though it may be as many as 11) and therefore known as a 'drop cap'. The text is indented to fit round it, following the shape of the letter. Alternatively it may be a 'raised cap', standing above its line, or a combination, such as one line raised and four below.

Increasingly common, though, is to insert a quote from the feature in bold type centred or sandwiched between two horizontal rules, or with a vertical rule down the left hand edge. For example:

'It wouldn't do if everyone
was as ambitious as
we are. But then we want
something more, something
extra out of life'

RONALD REAGAN HAD THE choice of labeling himself a liar or an incompetent. He could have admitted what most people suspect—that he knew and approved of the plan to use the ayatollah's money to fund the rebels in Afghanistan, Angola, and Nicaragua—the latter diversion an apparent violation of both

Peter Ustinov is a man of a thousand faces and accents. But the face and accent he most likes are those of Belgian detective Hercule Poirot.

"He's such an ass," Ustinov says delightedly about the character he played in 13 At Dinner, Evil Under The Sun and Death On The Nile.

The 63-year-old actor has retrieved Poirot from the back of his closet for a fourth outing, a TV production of Agatha Christie's Dead Man's Folly.

Harmon didn't work hard in the classroom, though, and when he graduated from high school, he couldn't get into any of the better colleges. He went to a community college for two years, improved his grades, starred on the football team and was wooed by several major universities. He chose UCLA, a ten-minute drive from the family home.

Then last September, after a successful launch into the Japanese fashion market, Peter and Adele headed for London

Figure 31 *Drop caps of 6, 10 and 14 lines, and a raised cap of 9 lines*

'Our love has grown
and grown . . . now
Ross and I just can't
wait to be married!'

'Howard wasn't very
romantic – he once
gave me an umbrella
for Christmas!'

Captions, continuations and rules

Picture captions will be schemed at a length determined by house style. The
best place for them is underneath the pictures to which they refer, ranged
left or right or justified with the last line centred. Second best is beside the
pictures, and ranged left or right against them. A single block of captions
referring readers to pictures, *above left*; *above*; *above right*; *far left*; *left*, and so
on can be hard to follow, while the practice of captioning pictures clockwise or

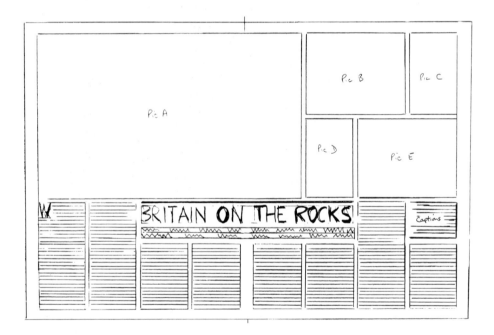

Figure 32 *Example of a simple layout*

anti-clockwise can be even more puzzling. A helpful designer will mark on the layout for the subs how many words or characters the captions need.

An artist will also insert continuation lines inviting the reader to turn a page for the remainder of a feature. These are normally set on a separate line at the foot of the last column on a page, perhaps a line of 9/9½-pt italic ranged right and saying *Continued overpage* or *Continued on page 00*. At the top of the turn page should be a line ranged left in the same type reading, *Continued from page 00*. Symbols such as arrows may be used instead, and symbols may also be inserted to denote the end of a feature.

Rules must also be placed. To separate one feature from another, or from an advertisement, it is common practice to use a ½-pt solid rule, a line bleeding off top and bottom in the case of a vertical separation, or from side to side in the case of a horizontal one.

Figure 33 *Layout for a feature on Rex Harrison in* TVTimes. *The Illustrations are as they are to appear; the heading and the text are cut from old features and are only to indicate position and size. All type sizes are marked on the layout*

Myths of the master of style

*This Wednesday on ITV, veteran actor Rex Harrison gives a rare interview in which he looks back on his distinguished career. Here, **Patrick Garland,** who conducted '...A Damned Serious Business', assesses the true achievement – and the legendary style – of one of Britain's greatest stars.*

Rex Harrison, like another 'incomparable', his hero, Max Beerbohm, is one of Britain's last authentic masters of style. It was appropriate, when we made our film about his distinguished life in the theatre (ITV, Wednesday), that he was staying at the Ritz in his customary fourth floor suite overlooking Green Park.

'I always try to stay there,' he explains, 'because it's handy for the things I like to do and the places I like to visit when I'm in London.

'The old pub [as he calls it] is near my favourite theatre, The Haymarket; is only a walk away from my club; is close to Wiltons for my grub; a stone's throw from Lobbs for my shoes; and close to Locks for my hats...'

Rex Harrison seems to live in the minds of many of his admirers as a legendary brand name, such as Rolls-Royce, Albany or Château d'Yquem – indeed, he is synonymous with things exclusive, elegant and stylish.

People assume he was born into the world as a miniature Professor Higgins, complete with tailored suit and tweed hat, so it comes as something of a shock to discover he is not a native of Mayfair, but of the Liverpool suburb of Huyton.

In those days, Huyton was a tiny village, and Harrison often visited his grandfather's lovely old Georgian house, Bellvale Hall, with its large cricket field, carefully mown croquet lawns, deep lakes, numerous tennis courts and even a rookery.

Somewhere in the past, perhaps after World War One, his family fell upon hard times, and he remembers his aged grandmother 'bowling around in an electric bathchair complaining – "Have to eat hash, have to eat stew, no money, no money, no money..."'

Reginald, as Harrison was christened, was brought up after the war in a semi-detached house in Sefton Park, and went, via a local kindergarten, to Liverpool College.

There, like so many young people before and since, he was inspired to act by an amiable teacher – in this case, his Classics master, Fred Wilkinson.

It was about this time that he decided, rather precociously, that none of the names his family called him by — Reggie, Bobby, Baa – was quite the thing, so instead he chose the name Rex, which he first heard when somebody was calling their dog. In spite of parental reluctance, Rex he has remained ever since.

The second assumption even his greatest fans make is that his celebrated individual style was somehow part of his professional armoury from an early age. Emphatically it was not, and it came as something of a revelation to discover that Rex Harrison endured rejection and hardship in his early years in the theatre.

In the end, he spent more than 10 years touring with 'fit-up' companies around the provinces – from the ends of piers out of season to northern industrial towns such as Rochdale and Wigan.

'Actors and fish' was written all too readily on the railway carriages when the countless regional tours of those days embarked for new destinations each Sunday from Crewe station.

It was a bohemian life, underpaid, long-houred and ill-fed, dependent on the generosity of landladies and the fellowship of other actors.

But it was there – and not in the West End theatres — that the youthful Rex Harrison was taught his craft.

'I learned my job the hard way,' he explains, 'by playing to different audiences – and they *were* different – every single night.'

And he learned the celebrated style from watching, on the nights he was not performing himself, marvellous actors such as Ronald Squire, Charles Hawtrey and Gerald du Maurier.

Barely remembered today, these are the craftsmen who had a lasting and mesmeric influence on the young man watching so intently from the gallery rails.

The glamorous and

Baby Rex Harrison, aged two, in 1910 and (above) debonair in 1939.

romantic side of Rex Harrison's life has attracted a lot of attention over the years.

As he now approaches his 80th birthday, debonair and willowy as ever, I, for one, believe the attention granted to his personal life has overshadowed the true quality of his work.

In ...A Damned Serious Business, the purpose is to re-focus the spotlight where *he* feels it truly belongs – on his years of hard work perfecting a remarkable style, and on his magisterial authority. We look not only at the world of the musical and high comedy (where he reigns supreme) but also at his marvellous performances in the plays of Chekhov, Pirandello and Bernard Shaw. The charm and talent of the man are well illustrated by his personal recollections, and by dazzling excerpts from his finest performances.

Figure 34 *The feature as it actually appeared in* TVTimes

Rex's fair ladies

Now heading for his 80th birthday, Rex Harrison's thirst for life and love is undiminished. He has taken the marriage trail six times, starting in 1934 with Collette Thomas. In 1943 he married German actress Lilli Palmer but was to meet and fall in love with Kay Kendall who, he discovered, was dying of leukaemia. Harrison asked Lilli Palmer for a divorce so he could marry Kay in 1957. Kay died three years later. Harrison's fourth marriage, in 1962, was to Rachel Roberts, and after that was dissolved in 1971 he married the Hon Elizabeth Rees Harris. This ended in 1976 and two years later Harrison wed Mercia Tinker, 30 years his junior.

Left: Rex Harrison as most people think of him – as Professor Higgins in 'My Fair Lady' (1964).

The many wives of Rex Harrison: 1 Collette Thomas. 2 With Lilli Palmer whom he left for Kay Kendall (3). Rachel Roberts (4) was next, followed by Richard Harris's ex, Elizabeth. 6 Current wife, Mercia Tinker.

Final layout

The final layout should show the placing of body copy, the size and positions of pictures, headlines, standfirsts, rules and bars, and any advertisements. The page number should not be forgotten. The layout may be presented in one of three main ways. The simplest is to draw rectangles or squares where pictures are to be placed, marking them A, B, C, onwards, and identifying the appropriate pictures for the printer by marking the same letters on the backs of the prints or the sleeves of the transparencies. The headline will be roughly lettered in the appropriate place, and columns of text indicated by squiggled lines.

Many small magazines are produced in this way, but offices with more staff provide precise layouts. Outlines of the figures or details in pictures are traced on the page at the correct size with the aid of a Grant projector, which will enlarge or reduce artwork. Headlines are lettered accurately and every line of type is ruled in.

A third way is to create dummy pages by pasting monochrome prints or photocopies of the pictures, cropped and sized, in position on the page. If the pictures are not available, other pictures of the same size will be inserted. Headlines, if already set or lettered, will be photographed or photocopied and pasted in position, or a gobbledygook heading of the right size and typeface will be cut from a back number of the magazine and pasted in position. Text will also be pasted in, but again may be gobbledygook, cut from an old copy of the magazine. Incidentally, art departments use Cow Gum rubber solution for the purpose, applied sparingly, because it does not cause pictures to cockle and allows them to be peeled off easily and stuck down elsewhere. The whole will then be photocopied.

This system can be confusing to those outside the art department. One automatically tries to read meaningless text, possibly about foreign royalty, juxtaposed with pictures of weightlifters, who may be the subject of the feature, before realizing it is there purely for display purposes.

The layout, clearly marked with the issue number or date, page numbers, and the pictures and artwork, may then go to the subs. However, if time is short (and it often is), the parcel may go direct to the printer or a reproduction house, after photocopies have been made for the subs to work on.

Computerized layouts

By the second half of the 1980s computerized designing, initially introduced by advertising, and then used experimentally by newspapers, was moving into magazines. Artists sit at video display units, whose screens will allow a spread of two A4 pages side by side, though artists can zoom in to work on a small section and pull out again to see a page or a spread. A hand-held control known as a mouse can move text and graphics around and alter column widths.

Designers begin by inserting the page size and placing vertical and horizontal guidelines on it to establish where various elements are to go. Text from a word processor can be inserted, typefaces and sizes and variations of leading inspected and varied at will. For instance, an artist can change three columns of 10-point type to two columns of 12-point with four quick clicks of the mouse. Graphics can be inserted from libraries on disc, offering hundreds of illustrations suitable for gardening, motoring, cookery and other types of features. These graphics can be stretched or squashed and pasted in where required. Fancy rules can be inserted with two clicks of the mouse, and artists can also command lines, squares and circles or create their own freehand designs. The final design for a page can be printed out from a screen as hard copy for use in the traditional way, or retained as an electronic file for further computerized operations and for ultimate transfer to a printing plate.

Computer technology saves tedious work, but most artists accustomed to roughing out designs with pencil and paper have found that it tends to inhibit their imaginations by enforcing modular or regular shapes; and it will not, of course, make a barely competent designer into a brilliant one. The need for skill and flair remains.

8 SUB-EDITING

From the art department the layout, words and pictures reach the sub-editors – in theory, at least. Often, owing to pressures of time, some pictures will not yet be in the office, or words will be in the process of being rewritten.

Subs and writers are traditional antagonists. Writers regard subs as butchers who delete the best passages in a feature, muddle the point, introduce clichés and destroy rhythm. It is no thanks to the subs, they say, if a feature still reads reasonably well. To subs, on the other hand, writers are practically illiterate, careless with spelling and syntax, frequently missing the point of a feature, indulging in clichés and mixing metaphors; and if a feature reads reasonably well it is mostly due to the subs.

In truth, good subs can trim so skilfully that writers are hard put to it to find where the cuts were made. They can save writers from errors and improve their work. There are also bad subs who turn sensitively written, original features into slick, hackneyed, formula writing.

Writers have the glamour assignments. Subs are expected to be the reliables of the office. They should be neat with corrections and pedantic with grammar, and have orderly minds, a well developed sense for what is new and important, and a large fund of general knowledge. That does not mean necessarily being familiar with Greek legends and knowing the origins of World War One; possibly more useful today is to be knowledgeable about pop music and other interests of young readers, who are sought after by all manner of publications. It helps to have a range of ages and views represented on the subs' desks. They need a working acquaintanceship with the law, and a healthy scepticism about miracle cures and products and all nine-day wonders; they need to be equally suspicious of stories of the oppression of innocents. The buck stops with the subs, for they bear the ultimate responsibility for mistakes in spelling, syntax and checkable facts.

In offices using direct input the way in which they carry out their work has changed, though the nature of it remains the same. The differences are explained at the end of the chapter (page 136), after consideration of traditional methods of handling hard copy, which is the lot of most subs.

Duties of a sub

The chief sub-editor will assess the complexity of a job to be done and elect a sub-editor to handle it. The sub's first action will be to read through the feature to see how much work is required on it, whether the writer needs to be contacted for clarification of any points or additional material, and whether any rewriting is necessary. In theory, of course, a feature should be right when it has been passed by the features editor, and a sub should need to do little more than tick it, as subs call the basics of marking copy for setting, but theory and practice often differ.

The next step is a word count to see that the length matches the space provided on the layout. A helpful artist may have indicated the number of words provided for on the layout, which may mean, in the interests of design, that some words may need to be cut or added. The sub may have to fill out or, if the piece is very short, ask the writer for more words. The sub then attends to any rewriting that may be necessary. Perhaps the intro has missed the point; the editor wants the feature to nose in on a particular angle. Or it may be, if the feature has been in the office some time, that it needs updating. It may be worthy but dull and need brightening. It is hard for a feature writer who has written a feature in a particular way to rethink it, and it is always easier to rewrite someone else's work than one's own.

The sub must excise clichés, unscramble mixed metaphors and correct grammatical mistakes, one of the most common of which is mixing singulars and plurals as in, 'Scotland Yard is investigating; they are questioning neighbours'. Whether Scotland Yard should be singular (as an organization) or plural (because it consists of officers based there) is debatable but it should not be both in the same sentence. The same problem arises with councils, corporations and football clubs, and this is an area in which the chief sub normally lays down rules.

The sub should watch out for double meanings. A distinguished writer once wrote an intro which read, 'What a pity Lady X cannot be stuffed'. This was changed in print to, 'preserved for posterity in wax'.

The sub must watch for possible libel, obviously a greater risk if one is exposing the high expenses of a charity, the poor examination results of an expensive school or the extramarital adventures of an MP than in features about sailing or tennis – though those subjects are not necessarily free from peril. A sub who scents danger should take up the question with the chief sub, who may refer it to the editor or legal reader.

Some publishing houses have legal advisers on the premises, and in the case of magazines specializing in scandal stories all copy may be read by them as a matter of course. On more sedate magazines, perhaps concerned solely with coin-collecting or chess, copy will normally be referred to lawyers only when journalists are anxious. There may be an arrangement to call a solicitor or barrister for advice, although an experienced journalist should be knowledgeable on laws that affect the press. What is needed from a magazine lawyer is advice on how to couch information or allegations safely, rather than a recommendation to delete them, and an able lawyer will make helpful suggestions. In the end, however, lawyers only advise; an editor may ignore the advice and publish, but it requires courage and sureness to do so.

The sub should make sure that nothing it is unsafe to assume is assumed. It is reasonable to assume in a New Year issue that Christmas was celebrated on December 25 but it should not be taken for granted that other events scheduled to take place in the weeks between an issue going to press and its appearance on bookstalls will actually have occurred. A case that should be remembered is of the women's magazine that went to press with a royal feature, written in advance, which described the Queen's bearing at a trooping the colour ceremony. When the magazine appeared, the ceremony had indeed been held, but without the Queen, who had been taken ill. There are enough hazards resulting from long lead times without creating more. During the writing of this chapter a magazine published the story of a day in the life of a personality whose death had been widely reported in newspapers before the magazine was on sale. That could not have been foreseen (though it is risky to feature the aged and sick) but it is not sensible to invite problems. Always leave a get-out. 'The ceremony due to take place last week', or 'The television series scheduled to start last week', may be clumsy but is safer.

Provided there will be a byline on the feature there is no reason why the writer should not express opinions. If there is no byline, and in news columns, subs should delete personal bias and animosity, whether against left- or right-wingers, employers or employees (unless, of course, the magazine is a political organ).

The sub then begins a process of checks – on spelling, punctuation and grammar, and on all verifiable names and dates – using reference books cuttings and telephoning authorities where necessary. American magazines have large fact-checking departments to do this, all modelled on that of *The New Yorker*, famous for its genteel and fastidious prose, according to novelist Jay McInerney. He has described life in the department in the first half of the 1980s in an article in *The Sunday Times Magazine*:

> I was one of seven fact checkers occupying a desk in an office lined wall to wall with reference books. It was our job to read an article and underline in pencil everything that was a matter of fact as opposed to a matter of opinion and then to verify every single matter of fact. If, in an article about Umbria, a writer said that 'the basilica of S Maria degli Angeli was designed by Allesi in 1569,' the fact checker would have to make sure there was such a church, that it was designed by Allesi, that it was begun in

1569. And he would have to verify that everything was spelled correctly. If an article mentioned the late Ernest Hemingway, the diligent fact checker would look in the encyclopedia to make sure that Hemingway was dead. When a living person was quoted it was the fact checker's job to call up and ask the quoted person if he or she did express the sentiments or facts conveyed in the quote. Unfortunately, people often change their minds after they hear themselves quoted. If this happened, the writer would usually get mad at the fact checker.

Sub-editors on British magazines are unlikely to tempt fate by giving an interviewee an opportunity to reword quotes, unless there are doubts about the writer's accuracy, but they are expected to verify facts, and must also ensure that copy conforms with office style.

House style

A magazine has to be consistent in its spellings and in the way it sets out dates, numbers and other matters. Office rules are commonly listed in a style book, compiled by the chief sub. (This is one of the first tasks when starting a new magazine.) The first section is likely to deal with spelling. *Organise* or *organize*? *Connection* or *connexion*? *Jail* or *gaol*? *Gipsy* or *gypsy*? *Airplane* or *aeroplane*? House rules usually decree following a particular dictionary, such as the *Concise Oxford*, adopting the first version where alternatives are offered, though they then frequently list exceptions, such as using 's' rather than 'z' in a word like *epitomise*. Style books are riddled with exceptions.

Some foreign names are spelled in different ways in different publications. For example, *Gadhafi* and *Qadhaffi*. A magazine normally elects to follow the spelling used by a particular newspaper. With British names spelling should not be a problem, but there are other difficulties. Some magazines, particularly trade papers, use people's names in full when first mentioned in a feature, and subsequently merely the surname. This is consistent, but some readers find it offensive to refer to a woman simply as Smith or Jones. The staff of a television magazine are instructed that male stars should normally be referred to by their surnames and women by their first names (which is obvious sex discrimination) but then they are told to make exceptions in the cases of popular comedians such as Benny Hill, on the grounds that the public always think of them by their first names. This is true but it makes the rules illogical.

Certainly in a friendly piece about a male game show host it seems natural to refer to him by his first name, but if attacking him for the crassness or vulgarity of his show, the surname seems more appropriate. With a girl singer in a pop group the first name comes readily, but with a mature opera singer it seems too familiar. With politicians also the first name seems over-friendly, the surname cool, while using the prefixes Mr, Mrs and Miss or Ms seems rather formal in a popular magazine; and there is also the problem of knowing which women wish to be known as Mrs, Miss or Ms.

In the 1960s a television magazine used to award prefixes to behind-the-camera people such as producers and members of the boards of production companies, but omitted them when referring to performers, a solution which looked most unhappy when the caption to a picture juxtaposed Jim Box and *Mr* John Cox. There is no solution which will please everyone, seem right on all occasions and also be logical and even-handed, and it seems one case where consistency has to be subordinated to commonsense decisions.

Most other matters can be more arbitrarily ruled on, and what follows is a set of typical style rules based on ones used in several offices. They can be argued about, for attempts to establish common rules have failed and there are few rights or wrongs. The use of single or double quotation marks, for instance, is simply a question of preference and what matters is being consistent. For that reason, these rules are not necessarily followed in this book, for book publishers also have their style rules; what follows is intended to spotlight some of the matters on which rules are needed.

- **Foreign words**. Those which have become anglicized, such as cafe, communique, elite, naive and fete should be set in Roman type without accents, but words which are still regarded as foreign, such as *déshabillé* and *pièce de résistance* should be italicized and accented.
- **Capitals**. An initial capital is used where a title is unique, such as the *Prime Minister* (but *prime ministers* when referring to a number of them); the *Government*, meaning the one in power, but *successive governments*; and *the Church*, meaning the establishment, *a church*, meaning a building. Words where the origin is now remote, such as *french beans*, *french polishing*, *wellington boots*, *yorkshire pudding*, *platonic* and *dutch hoe* do not need capitals. The seasons take lower case (*spring* and *autumn*); so does the *northeast* of England, but capitals should be used for the *North Country* and *the Far East*.
- **Punctuation**. Introduce quotations with a colon and use single quotation marks. For example, *He said: 'Do it like this'*. Introduce quotes within quotes with a comma, and use double quotation marks. *She said: 'The Queen told me, "It's fantastic"'.* Enclose punctuation within quotes except where a quote is not a full sentence, when it ends with the point outside. *He said it was: 'a storm in a teacup'*. Commas and dashes should be kept to the minimum required to avoid sentences being misread, or to indicate pauses. Hyphens should be avoided; if words can be joined without looking odd, or marring the sense, this should be done. Words such as *motorcycle*, *crossfire*, *showcase*, *wildlife*, *quizmaster*, *newsroom*

and *bookstall* do not need them; *old-fashioned* and *re-employ* do. Lists should be introduced by a colon. Marks of omission consist of three full points closed up on the previous word and followed by normal word spacing, like this . . . When a question is posed, the question mark is substituted for the third full point. Do not add a fourth point at the end of a sentence. Possessives of words ending in 's' should have an apostrophe 's': *Jones's car* (not *Jones' car*). Headlines and straplines are not followed by full points, but captions and standfirsts are.

- **Numbers**. Spell out numbers one to nine and use figures for 10 to 999,000 – though when starting a sentence a figure should be spelt out. (*Nineteen-year-old Mary Smith . . .*) Millions are rendered as one million and 10 million rather than as seven-figure numbers, but numbers in between should be in figures, 9,501,000 (or 9.5 million). Four-figure numbers should be without a comma (9000); five figures or more with a comma (13,000). When a sentence contains a mixture of large and small numbers (*between 8 and 12 days*, or *odds of 10 to 1*), all should be in figures. Vague quantities such as *around five thousand* should be spelled out. When followed by units of measurement figures should be used: for example, *6ft 4in tall*. Percentages should also be expressed in figures as, for example, *15 per cent*. The symbol % should not be used in features, though it is acceptable in tables. Dollar signs should not be used; write dollars. Use hyphens when referring to a *14-year-old boy*; alternatively write *a boy, aged 14*. Hours and minutes in times are separated by a full point (*11.45am*). Use *Henry the Eighth*, not *Henry VIII*, and *World War Two*, not *World War II*.

- **Abbreviations**. Set them without full points. TV, RAF, USA, CID and BBC need no explanation. Less familiar abbreviations should be defined on the first appearance in a feature: *CIA, America's Central Intelligence Agency*. With weights and measures, abbreviations should be closed up on figures; for example, *5ft 9in tall*. Note the use of *in*, not *ins*. Use *ft, yd, oz, lb, km, hr, min, sec, mph, mpg*, but *stone* rather than *st*.

- **Dates**. The normal form should be *22 November 1963*, in which the figures are separated without need for a comma. The *25th of December* is acceptable when referring to a familiar date or when quoting someone. In historical articles *BC* should follow a year and *AD* precede one. Render decades as *the 1980s* (without an apostrophe) or the *Eighties* (with capital) but not as *the '80s*. *In his 40s needs no apostrophe*. Use *sixteenth century* rather than *16th*.

- **Titles** of books, films and television programmes, and names of ships should be set in italics rather than placed between quotation marks.

- **Addresses**. There should be no comma between a house number and the name of the road. *Street, road* and *avenue* should not be abbreviated. They should be joined to the name by a hyphen and given a lower case initial: write *10 Downing-street*. No point should follow an abbreviation of a county such as *Herts* (except, of course, at the end of a sentence). Base British place names on *Bartholomew's Gazetteer*, foreign place names on *The Times Atlas*.

As queries arise – for example, should *vice president* be hyphenated? – and are settled, it is useful to write the decision in an alphabetically tabbed notebook kept in the subs' department for future reference. In this way you can build up a valuable reference work.

Trade names

Brand names and trade marks are best avoided where possible, for they contain traps. Referring to a person 'hoovering' a carpet is wrong, because Hoover is a brand name and requires an initial capital. Unless the person is specifically using a Hoover, and it is relevant to say so, it is preferable to refer to a vacuum cleaner. Jeep is another misused name. It is not a generic term for a four-wheel-drive, go-anywhere vehicle but the name of a particular American make, and so should not be spelt with a lower case initial, nor used for rival manufacturers' vehicles. These names are protected under various Trades Marks Acts, and misuse of them is liable to bring a formal complaint, because manufacturers have to safeguard their brand names if they are not to become generic terms.

Ansafone is a registered trade mark of the Ansafone company; telephone answering machines in general should be called just that. Autocue is a product of the Autocue company, and unless one is sure that an Autocue is meant, it is better to write of a television prompter. Band-Aid and Elastoplast are particular makes of adhesive strips and bandages, and Coke is a registered trade mark of Coca-Cola. These names should not be used with lower case initial letters; nor should Flymo, Trimphone, Tarmac, Teflon, Portakabin and Polaroid, and unless referring specifically to the following products it is advisable to use the words in brackets: Day-Glo (daylight fluorescent colour products), Dolby (noise reduction circuitry), Fibreglass (glass fibre), Kleenex (tissues), Jiffy bags (padded envelopes), Tannoy (public address system), Wimpy (hamburger), Xerox (photocopier), Photostat (photocopy), Catseyes (reflecting road studs), Jacuzzi (whirlpool bath) and Dictaphone (dictation machine).

On the other hand, some words are frequently given capital initials when they are not registered. For example, aspirin is an analgesic made by many companies, is not a brand name and takes a lower case first letter, as do hovercraft, derv fuel and melamine furniture. There is no sure way of guessing which are, and are not, registered, but lists appear quarterly in *UK*

Jean Jones

Sussex World 10
p 33

Cliff 1

8/9 pt Univers Light u/lc × 11 ems

3-line
D/c

The morning after his girlfriend phoned him and told him, "It's all
over," a 22-year-old London clerk got into his Volkswagen, ~~purportedly~~ ostensibly
to go to work. Instead he drove to Eastbourne and along to Beachy Head,
where he turned on to a ~~private~~ drive to the former Belle Toute
lighthouse, now a private home, on the cliff top.

A young architect watched helplessly from the house as the car
swung across the turf towards the cliff edge, crashed through steel
fencing and smashed on to the beach 450ft below. (run on)
The car was flattened by the impact and the driver killed
instantly.

It was one of the most spectacular suicides at Beachy Head, more
than 600ft high at its peak and the most visited, most deadly beauty
spot in Sussex.

That particular suicide was in 1960 but the toll of the notorious
headland does not diminish. It claims an average of 10 victims every
year. (run on)
Most of the deaths, about six out of 10, are clear cases of suicide.
In roughly a third the coroner returns an open verdict because the
victim gave no clear indication of intent to ~~top~~ kill himself or herself, but
inevitably these cases include some suicides. Accidental deaths do
occur, but are comparatively rare.

more

Figure 35   *A folio of subbed copy*

Press Gazette and should be pinned up in offices, and further information is obtainable from the Institute of Trade Mark Agents.

Marking copy

Any passages that have become an untidy jungle of insertions, deletions and changes should be retyped at this stage when subbing hard copy – that is, on paper – for it is asking too much of a compositor to set illegible copy accurately. The sub can then prepare the copy for the printer, using a number of conventional marks. The opening paragraph will usually start full out (without any indent), with the first word probably in capitals and, in many magazines, the initial letter an oversized drop cap. The sub will indicate what is required, encircling the initial letter and writing in the margin, say, '6-line D/C,' and underscoring the rest of the word three times to indicate capitals. It is commonplace to underscore only twice, which strictly means small capitals. As these are rarely used – being reserved mainly for letters after a name, such as QC, MP, which would otherwise look clumsy – confusion rarely arises, but the correct way of indicating upper case is by putting three lines under the character or characters.

If subsequent paragraphs are to be indented, the sub will mark the start of each with a square bracket, [. If paragraphs are to start flush left, the sub marks the start with a bracket facing the other way,]. To make the requirement absolutely clear, 'np' (for new par) can be written in the margin and ringed, which is the conventional way of making clear to compositors that the mark is an instruction and not to be set in type.

Words to be set in italic are underscored with a single line; words to be set in bold are underscored with an undulating line. Again, for clarity, the sub can add 'ital' or 'bold' above the word, ringing the instruction. If there is an improbable spelling, e.g. *Robynson* or *Joanes*, it is sensible to ring 'spelling correct' or simply 'OK' in the margin, otherwise a helpful compositor is likely to alter it to the conventional spelling.

Words to be cut are crossed out and a deletion mark, a Greek δ, is placed in the margin. If the sub has crossed out anything in error it is underscored with a dotted line and the instruction 'stet' (meaning 'let it stand') is ringed beside it. The sub should check the catchlining, making sure that no other feature has been allotted the same word, and renumber the folios, ringing them, and also placing 'mf' at the foot of each page. Clarity is all important; when there is any possibility of an instruction being misunderstood, spell it out in the margin, and ring the instruction.

Marking for type

The sub then returns to the top of the feature and marks it for type. This is done in the following order: the type size, the typeface and its fount, whether it is to be set in capitals or lower case or the conventional mixture of both, whether it is to be ranged left, right or justified, and finally the width.

The artist should have indicated on the layout what is required. Suppose it is to be set in 9-pt Times Roman upper and lower case, justified in columns of 9 ems wide; the sub writes '9-pt Times Roman U/Lc justified × 9 ems'. On a magazine where this is the normal setting, this may in practice become abbreviated to '9 × 9', but it is never wrong to make instructions perfectly clear. When in doubt, specify.

If copy is to be unjustified and ranged left, with a ragged edge on the right, like typescript, the sub may mark it: '9/10-pt Times Italic U/Lc unjustified, R/L on 9 ems'. There may be more complex measurements to indicate.

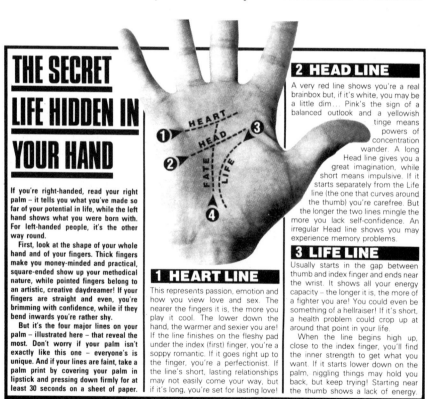

Figure 36   *Example of a bastard measure in* Sunday; *copy has been set to fit around the thumb*

Perhaps the first paragraph is to be set in larger type across two columns (which means two columns of 9 ems plus the 1 em margin between them); then a sub may mark, 'First 10 lines, 12-pt Times Bold U/Lc × 19 ems, then 9-pt Roman × 9 ems'. Alternatively, which is preferable, the sub will write out the matter to be set in larger type on one folio, marking it for 12-point, then mark 9-pt at the top of the rest. It is easier for comps, whether using old technology or operating a VDU keyboard, if subs avoid showing more than one type size or typeface on the same folio.

There may also be 'bastard' measures (abnormal column widths). Perhaps there is a cut-out picture in the centre of a page and type has to follow the lines of the body on either side of it with the column widths decreasing by steps; then the sub will annotate it appropriately. There are special arrangements for 'skewing' type in this way in modern computerized systems.

The position of crossheads in the copy can be indicated by the letters A, B, C and so on and a ringed instruction to create a space: 'Leave four lines #'. Assuming they are in a different typeface or size, they should not be inserted in the feature but written out and keyed on a separate folio. With photosetting they can easily be inserted on the page and positioned accurately at the paste-up stage.

Headline writing

Having dealt with the copy, a sub turns to the headline. It may already have been decreed by the editor and have been provided by the art department in the form of Letraset or artwork, and therefore need no further work; if not, it will be up to the sub to devise a headline and have it set. The artist will have indicated on the layout, either in pencil or in gobbledygook, the position of the headline and the size and style of the type, which may often be standardized. The main problem is the length required, which limits creativity.

Conventions are that punctuation – especially exclamation marks – and abbreviations should be avoided as far as possible. Names of persons are preferred to place names. The past tense is also undesirable; words should be active and vigorous. That much magazine headlines have in common with newspaper headlines, but it is comparatively easy to compose a headline for a major news story such as the murder of a statesman. It can be more difficult to write a headline for a feature, for there may be no obvious news angle. However, a headline should not be a mere label. 'Fish recipes' is unexciting; one magazine sub headed such a page, *Tasting the riches of the deep*. 'Angling' has nothing to commend it either. *Casting upon the waters* was the headline a sub devised. Here are two other examples from a pile of magazines: a feature about a woman shepherd was headlined *One woman and her flock*, and one about resident clerks of the Foreign Office *Nightshift at the FO*. (The last one does, however, indicate the dangers of using abbreviations; not all readers would recognize the meaning of FO instantly.)

It is often helpful to ask, what is the writer's main point? In a feature about trawler fishing it may be that the writer claims that it is 'The most dangerous job going'. That makes a reasonable headline.

Headlines sometimes pose questions, e.g. *What's wrong with our cricket?*, though it would be more positive to headline what the writer says is wrong with it. Sometimes they are designed to titillate, e.g. *Sexy Suzy's Bedroom Secrets*, but many feature headlines are a play on words. Examples abound in all types of magazine:

Waste measurement (about refuse).
On course for success (golf).
Man with a porpoise (on a dolphin expert).
Philately will get you nowhere (stamp collecting).
The Pryce of tragedy (actor Jonathan Pryce).
Honest john (a new loo).
A novel way to attract young people (fiction for youngsters).
A National institution (the Grand National horse race).
Manor from heaven (a stately home).
Stately gnomes (garden gnomes).
Punching judies (women boxers).
Driving yourself mad (rush hour traffic).

More are a play on familiar phrases, film and song titles. *Gone with the Wind*, *Close Encounters of the Third Kind*, *Charlie's Angels*, *The Avengers*, and *Softly Softly* were all exploited in their day, and the fashion continues. Examples:

Blowing in the wind (parachuting).
Deep in the heart of Geldof (on the pop singer).
They'll take Manhattan (American property developers).
Memories are made of this (a theme park).
His kind of town, Chicago is (on Saul Bellow).

Possibly the hardest features to headline are service columns on hobbies and products, not least because they are usually short and the headlines must also be brief. Again, subs commonly find inspiration in word play. Examples:

Doc brief (advice by a doctor).

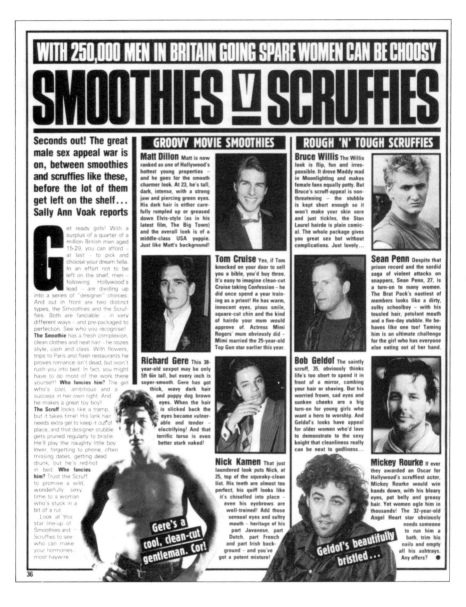

Figure 37   *Example of strap, heading and standfirst in* Sunday

Horribly successful (horror fiction).
Shady deals (sunglasses).
Face values (watches).
Do yourself a flavour (ice creams).
Finger on the pulses (vegetarian diets).
L'eau life (Belgian mineral water).
High filers (Filofaxes).

Straplines and standfirsts

Sometimes a complementary or explanatory strapline is placed above the main headline. For example, on a feature about the quarantining of animals:

Six months inside, no remission – and society is safer for it
VISITING TIME AT THE PET PENITENTIARY

A strap may also be accompanied by a standfirst, which is, as the name suggests, an introductory paragraph that stands before a feature. Its main purpose is to explain what the feature is about, or the topical reasons for its inclusion. It also frees writers from having to carry explanatory matter – such as the opening date of an exhibition or film – in the first paragraph, and allows them to devise an arresting opening. Here is an example of strap, headline, standfirst and opening paragraph from a feature in *Sunday* Magazine:

Inside a perspex tank, connected to 9ft of plastic tubing and a mass of monitors . . .

A TINY HEART BEATS

For Alexis and Graham Curtis, both a dream and a nightmare began when she gave birth to the daughter they had longed for. But their Michelle weighed in at only 44 ounces – and the doctors gave her just 10 minutes to live. But then in her first few weeks the tiny tot had her life saved twice by the skill of staff at London's Guy's Hospital where today her battle against the odds goes on around the clock.
Alexis Curtis walked over towards the perspex incubator and then so slowly and carefully threaded her hands in through the mass of tubes and drips that completely swamped her baby daughter's tiny, delicate body. Then she picked up her child and wept.

It is more common now, though, to use only a standfirst and omit a strap. Here is an example of headline, standfirst and opening paragraph from a feature in the *Sunday Express Magazine*:

A SIGN OF THE TIMES
Gone are the days when best selling authors could rest on their laurels, raking in the royalties. Book-signing sessions have given a brand new meaning to writer's cramp.

Barbara Cartland loathes it. Jackie Collins dreads it. Margaret Thatcher was unsure about it. But Princess Michael adored every minute. In the movie-star world of high-profile writers, no longer can the author sit at home in perfect isolation waiting for the reviews to drop on the mat . . .

Here are two more standfirsts taken at random from magazines:

CANVASSING THE QUEEN
A major exhibition of paintings of the Queen opens on Friday. No other living person has been portrayed so often as our monarch. But what of their merit? How do they rate artistically?

WELLIE CLASSY
They can be short, squat or long and fitted; they come in all the colours of the rainbow and they're found on the doorstep of every English home. They're worn by people as famous as Princess Anne and as cuddly as Paddington Bear. Yet the trusty, practical Wellington Boot is no longer what it used to be.

Bylines

A writer's byline is frequently incorporated in the standfirst, as in the following example:

SUPPORT SYSTEMS
Fifty years ago British women didn't wear bras. Today they buy 60 million a year. Jean Scroggie talks to bra fitters, designers and manufacturers about the changes in shape, fabric and style.

Sometimes the photographer's byline is added at the end of the standfirst. The practice of placing bylines at the head of a feature is merited when the writer and photographer have famous names, which are, in themselves, an invitation to read on. A byline on a particularly opinionated feature also needs to be at the top, so that readers know from the start whose opinions they are agreeing or disagreeing with. On other features, when the names will mean nothing to most readers, they might just as well be placed at the foot, a practice known as a 'sign-off'.

But all features should carry bylines, not necessarily to publicize or reward those responsible, but so that readers can form some judgment about the authority of the feature. A neat solution is to box the names of writer and photographer at the foot of a column on the first page of the feature.

Captions and credits

The author's byline (and photographer's, if applicable) are written out in copy or on screen. There may also be photo credits to include. These are sometimes printed sideways in small type along a vertical edge of the pictures to which they refer and aligned with the bottom of the pictures if they are unbled, or the type area if bled.

Subs also write picture captions. These may be simple label captions, such as *William Smith* or *Westminster Abbey*, or they may be of two, three or four lines. They are sometimes required to fill the space to the letter (which, without a computer, requires character counting). If there is more than one line, the last line may be centred. Longer captions should complement a feature, not merely repeat information in it, and should add to what the readers can see for themselves. There is no merit in telling readers that a picture shows the Queen on horseback; they can see that. But where and when were the pictures taken, what is the horse, how often and where and under what circumstances does she ride it? A caption should pull its weight, add something. Too often, captions are written in clichés. Faced with a picture of a police constable some subs automatically begin a caption: ''Allo, 'allo, 'allo, what's all this, then?'

One difficulty in writing captions in magazine work is that subs often have to work from photocopies of pictures, the originals having left the office for a repro house or contract printer, and this can make it difficult to identify some of the persons in a group or exactly what is taking place.

Final work

All that remains for a sub to do, after editing and checking has been carried out, is to mark up for type everything that requires setting. The artist will have indicated on the layout what is required. Straplines and bylines may be in a 14-point italic version of the headline type. Captions will usually be set in an italic or bold version of the body type used for the feature, and slightly bigger or smaller than the feature – possibly $9\frac{1}{2}$/10-point italics. Standfirsts may be in 16/17-point italic and picture credits in 7-point Roman small caps. On rigidly unchanging magazines, typefaces and sizes used may, by arrangement, be known to the subs and typesetters simply as A, B and C.

The whole parcel is then clipped together, folios catchlined and numbered from start to finish, and goes to the chief sub for approval and possible amendments; it may also be submitted to the editor if it is an important feature, or if the chief sub feels the editor may not be happy about a headline or intro. On some publications executives of different ranks use different coloured inks, so that, in theory, everyone will know the author of a mark on a piece of copy or proof. Green may be reserved for the editor, red for the deputy editor. One feature writer caused confusion by being the only man on the staff of a magazine who did not know of this system. When he began making amendments to his copy in green ink, his marks were treated as holy writ by subs until an apparent schizophrenic clash between green marks led to his unmasking.

Finally, copy, pictures and layouts go to the production editor, who will normally by this time have been demanding them, and trying to hasten their progress, because contract printers impose 'lateness charges' if copy arrives behind schedule, and the production editor is held to account for them. The production editor will log the feature out on a progress chart in case of later dispute with the printer, and make it ready for dispatch, ensuring that all is complete. The last action taken before it leaves the premises is photocopying everything in case of loss.

Subbing on screen

For subs working with direct input, much of the labour described in this chapter belongs in the past. Perhaps the biggest benefit to them is that they no longer need to count words or characters, because the computer will give them counts, and with the magazine's standard typefaces and sizes formatted in the computer, and automatic hyphenating and justifying, they can see on screen immediately whether copy fits or whether it needs lengthening or cutting. They have no need to await proofs anxiously to discover whether they have done their work well or badly; they can ensure that everything is correct.

Subs using new technology work at editing terminals, similar to writers' terminals but with additional command keys. Copy on the screen is 'clean', without any inky or indecipherable insertions by the writer or executives. When it leaves the subs, it will be equally clean. Leafing through a dictionary is unnecessary; the computer has one which will monitor spellings and check that they conform to house style. When rewriting copy, subs can use a split screen facility and have the original on one side of the screen and the new version on which they are working alongside. This facility is also useful when the need to merge two pieces of copy into one arises.

When the work is finished, it can be inspected by the chief sub on his or her own screen. When it is approved, it has merely to be routed through a photosetter to be printed out as text.

9 AN ABC OF MAGAZINE CONTENTS

While interview-based features are probably in the majority on all types of publications, which is why the emphasis has been on them thus far, the range of other ingredients in magazines is wide. They can include *investigations*, which may look into such scandals as the selling of time-share apartments in Spain or the materials and workmanship in a new flyover. They can include *stunts*, in which a writer may be sent to tackle a job – as a traffic warden or good food inspector – for a day, or is dispatched to test the honesty of shopkeepers and cab drivers by pretending to be a foreigner with a fistful of money but no grasp of the currency or language.

The most common elements of magazines include the following, arranged in alphabetical order.

Advice columns

Advice columns are found in all types of magazines, though the nature of them varies according to the publication. There are advisers on subjects from financial investment to sexual technique but the most popular are the 'agony aunts' of the mass circulation women's magazines. There are cynical members of the public who believe that the letters answered are written in the offices of the magazines, but this is unnecessary. Letters flood in: 'I want to change my sex life', 'He's harsh with my daughter', 'My dull lover'. One aunt gets 200 letters a week and has three assistants to help deal with them. The job calls for broadmindedness, maturity and commonsense. Correspondents do not want to be lectured on their morals, yet the adviser has to be responsible and cannot, for example, encourage a teenage girl in an affair with a middle-aged married man.

Here is a typical letter published in *Chat*, with the answer from Maggie Comport:

My dad hates my boyfriend

I am 15 and have been going out with my boyfriend for three months. I see him most days and sometimes stay with him for the weekend. My parents thought I was with friends but have now found out and realise I am having sex with him. My dad went mad and wanted to hit my boyfriend. Now we want to get engaged and for me to come off the Pill.

Your dad went mad because he'd trusted you and you let him down and because he is worried sick about you. He is rightly furious with your boyfriend who is actually breaking the law because you are having under-age sex . . . Try to make it up to your family for deceiving them and get your boyfriend to talk to your father about your relationship.

The letters published represent only a fraction of the number received, all of which are usually answered individually by post. On *Woman*, for example, the aunt cannot answer them all personally but reads them all, picks those for publication and personal attention, and marks others with comments before passing them to her staff for replies. Many of the writers are desperate for advice or help, and tardiness could have unhappy results. Fortunately, from the staff point of view, many concern the same subjects, such as bed-wetting, masturbation, incest, premature ejaculation and snoring. 'There are always new problems but basically they fall into a number of main categories', says one aunt. 'Some mornings you come in and shout, "Oh, no, not another orgasm letter".' Many can be answered by a secretary after a look at replies to similar letters in the past, and others by sending or recommending books or leaflets. Some offices hold supplies of leaflets on such subjects as the menopause. In other cases it may be necessary to refer a correspondent to a doctor or clinic.

It is sad that so many, young and old, cannot talk to members of their family circle or consult their own doctors. But there is manifestly a need for a wise and unshockable outsider who can be consulted anonymously.

Inevitably there are hoax letters. 'You'll get a bunch of schoolkids or students getting together and sending in a joint effort, or sometimes people send a letter in under someone else's name', says an aunt. It would be next to impossible to check their authenticity and maintain confidentiality but as anonymity is preserved and names are not published, no embarrassment is caused by treating them all as genuine – except of course to an innocent male who, as a result of a hoax letter, receives an unsought leaflet in the post telling him how to get a vasectomy.

Medical columns, answering such questions as, 'Why are my baby's eyes swollen?' and 'Why can't we conceive?', are, of course, written by doctors, or in some cases nurses, and from the editorial point of view the main problem is checking medical terms.

Legal and financial columns are usually written by lawyers (or journalists with legal training) and financial journalists.

Here are two typical letters:

My boyfriend was mugged two weeks ago. His face was scarred and one of his arms was broken. Can he get compensation?
Yes, he can. The Criminal Injuries Compensation Board is a state-run body that compensates victims of violent crime.

I wish to sue a builder who recently did some work for me. There is very little money involved (£450). How do I go about this?
You should go to your local county court office and tell them that you want to make a claim for under £500.

Backgrounders

One function of many magazines is to investigate and analyse the background to events that have occurred or, on occasion, are about to occur, because they can normally do this at greater length and in a more considered way than daily newspapers or television. These 'backgrounders' examining the how and why of events, setting them in perspective and explaining underlying causes, are often the main features in news reviews.

On modest publications they may consist of a single feature, the work of one expert. On major news magazines they may entail massive and expensive effort, as was seen in the coverage by the American news magazine *Time* of the stock market crash of 1987. In its *Letter from the Publisher* Robert L. Miller told how the coverage was organized:

It was the day after the end of the world, and Charles Alexander's lunch of salad and Pepsi Free sat untouched on his paper-strewn desk. Alexander, the editor of *Time's* Economy and Business section, had spent the past nine hours blocking out this week's 24-page cover [story] on the cataclysmic demise of the five-year-old bull market. Just after the market closed on Black Monday, editorial queries went out to an army of more than 25 *Time* correspondents in 20 financial capitals around the world. Before long their reports would begin hitting the in-baskets of 30 editors, writers and reporter-researchers in New York City. As co-ordinator of the magazine's coverage of the Crash of '87, Alexander for the rest of the week would find his meals as elusive and unpredictable as the stock market . . .

The 508-point drop in the Dow Jones industrials on Black Monday was such an unsettling event that a major examination was in order. Under

Alexander's supervision, *Time* directed its considerable resources at determining why the bubble burst, where the financial markets were headed, and what the implications of the crisis were for both the global economy and the wallets of individual consumers.

The coverage began with an introductory spread. Then came a nine-page feature on what happened in markets around the world, followed by a three-page hour-by-hour diary, two pages of interviews with investors, two pages on the brokers, three pages on America's budget and trade deficits (an underlying cause), a page on so-called yuppie brokers and bankers, and two pages on the Wall Street collapse of 1929. Incorporated were coloured and tinted panels and boxes featuring interviews with the US Treasury Secretary and Federal Reserve Board chairman, and pieces on the use of computers in the financial organizations, investors who emerged winners, and possible methods of reducing the US deficits. Later in the magazine, in its US section, there was a feature on the reaction of Presidential candidates and a *Time* poll of members of the public on how the crash had affected their finances and would alter their spending.

Book adaptations

Adaptations from books, whether fiction or non-fiction, can be circulation builders. A magazine will usually buy rights from the publisher to run an agreed number of instalments and words on dates coinciding with, or immediately preceding, the book's publication.

In the case of non-fiction, such as an autobiography, unless the instalments are of great length, it is rarely a good plan to attempt simply to condense the whole book, which will destroy style and result in a jerky read. If the agreement is, say, to publish three instalments of 1,500 words each, it is far better to find three separate chapters to lift, or to select three topics or themes, such as 'my marriages', 'my money', 'my secret fears', picking material from various parts of the book if necessary. Bridging links between passages from the book are best avoided if possible, but it may be necessary to insert them – in italic to make the distinction plain.

Often it is a good idea to run two or three separate pieces in each issue – perhaps a main story and one or two anecdotal sidebars or boxes. This can be easier than trying to marry the extracts into one narrative, and makes the pages look more attractive and less daunting to read.

Serializations of novels are dealt with under the heading *Fiction*.

woman HELPLINE

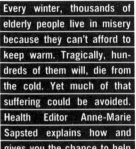

Every winter, thousands of elderly people live in misery because they can't afford to keep warm. Tragically, hundreds of them will, die from the cold. Yet much of that suffering could be avoided. Health Editor Anne-Marie Sapsted explains how and gives you the chance to help

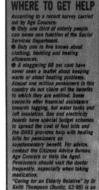

ast winter was a bitter, bad one for all of us, but particularly for the senior citizens in our community. In fact, during the cold snap of February and March at the start of this year, hypothermia caused, or helped cause, the deaths of some 320 pensioners.

That's going on for half the number of over-65-year-olds who perished in this way throughout the *whole* of 1985—a total of 705— according to the Office of Population Censuses and Surveys, who compile such figures.

In short, cold kills the elderly. And it's a problem that's getting worse every year, according to Malcolm Wicks, director of the Family Policy Studies Centre.

"The trouble is that we still think of Britain as having a mild climate. Every two or three years we have a bad winter, and it takes everyone by surprise. After that we forget about it."

But it is a problem that is growing all the time. For between now and the end of this century, there will be a rapid increase in the numbers of people in their late seventies,

eighties and nineties. Indeed, between 1971 and 1981 alone, the number of people aged 75 or over increased by 20 per cent; this meant an extra 516,000 people.

"We just don't look after elderly people properly," says Malcolm Wicks. "The sort of advice we are giving to the old on how to cope in winter is rather like the advice we give to a party of mountaineers about to set off on an expedition to Everest! It does suggest that our society has not got its priorities quite right.

"But having said that, there is a serious problem and there is a lot we can do."

Quite obviously the main problem in winter is keeping warm. And given the enormous rises in the cost of fuel in recent years, this can be very difficult to overcome.

Over 95 per cent of our elderly population live on their own or in family homes. So what are the signs to look for in an old person who's having difficulty coping?

Self neglect among the elderly is not uncommon, and is very often because of loneliness and depression. After all, if you don't

have anyone to care for you, there may well seem little reason to take care of yourself.

Of course, there are those who have always isolated themselves and who survive in what we might think are the rather squalid conditions they are quite used to and apparently find perfectly acceptable. But, for most people, self-neglect is often a symptom of illness rather than a way of life and the. danger is that it becomes a downward spiral of hopelessness and despair.

Some of the danger signs are:
● A smell of urine
● Untidiness
● An attitude of neglect, acceptance, hopelessness and lack of motivation
● Dirty washing accumulating
● Clothes changed infrequently or a person wearing night clothes all day
● Not taking prescribed medicines or hoarding drugs
● Mental confusion, often about the time of day or day of the week

WHERE TO GET HELP

According to a recent survey carried out by Age Concern:
● Only one third of elderly people can name one function of the Social Services Department.
● Only one in five knows about clothing, bedding and heating allowances.
● A staggering 88 per cent have never seen a leaflet about keeping warm or about heating problems. Almost one million pensioners in this country do not claim all the benefits to which they are entitled. Some councils offer financial assistance towards lagging, hot water tanks and loft insulation. Gas and electricity boards have special budget schemes to spread the cost of fuel bills and the DHSS provides help with heating bills for pensioners on supplementary benefit. For advice, contact the Citizens Advice Bureau, Age Concern or Help the Aged. Pensioners should visit the doctor frequently, especially when taking medication.

"Caring for an Elderly Relative" by Dr Keith Thompson (Dunitz, £3·95) is an excellent and sympathetic guide.

YOUR CHANCE TO HELP

You can help a needy old person—and ensure they don't suffer from hypothermia this winter —by nominating them for our special Benylin Emergency Survival Blanket, plus a selection of leaflets. 10,000 free blankets are available.

The blanket is made by J S Clayton & Co and provided by Warner Lambert Health Care, the maker of Benylin cough remedies, and can be used to help retain body heat in a number of ways. In bed it can be put shiny side up between the upper sheet and blanket, or shiny side down between the bottom sheet and underblanket. It can also be wrapped around the shoulders like a shawl or around the legs. There are also a number of useful leaflets about coping with the cold. *Hypothermia—the Chilling Facts* (Damart); *Advice for Senior Citizens* (British Gas); *5 Ways To Keep Warm This Winter* (Help the Aged); *Advice for Elderly People; Easy Ways To Pay; Using Energy Wisely* (Electricity Council).

If you know someone who would benefit from a blanket, just fill in the coupon below and send it, glued to a postcard, to the address on the coupon —you can nominate yourself or an elderly friend or relative. Those named in the first 10,000 postcards will be sent a blanket plus the leaflets.

PLEASE CUT ALONG BROKEN LINE

NAME...

ADDRESS..

.... Post code...................

Send to: Help the Old Fight the Cold,
PO Box 91,
Southampton SO9 7FT

Closing date: December 19, 1986

Figure 38 *Example of a campaign – on behalf of the aged – from* Woman

Campaigns

Campaigns may be contained in a single issue or run over a period of months or even years. They may be against food irradiation, the sale of lethal knives or for better pensions or sports facilities, but are frequently run in support of charities, and combine happily the merits of being readable, getting the publication talked about and achieving good. For example, *Be my parent*, a campaign in *Chat* in 1987, was for a scheme run by British Agencies for Adoption and Fostering to find homes for 17,000 children in care. Typical copy read:

> How big is your heart – and your home? Are both large enough to make room for a ready-made family . . . Paul, seven, brother Lee, six, and sister Kelly, five, desperately need a permanent home together. They need warm, loving parents (preferably one Asian) with whom they can grow up happily.

A magazine should, however, be very sure of the worthiness of a cause, and of those promoting it, before giving them backing.

Competitions

The best type of competition from the staff's point of view is one that stipulates that winners will be the senders of the first correct entries opened on a certain day: for example, 'The first correct entry examined after the closing date will win a TV set, the next two correct entries will each win radio recorders and the following seven correct entries will win cassette players'. With luck, staff may need to open only ten envelopes and there can be no complaints from readers who sent in correct entries but did not win. Stipulating that entries must be on postcards saves opening envelopes but reduces the number of entries, as readers rarely seem to have postcards in their homes.

The worst type of competition where staff are concerned is one in which all entries, possibly photographs or children's paintings, have to be examined and judged. This can mean sacks of mail piling up in the office, creating an obstruction and a fire hazard. It can mean conscripting everyone who may not be busy, from secretaries to subs, and hiring temporary staff as well, to open envelopes and make a preliminary selection, throwing entries into sacks labelled 'possible winners', 'mediocre' and 'hopeless'. This is why some magazines now have all entries sent to a specialist competition firm which will, for a fee, select the winners.

If a competition is simple and could lead to hundreds or thousands of correct entries, it may be necessary to devise a tie breaker, which is commonly to devise a slogan or to complete a sentence relevant to the subject of the competition or the nature of the prize. Most slogans submitted are dreadful, but they have to be judged, and it helps to give importance to a competition to have some expert judges – perhaps two television stars for a competition about show business, or a naturalist and a wildlife photographer for one about animals. They cannot be expected, and are unlikely to be willing, to sift through all the entries, and will usually be presented with a short list of possible winners from which to make a final selection.

While competitions in highbrow magazines can command large entries even though the prizes may be merely book tokens, the number of entries in competitions in mass circulation magazines tends to depend on the desirability of the prizes, and readers become blasé about offers of cars and holidays in the sun. However, it is possible to be too imaginative in devising prizes. A comic offered two lion cubs as a prize in a wildlife competition. Of course, the child who won them would not get to keep them; they were to go to a zoo where a plaque would be put up naming the young reader as the donor. He or she would also get a ciné camera to film them. Unfortunately, owing to bureaucratic delays in shipping them, the cuddly cubs had grown into large and less lovable animals by the time they arrived in Britain.

Deals can usually be made with manufacturers to obtain major prizes at a greatly reduced price in return for the publicity the products receive in the magazine. Cheaper articles such as records, suitable for consolation prizes, may often be obtained for nothing.

Competition rules

Framing the rules of competitions calls for consideration. There should be a coupon, otherwise many readers will forget to provide their names and addresses, and the coupons or entry details should include the address to which entries are to be sent – despite which, some readers will contrive to turn to the imprint at the back of the magazine and send their entries to the printer. The closing date by which entries must be received should be stipulated, along with the method of determining the winners (first correct solutions opened, or by judging of all, in which case the judges should be named).

Sometimes only essential rules are published, and readers are told that the magazine's standard competition rules apply and that they can be obtained by writing for them. Standard rules run commonly along these lines:

1   This competition is open to anyone resident in the UK except employees of the publishers, printers and companies directly connected with the competition, and the families of those employees.
2   Entrants may send as many entries as they wish, so long as they are on coupons cut from the magazine, but no entrant may win more than one prize.

3   There can be no alternative prizes, nor cash substitutes for prizes.
4   Proof of posting does not constitute proof of delivery.
5   The editor's decision is final on all matters relating to the competition and no correspondence can be entered into. No entry can be returned.
6   Winners will be notified by post. A full list of winners will be available on request.
7   Any person entering agrees to abide by all the rules; entry implies acceptance of them.
8   Entrants under 18 need parental consent.

Care needs to be exercised to see that the same person does not win competitions twice within a few weeks, or other readers will complain. Such wins can easily happen, since there are many almost professional competition entrants, who, through experience, send in better entries than most.

Particular care is needed with children's competitions for poems, essays or stories. Children cheat. Adults do too, but children are more blatant about it. If prizes are offered for letters about amusing personal experiences, there will probably be a dozen telling the same story, such as how the writer was delivering newspapers and putting a copy of the magazine through a letterbox when the owner of the house – frantic to see the new issue – snatched at it from the other side, and the writer's hand was pulled through the slot and trapped by the flap. Most of the letters will use identical words. Research will establish that the story has been copied from a comic on sale the week before.

It is harder to detect cheating in a poetry competition, when many of the entries will have lifted from books of verse, some of which may be obscure. Rules that entries must be original have little effect. A part answer is to require a parent to certify that the entry is the child's unaided work, though parents may well be deceived by their offspring.

Ideally a national magazine likes winners to come from different parts of the country. If the prize comprises the winners travelling – to London for a presentation, or to Paris on a holiday – winners from Scotland or Wales will cost more in expenses, but this should not be of concern.

Contents pages

One of the last tasks with every issue is compiling the contents page, because it cannot be completed until the pagination is finalized. Most often the contents get a half-page, though sometimes a page, sometimes only a single column. The main purpose, of course, is to index the contents (usually with the headline and a few words of explanation), but if they are all listed in order, regular and unimportant features will detract from special features, so most magazines split the list into two parts. For example:

SPECIAL FEATURES
13 The Ku Klux Klan today: a special report.
22 Say cheers. Meet the champions of British cheerleading.
26 Perfume wars. What's brewing in Grasse.
38 For my next trick. Secrets of TV's top magician.
44 The tempting charms of the Veneto. The wine and food of one of Italy's most ravishing regions.
58 Gone missing. Bringing runaway children home.
DEPARTMENTS
8 TV and movies.
62 Pick of the paperbacks.
66 Crossword.
70 What the stars have in store for you.
74 Competition. Win a family holiday in Spain.
76 Special offer – green waxed jacket.

Some magazines divide contents further, listing them under sideheads such as FICTION, ARTICLES, SERVICES. Page numbers may, of course, appear after the title of a feature rather than before, and the layout can be dressed up, according to space offered, with a picture from each major feature or with brief notes on the writers. Some magazines also include 'The editor writes', a panel in which the editor tries to create a family feeling among readers, or 'A letter from the publisher' explaining the distances writers and photographers travelled and the ordeals they survived to prepare the issue.

The contents page may also be used to list the names of the editor and editorial and advertising executives. Some magazines go further, listing the entire staff, including secretaries and the receptionist, which no doubt pleases them and their mothers but has little other merit. Some trade magazines also list direct telephone numbers of staff writers, a questionable practice, because it can expose them to calls from cranks and bores at the most inconvenient times, such as when they are racing to complete a feature.

Covers

Possibly the single most important element of a magazine is its cover and this always rates – or should rate – the editor's personal attention. It is particularly important for magazines which have to sell on bookstalls, as opposed to those given away or sold by subscription. It has been estimated that three-quarters of the sales of women's monthly magazines are impulse buys, and that customers buy fewer than 6 of the 12 issues in a year. So a cover has to be striking and different, in order to stand out from competitors.

Figure 39   *Covers and cover lines.* Woman's Own *is an example of a busy multi-picture cover and* Time *of a totally typographical cover*

continued

Figure 39 – *continued* TV Times *cover combining photography and cartoon. The* Cosmopolitan *and* Bella *covers each carry nine separate cover lines, the* Sunday Express Magazine *just one*

October 1987 • £1

Those things
you do
to your mind
and body
Results
of our giant
health survey

What you
can learn
from the
lousiest job

Why it's hard
to say no to
Jack Nicholson

Beating the
guilts,
planning for
passion
and other
help for
working mothers

How to
live with
a man
and still
love him

The word is
BUZZ!
Cosmo's very
own soap
opera starts on
page 204

The mood on
campus now

Have you lost
your sex life?

More powerful than
'The Women's Room'
— an extract from
Marilyn French's
great new novel

continued

2–8 Nov, 1987 **29p**

Bella

NEW! only 29p **Dining a dozen**
Recipes for success

Those little Windsors
Leading the Royal brat pack

Beautiful rooms in shades of blue

Eat all you want – and still lose weight

Fashion's velvet touch

Porn boom
Can you protect
YOUR child?

Get knitting!
Twinsets go trendy

Will Charlton Heston run the USA?

Real life drama
The woman who collected husbands

It can be text or an artist's illustration, but is most often a colour photograph, and for maximum impact it should bleed on all edges rather than have a border. Trade magazines may show equipment, e.g. a camera or a car, and travel magazines may show an Egyptian pyramid or a villa in Spain. But the most eyecatching covers consist of faces, and the greatest impact comes from one face rather than two. Split covers featuring several separate pictures of subjects, whether of people, products or places, tend to dissipate impact, but it is not always easy to obtain pictures of the top quality sought for a cover, and some variety is called for occasionally.

It is unfortunate when two magazines on sale at the same time have similar covers, but it can happen easily. For example, magazines are unlikely to be able to induce members of the royal family to pose for exclusive pictures, and so there is a danger of having almost identical pictures at the time of an anniversary. On these occasions the obvious cover picture from an agency's files is not necessarily the best choice.

Cover lines

Cover lines – the words on a cover – are there primarily to snare the casual browser at a bookstall, and so, like cover pictures, are important on bookstall magazines but less so on subscription publications and giveaways.

A common error is including too many lines in an attempt to list every major feature inside on the principle that everyone will find at least one of interest. None of the lines then has much impact. For instance, here are cover lines from an American health and fitness magazine. There are seven of them in a mixture of caps and lower case and of type sizes and styles.

THE BIGGEST FITNESS CHANGE IN 10 YEARS
How to give up one food, lose 5–52 pounds
SENSUAL SKIN. Personalized map to the best body care
SAFE SEX. CANDID GUIDE TO DISEASE-FREE LOVEMAKING
10-minute terrific tummy-trimmer
BRUISED FRIENDSHIPS. How to ease hurt feelings
GLORIOUS HAIR. Breakthroughs in body and shine

It is probably better to identify one major selling point and promote that, rather than trying to interest everyone. Another error, often linked, is not making clear which cover line refers to the cover picture. A picture of a woman may be accompanied by cover lines reading:

The little girl who grew up to marry a prince
What you've always wanted to know about Julie Andrews

Who needs to get married?, asks Mary
A mother's lone fight for her daughter's life
The housewife watchdog
The woman who talks to plants
Knit it today, wear it tomorrow

Readers looking at the picture cannot be sure which of the lines refers to it. The subject of the picture does not look like Julie Andrews, so is she the princess, the mother, the housewife or the woman who talks to plants? Only a search through the magazine establishes that she is a model wearing the quick-knit sweater. The line referring to the cover picture should stand apart from the others, possibly on a flash or colour panel, and preferably should also be in a different typeface, or in caps where the others are in upper and lower case.

A last vitally important job on the cover is to make sure that it bears the correct date.

Diaries

Only journalists call them diaries; readers generally – and understandably – call them gossip columns, and they should in fact be about people, rather than places or things. While the point of a paragraph may be that a painting discovered in an attic is about to be auctioned, the story should focus on the finder or the artist. Likewise, if ownership of a stately home is about to change hands, a diary paragraph should centre on the owner or resident, rather than the history or furnishings.

A diary is best written by one person, so that a consistent style is established, though it may benefit from contributions from others, rewritten by the diary editor. Features that have not quite worked out, or for which there is no space, may be trimmed down to make acceptable diary stories. However, the diary should never be used as a dumping ground for the names of competition prizewinners or puffs for good causes to which the proprietor or editor has rashly promised some support. Even worse damage is done to a diary when it is used to accommodate corrections and apologies relating to other parts of the magazine. The diarist should be prepared to fight to keep these out; they should in fact be placed elsewhere.

Do-it-yourself features

All do-it-yourself features, in which can be included cookery columns, must be checked carefully. When magazines list the wrong quantity of an ingredient in a recipe, following the instructions can make a meal unpleasant if not worse; and readers become annoyed when they find that a dish supposed to take 20 minutes in the oven actually requires a full hour. All recipes, including those offered free to magazines by food manufacturers, should be tested by a responsible cook before publication.

Giving inaccurate information can, on occasion, be actually dangerous. Coal-conserving briquettes made by a method detailed in one magazine could have exploded, and the embarrassed editor had to give the story to radio to broadcast an urgent warning to readers.

Fiction

There are some all-fiction magazines, others that use fiction regularly, some that run it occasionally, and others that never carry it at all. Fiction in magazines is diminishing. Lee Eisenberg, editor-in-chief of America's *Esquire*, which for some years has published a summer issue devoted almost entirely to fiction, wrote in its August 1987 issue:

> We live in a time when hardly any national magazines give enough of a damn to publish fiction – quality, pulp or otherwise. They refrain, they say, because fiction 'doesn't sell' and because their printouts tell them that short stories rank last in their reader polls. As far as our experience tells us, they ought to can the pollsters. Our first summer reading issue proved to be one of the best selling numbers of 1984 and ever since the letters from readers and the goodwill that has been returned to us by the writing community have more than paid us back for our risk.

Those that run short stories have clear requirements. Some will buy only fiction by famous authors; others prefer the work of new writers. One magazine will buy 3000 words with a happy ending, another 1500 words with a twist in the tail. Some are concerned with old-fashioned hearts and flowers romance, others with contemporary sexual mores. For some the characters must be ordinary, working, British people – no foreign millionairesses or aliens from outer space – while others prefer the exotic.

The rules, written or unwritten, of a publication commonly cover, apart from length:

1 Number of characters, male and female.
2 Ages of the main characters and their professions (airline pilots and surgeons, or shepherds and village postmistresses; single working girls or mothers with young children).
3 Names (Fred and Betty, or Rupert and Fiona).

4   Backgrounds, foreign or domestic.
5   Endings, happy or hopeful (rarely downbeat).
6   Narration, first person or third person. (Confession type stories are normally told in the first person but some fiction editors bar first-person stories.)

While there are probably no staff fiction writers, it is not unknown for a staff feature writer to be asked to produce a short story on a given theme – such as an untold adventure of a soap opera character (by arrangement with the producer and TV company). Given the leading characters and their known habits and backgrounds, the writing is comparatively easy.

Schools of writing teach complicated systems of plotting stories which seem akin to practising carpentry. There is a Theme to be set out and a Key Character (the hero or heroine) from whose viewpoint the story is told. The Key Character has an Objective, such as winning a girl or getting a job. There are Antagonists, and Conflict Tests leading to a Black Moment when failure seems inevitable, followed by a Final Triumph.

Such systems may be of help to some, but probably most successful fiction writers begin with a strong original fragment of plot, characterization or theme and develop a story forwards and backwards from there. They create a character and see how he or she behaves, invent a plot and devise characters to participate in it, start with a climactic scene and work backwards to what led to it, or choose a theme and find a way of illustrating it.

Newspaper cuttings of stories about, say, a ferry disaster, a pools win or a divorce, can inspire ideas. So can the problem pages of women's magazines. Fiction writers need to note them as they occur. They also need to note characters – among people encountered on trains, in shops and on holiday. In any story there should always be one with whom readers can identify, and even the hero or heroine should have some weakness or flaw.

The hardest part of fiction writing for reporters or feature writers is probably the dialogue; for stories should be told as far as possible in dialogue. It need not be natural – people tend not to finish sentences, to overlap each other's words – but it should be credible. Few people talk like those quoted in newspaper stories and sometimes features. Nor do they make long speeches. Ending quotes with *he chuckled*, *he smiled*, and *he laughed* should be avoided; there is nothing wrong with *he said*. Descriptions can also be difficult for journalists, because their training has been to pare and pare again; in fiction, unless he or she is writing ultra short stories, a writer has space to develop character and atmosphere.

Fiction intros

A good opening is as important in fiction as in a feature and an opening sentence can sometimes suggest a story, though short stories need a good ending too, even more than features. Different types of intro (and different types of story) were well illustrated by entries in a *New York Magazine* competition in 1987 in which contestants were asked to devise opening sentences. They were parodies, but they show the range admirably. These were just some of them:

> When the Earl of Studley was born, his secret stayed within the castle walls. That he was inordinately clumsy was know only to his parents and a few members of the household staff, who were pledged to silence on penalty of death.

> It was the summer she had trouble getting her first service in. It was also the summer she started calling him Harold.

> The thing lifted its oversize head and stared down as the girl's body twitched in one last convulsive gasp of life. When it was sure she was dead, the blood-caked mandibles of its maw distorted into a scarlet grimace.

> Settling into her chaise, Miss Stephens noticed Mrs Gray across the pool, asleep at 10 in the morning – no doubt a result of the three empty Bloody Mary glasses by her chair.

> 'Don't frown', Larah told herself. Frowns cause little wrinkles around the mouth, and she was not going to give Hamilton the satisfaction of seeing her age before his eyes.

> Jack seemed so pleased to be out of our three-room apartment and settled into a house of our own that I didn't tell him how lonely I felt being five miles from the nearest neighbour. Nor did I tell him about the voices of crying children I sometimes heard coming from the attic late at night.

> I hadn't seen her in ten years, but there she was – stepping out of the taxi in front of me. I recognised her immediately: the porcelain skin, that sleek crop of blonde, thick hair. My fingers itched to caress that hair as they had once done years ago.

> Crouching naked inside the birthday cake, Susie Steinberg was beginning to have second thoughts.

Adolpho Mitsuhashi was discovered at precisely 3.05am on the floor of the Meredith Hotel with a bullet hole in his head and his left thumb missing.

What were the odds of four out of nine F-111 laser guidance systems suddenly failing? Mere coincidence? An act of Allah?

Arachnid. Even the word is alien and forbidding. Of 278 species of spider only 78 are know to be poisonous and only 17 poisonous to the point of death.

As dawn broke over the Watergate Hotel, John Randolph Stryker, the president of the United States, sat up in the disarrayed bed and reached out to stroke the honey-scented hair of the wife of the Soviet premier.

Small slivers of sunshine intruded their way through the venetian blind and one came to rest on Yetta's sleeping eyes. She awoke slowly and a smile came to her lips.

Until experiencing the wondrous adventure I shall describe in detail, I was as sceptical as the average intelligent person about reports of extra-terrestrials here on this planet.

Serializations

A novel may run to around 100,000 words, yet one women's magazine frequently serializes such books in six instalments of 5,000 words each. Another prefers four generous instalments of nearly 14,000 words each. For both it means cutting a great deal. The simple, but wrong, way of reducing a book to half its length would be by discarding the first or second half, or by throwing away every second page. The pace and style would, of course, be ruined. It would be just as much butchery to slash all descriptive paragraphs or dialogue.

Yet the fiction editor of one of the magazines says, 'We claim to get the whole story in'. Her method, when seeking, say, six instalments, is to divide the book into six sections, the first five of which have cliffhanging endings and the last one, of course, the denouement. She then cuts as necessary, removing firstly any confusing sub-plots, or anything irrelevant to the advancement of the story in the six episodes.

Sometimes this necessitates changing the continuity of a book. A flashback may be confusing to someone reading in instalments, and it may be better to tell the story chronologically. Equally, there may be an explanation in a late chapter of something that happened in an early one, which in a serialization is better explained at the time. The skill of those who do the work was vouched for by Noel Barber, author of several extremely long best sellers which have been serialized, who said, 'I know my books have been cut for magazine serialization but I have never been able to spot how it has been done'.

Occasionally magazines take a single extract of perhaps 2300 words from a novel, but this is only practicable when there is a passage that can stand on its own. Fiction editors have to be clever at spotting quickly how a novel can best be used within the formula of their publications.

Horoscopes

Horoscope columns are so popular that countless newspapers and magazines offer them, even though many people who admit to following them avidly add defensively that they do not really believe them. Horoscopes commonly consist of a main forecast for those whose birthdays fall in the period of sale of the magazine, and shorter ones for others, and they may run like this:

LIBRA (Sept 24–Oct 23). Events today may bring a much desired ambition into the realms of possibility.
SCORPIO (Oct 24–Nov 22). It is a blissful day for affairs of the heart. You are in an extra-amorous mood, ready to sweep a loved one off his or her feet.
SAGITTARIUS (Nov 23–Dec 21). Work will be causing you sleepless nights this week, and ironically your problems will stem from too much success.
CAPRICORN (Dec 22–Jan 20). Secret fears may be preventing you from feeling on top form so perhaps you should open your mind or your eyes to the fact that there is a lot you can do if you really want to change a situation.

The true astrologer claims to cast a horoscope, which is, in effect, a map showing the position of the sun, moon and planets within the twelve houses of the zodiac at the moment of the subject's birth, and then by observing their positions and interrelations foretells the outlines of a person's character and future. While magazine astrologers cannot, of course, cater for individual readers, many make frequent references to planetary movements. For example:

ARIES (Mar 21–April 20). The sun swings into your sign on Saturday, bringing a bumper helping of luck.

GEMINI (May 22–June 21). Watch out for mix-ups over messages as your ruling planet Mercury is travelling backwards.

VIRGO (Aug 24–Sept 22). Today's full moon falls in your own sign and warns you against a slick trickster.

Apart from such generalized predictions, horoscope columns may also offer predictions about particular people and events, and are sometimes startlingly accurate, though it is not unknown for a seer to admit to editorial staff that they have been based on mundane information or guesswork rather than on astrology: for example, a forecast that a named film star would become pregnant, made after hearing from friends of the star how anxious she was to have a child; and a forecast that a statesman would suffer ill health, deduced from the bearing of the man when seen in a newsreel.

Horoscopes need reading carefully by subs; more than one magazine astrologer has muddled word processor files and recycled identical forecasts for different birth signs in successive weeks. After such debacles a writer or sub with no previous experience of foretelling the future has sometimes taken over a column from a famous astrologer, and no readers have complained that the new stargazer was any less accurate or intuitive.

In our next issue

A late task, sometimes the last on a particular issue, is to write the blurb for what is commonly known as the NMI (for next month's issue) or NWI (next week's issue), which by this time should be well in hand. This is designed to persuade the reader to buy a copy of the next issue. The writer or sub landed with this chore soon appreciates how skilled is the work of advertising copywriters. The greatest difficulty is to avoid clichés such as *Watch out for . . . Don't miss . . . Calling all kids . . . You'll be thrilled by . . .* and the like. There is much to be said for merely listing coming features, as attractively as possible, without hyperbole.

Letters pages

Readers' letters pages are often the most widely read in periodicals. A topic such as 'a kindly act I came to regret' or a controversy about the etymology of an expression can run through many issues. Sometimes a modest payment is made for the 'lead' letter, sometimes for every letter, though it hardly seems necessary. It brings in some well written letters from amateur or semi-professional journalists seeking to earn a few pounds; unfortunately it

NEXT WEEK
FLOYD AT LARGE

Keith Floyd, star of BBC 2's *Floyd on Food*, joins the *Sunday Express Magazine* next Sunday when he begins a witty, informative, entertaining and exclusive monthly column.

Described by Egon Ronay as 'breathlessly rumbustuous, pure entertainment' Keith Floyd will cast a critical eye over fashionable fads and fancy foods.

Next Sunday, Floyd at Large celebrates the glorious simplicity of good French cooking with three traditional country recipes.

SUNDAY EXPRESS MAGAZINE

It adds so much to Sundays

Figure 40 *Two ways of handling the blurb for the next issue; a busy approach in* Woman *and a straightforward one in the* Sunday Express Magazine

also encourages persistent letter writers whose views and names and addresses soon become familiar to other readers. Letters from regular correspondents should be used sparingly, even though they may be above average.

However, readers' letters pages sometimes need professional assistance. Some weeks most of the letters received will relate to a feature in a past issue, and because of the printing schedule they will seem very old by the time they can be published; or they will be on topics which have already been exhausted; or largely the work of cranks, whose efforts are usually immediately recognizable by being written in green ink and continued around the margins of the notepaper. On occasion a writer or sub may solicit letters from celebrities, or persuade other writers to contribute letters in order to get some punch and freshness, introduce some topicality, and avoid the chore of deciphering scrawling handwriting. It is customary to append the names of towns in far parts of the country to make the readership appear widespread.

Having commissioned letters also prevents the magazine being hoaxed. Ideally, the authenticity of all letters should be verified, the simplest method being to telephone the writer and say that the letter is being considered for publication. This is sometimes too time-consuming, but doubtful letters should always be checked. A letter in praise of spanking should be automatically suspect; it may bear the name of a schoolteacher and have been sent by pupils. Similarly, a letter attacking blood sports may be found to bear the name of the master of a hunt.

Some magazines like to tail each letter with a reply or comment, but this is only warranted when a letter calls for a response. Footnotes added for no good reason are hard to compose and space-wasting, and can seem flippant or patronizing.

Lists

The most talented hostesses, barristers or surgeons . . . the most exciting cities, preachers or artists . . . the most boring buildings, couturiers or TV pundits . . . the most expensive schools, restaurants or cars . . . Magazines are addicted to lists of all kinds, usually fleshed out with descriptive notes.

Most often they list superlatives: the wealthiest women in the world, the most eligible bachelors, the most wanted fugitives, the fastest growing plants, the most endangered species, the most popular breeds of dogs, the safest airlines, the most puzzling unsolved mysteries, the greatest sporting champions, the television programmes with the largest audiences . . . Variations are arbitrary lists of the fashionable and unfashionable, under such titles as *What's in and what's out* or *What's hot and what's not.*

Make-overs

Take a reader, a homely female lacking fashion sense or style. Give her a new hairstyle, have her made up by a beauty expert, dress her in modish clothes, and then pose her for pictures by a fashion photographer. That is the basic formula for a type of feature known on women's magazines as a 'make-over', and sometimes arranged as a competition prize.

Makeover with Bella

Clare Rossiter (32)

Before

After

Three years ago Clare helped husband Chris start his own garage business in Kings Lynn, Norfolk. Even now with Tom, 4½ and Alice, 16 months, Clare still takes care of the books. At present they are building a house but, while her plans were shaping up, Clare felt her hair was shaping out. A style that lifted the weight of hair from her shoulders gave Clare a smart new look. Too much hair fell away from the centre parting so it was cut short enough to stop it sitting on her collar and clipped on top to lose the parting.

As Clare often had dark shadows under her eyes, a light concealer is blended in before applying Liquid Foundation in Natural. It is then dusted with Translucent Matte Finishing Powder and Hazlenut Powder Blusher for the cheeks. Eyeshadow Duo in Powder Cup is emphasised with grey Eyeliner Pencil. Lips are filled in with Spice Lipstick.

Photos: Rob Lee. Make-up: Ruth Fennel. Cosmetics: Swedish Formula. Hair: Elliott at Glemby. Shirt by Benetton.

Would you like a brand new look with a *Bella* makeover? Send your photograph, together with your age, address and telephone number to: *Bella* Makeover, 25 Camden Road, London NW1 9LL. Enclose SAE if you wish your photo returned.

Figure 41   *Example of a make-over, from* Bella

Men can also be given the treatment. Scruffy teenagers can be transformed into smoothly tailored and barbered city types; staid, prematurely aged businessmen can be made to look years younger with a tan (from a bottle) and a wardrobe of sports clothes.

The idea works well when an obvious improvement is wrought and a plain Jane or John displays a lively new personality. However, when the 'before' picture is arguably more attractive than the 'after', as sometimes happens, the experiment must be deemed a failure.

Variations are to make over several people from particular professions or occupations, such as members of parliament, librarians, nurses or novelists. Volunteers photographed before and after, or at intervals during, slimming programmes could also be classed as having been made over by magazines in that, if they are successful in losing weight, they look like different persons.

Merchandising

The public has a keen interest in new products and gadgets, which is catered for in many different types of publications, from trade magazines devoted to, for instance, office equipment, and compiled largely from the handouts of manufacturers' press representatives, to the upmarket women's glossies, spotlighting trends in fashions with colour pictures of models displaying them, and overleaf a list of where the new fashions can be bought and their prices.

The main requirement of a product if it is to be of interest is that it must be new. If products have already been seen in the High Street, it is too late to feature them. There should be news in 'merch', as merchandising features are known on women's magazines. The exception to this is in comparison tests – of lawnmowers or showerproof jackets or brands of marmalade. Considerable ingenuity is called for in projecting such features, e.g. in getting the players of a famous football team to be photographed testing showers, or getting celebrated authors to test and report on different word processors.

Magazines move further into merchandising when they carry special offers, designed partly as a service to readers and partly to earn revenue. Ideally, such products should be unavailable from any other source. If not, they should be offered at a price lower than obtainable elsewhere. It is embarrassing to offer, say, a holiday or a garden tool and find it can be bought as cheaply at discount shops; even more embarrassing is when a rival is found to be making a similar offer more cheaply.

Opinion columns

Writers of opinion columns are paid to parade their views and are expected to be opinionated and provocative about everything they discuss. Ideally, their views should be shared by most of the readers; it is the role of the columnist to articulate readers' often expressed, or perhaps never consciously felt, opinions. However, while everyone is against cruelty to children and animals, opinions vary, even among the readers of a particular magazine, on such subjects as education, cats, package holidays, television programmes, pop music and foreigners. The columnist should please most readers most of the time, but is entitled to offend some readers some of the time.

Columnists' views attract much mail, some of it offensive. 'You should be castrated with a broken lemonade bottle', wrote an elderly woman reader when a columnist mildly suggested raising certain speed limits. The columnist should never be tempted to write back rudely. To be recommended is a courteous letter on the lines of 'Thank you very much for your letter; it is always a pleasure to hear from readers'. There can be no complaint about the wording, but it is guaranteed to infuriate recipients because it implies that the writer has not troubled to read their abuse.

Quizzes

A quiz is a useful way of covering a subject so much written about that no new feature idea suggests itself. Quizzes are also handy for filling half pages. The main problem in compiling them is pitching them at the level of knowledge of the readers. Unless deliberately setting a brain teaser, it is not sensible to pose the almost unanswerable – which is easy to do, given that the compiler knows the answers before framing the questions.

Unless there is a major prize at stake, a quiz should not be too difficult, and in one set purely for fun it is often best to offer multiple choice answers, thereby giving everyone a chance at least to guess the right one. Ask the name of the river that flows through Paris and some readers will find it impossible to answer. Ask whether the river that flows through Paris is (a) the Seine, (b) the Rhone, or (c) the Loire, is easier; offering a choice of Seine, Danube and Mississippi is easier still. The level must depend on the educational standard of the readers.

Even so, answers must be carefully checked. One quiz asked the transfer fee paid for a footballer and offered three possible answers, none of which was correct and a reader complained to the Press Council.

Picture questions are useful for brightening the page, but should be chosen carefully to avoid disclosing answers. Showing a picture of Marlon Brando above the question, 'Who played *The Godfather* in the 1971 film?' gives the answer away. Showing a long shot of the wedding scene from the film or one of the mobsters would not.

Self-knowledge quizzes such as *How's your sec's life?, Are you a man or a wimp?* or *How do you rate as a parent?*, with marks to be added or deducted to give a score, are also popular. In these, as in other quizzes, it is customary to provide ratings at the end, with scores and ratings normally geared to make readers feel that they are brighter than perhaps they are. For example, *What Kind of* Financial *Fool Am I?*, a quiz encouraging readers to analyse their spending habits in relation to entertainment, drinks, clothes, unplanned buys, borrowing, hire purchase, savings and credit cards might offer ratings on these lines:

HOW YOU RATE

1   If you scored below 30 you are a financial delinquent, living in cloud cuckoo land. Be warned. A day of reckoning will come.

2   31–50. You have some financial savvy but you could manage your affairs better by more careful budgeting.

3   51–70. Congratulations. You are better than most at money management, and will never find yourself in financial straits through recklessness or foolishness. You should prosper.

4   71 or more. Are you by any chance a bank manager or an accountant? You are shrewd, but be careful not to become obsessive about watching the pennies. Go a little wild just once in a while.

Reviews

The main problems with reviews – of plays, records, books, videos, television and exhibitions – are production schedules, particularly on monthly magazines. Books present the smallest problem, advance copies or proofs usually being obtainable long before the publication day, which is decided well in advance and rarely changed. Therefore magazines can review them at the same time or soon after daily newspapers. Television presents the biggest problem, because there may be only one opportunity for viewers to see a programme, unlike films and plays, which may run for a considerable time. Consequently programmes are usually *pre*viewed rather than *re*viewed, because there is little merit in lauding a programme when the opportunity to see it is past. Unfortunately, even when programmes can be seen by a reviewer well in advance, either in a studio or by borrowing a videocassette to watch at home, schedules are subject to change until only a few weeks before transmission.

One thing all subjects of reviews have in common is that the brilliant and the awful are easy to write about, though in the latter case there is always a danger of yielding to the temptation of indulging in cheap cracks, such as reviewing a film called *Moment of a Lifetime* with a put-down such as *It ain't*. It is much harder to review the competent but pedestrian.

Perhaps the worst sin a critic or reviewer can commit is to disclose the ending, whether of a book, a film or a TV programme. Apart from ethical considerations, readers will not be grateful, and some will be enraged.

Strips

There are photo strips in which models are photographed, and drawn scripts in which an artist creates the pictures. Children's comics and some adventure comics for adults rely heavily upon them, but they also have their uses in heavier journals, e.g. in illustrating the chronology of a terrorist attack or the chain of command in a big organization.

Strips start with scripts, the writing of which calls for an ability to see a story in pictures. They are set out much like those for films. For example:

Frame 1. L/S (long shot): An airport. Night. Lights blaze from the control tower and buildings. A jumbo jet is about to land.
Title panel: NIGHT FLIGHT
Frame 2. M/S (medium shot): The aircraft is on the ground and steps are being positioned at the door.
Balloon from window: Wake up Maggie, this is England.
Caption: 14 March 1987.
Frame 3. C/U (close-up): A beautiful, well dressed woman in dark glasses is framed in the door of the jumbo, about to leave the plane.
Thinks bubble: Chin up, Maggie. They can't know you're here.

Supplements

Supplements bulk out a magazine, are good for circulation, and provide something to publicize; they can also be vehicles for extra advertising. They can be stitched inside magazines, inserted loose or banded to them with plastic or paper wrappers. The main thing against stitched-in supplements is that their natural place is in the centre of the magazine and this spoils the look of a centre spread until the supplement has been extracted.

Supplements may be complete in one issue; they can also be run through a number of issues to promote regular buying of the magazine, e.g. a who's who of characters in television soap operas, or a guide to home decorating or dieting, in which the weekly parts are removed, folded and inserted inside each other to form a booklet. Journalists asked to compile an encyclopedic four-parter should remember that if the pages are to be pulled out and inserted inside each other, it is not feasible to cover A to D in the first week and E to K in the second. The first week's instalment is likely to cover A to C and W to Z because it will form the outer section. The second week may contain D to F and S to V, and so on.

Some magazines incorporate sponsored supplements, sometimes virtually quarterly or half-yearly magazines in their own right; for example, a motoring supplement may be produced in association with one of the motoring organizations, a home-buying supplement with a building society, a photographic one with a film manufacturer, one on holidays with a travel organization. The merits are that the parent magazine gets an authoritative supplement for practically nothing or even makes a profit, depending on how much the organisation or firm can be persuaded to pay, while the latter gets publicity and will be able to buy cheaply a run-on of additional copies of the supplement for distributing by mail or over counters. It is important, though, that the final word should remain with the editor. While the material cannot be critical of the sponsor, it should not be a blatant advertisement.

However, at Christmas it has become commonplace for big chain stores to sponsor supplements which are effectively their catalogues. Magazines get income from them while the stores may get the design and production work basically free of charge. This sort of supplement should be clearly distinguished as advertising and not promoted as part of the magazine.

Publicists reckon 'advertorial' – sponsored material looking like editorial – as worth between two and ten times as much as an equivalent amount of advertising space, one reason being that readers assume the product or service is endorsed by the magazine, which is not necessarily the case. Editors reply that bad products are not given space, and liken the publicity to book review columns, which do not deal with meretricious books, or if they do, say they are bad. Journalists are, however, understandably wary about the influence of money on editorial pages.

Free gifts

Supplements are often promoted as free gifts and are generally welcomed; other types of free gifts are often unpopular with newsagents, particularly if they are unwieldy. Yet DIY magazines give away rulers, screw gauges and wallpaper roll calculators, audio magazines give away cassettes and anti-static cloths, teenage publications give away scent and lipsticks and unbreakable mirrors.

They are commonly taped to magazine covers – and need to be, for readers get annoyed when they open half a dozen copies from a rack in succession and find that none contains a gift because the gifts have been stolen by browsers or have dropped out and disappeared behind other magazines. However, no journalistic work is usually necessary, other than writing blurbs for the gifts.

Surveys

Surveys require reader participation, which is always desirable, and also provide good copy. For example, a survey on the desirability of vigilante groups asked:

1 Do you believe the maintenance of law and order should be left to the police? *Yes/No*.
2 Would the presence of vigilantes in your area make you feel more or less safe going out at night? *More/Less/No change*.

10 PRINTING AND PRODUCTION

The process of readying material for printing is known as 'origination'. Unlike newspapers, where this is normally all done in house, magazines generally rely on contract printing at other premises. Copy may be sent to a specialist typesetting shop, and artwork to a 'repro' (reproduction) house, and both brought together at a third establishment for printing; or all the processes may be handled by one firm. The first option can be cheaper and quicker, but if the printer's is a union house, it is often necessary for pre-press work to be accompanied by numbered stickers proving that it was carried out by union members.

Typesetting

Words have to be typeset by compositors, unless they have been directly input into a computer system. The 'hot metal' method is obsolescent now, but is still offered by jobbing printers for church and club magazines and similar small publications, and can give good quality. The two main kinds of hot metal machine, both developed at the end of the nineteenth century, are the Linotype, which casts complete lines or 'slugs', and the Monotype, which casts each character individually.

As an operator types copy on the keyboard of a Linotype, inserting spaces and word breaks to justify lines, the machine selects an appropriate matrix or mould for each character from a magazine and makes them up into a complete line, which is cast in molten metal (a lead alloy). A disadvantage is that if any correction is required a whole line has to be reset. Monotype setting is easier to amend as the characters are separate. A Monotype keyboard produces a paper ribbon perforated with a code of holes which then drives a 'caster' controlled by another operator, in which moulds of the characters are filled with molten metal and cooled before being placed in their line.

From these comparatively primitive, large and noisy machines were developed the 'cold type' photocomposition machines which succeeded hot metal as the standard system in the 1960s. They also depended on punched tape, but matrix cases contained negatives of characters on film, through which light was projected to print a positive of the image on photographic paper.

In modern digital machines punched tape has been replaced by a computer. A keyboard operator, sitting in front of a video display, selects a typeface and the type size in points or millimetres, the digital system commonly offering from 2-point to 96-point in half-point increases. However, a standard series of type sizes is usually formatted into the system and programmed on to keys for ease of selection. The computer will automatically set spacing, although it can be varied. At a keystroke it will hyphenate and justify lines, checking that word breaks are acceptable to a dictionary in the system, which includes 'exceptions', or words that do not hyphenate logically. For example, *ink-ling* is more acceptable than *inkl-ing*, which the computer would otherwise offer.

A laser beam or a cathode ray tube (CRT), like a small television tube, then scans and builds up each required character from type masters. Digital photosetters are faster and more reliable than the mechanical models and can reproduce perfect characters an infinite number of times.

The paste-up process

In hot metal printing each page of type is assembled, together with 'blocks', which are zinc engravings of photographs and artwork, and locked into a 'forme' from which a mould is made and molten lead alloy injected to produce a heavy printing plate.

In photocomposition the assembly of metal type is replaced by a 'paste-up' of text and illustrations on photographic paper, and this is the standard system today. Page compositors work at easels on graphed cards marked vertically in column widths and horizontally in centimetres and millimetres like artists' layout grids. With a scalpel a compositor cuts up the sheets of photographic bromide paper on which the photo-setting machine has printed the text, and sticks the columns on to the grid with a hot wax paste in accordance with the art department's layout. Black and white photographs, printed to the correct size on the same weight of bromide paper, are also trimmed with a scalpel – and can be turned into cut-outs, if need be, before being pasted in position, along with headlines and other matter. (Colour pictures are handled in a different operation.) The page compositor applies adhesive tape rules, and on instructions from the subs can also literally cut overmatter.

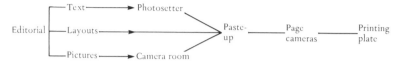

Figure 42   *Path of material from the editorial office to printing*

Computer enthusiasts regard the process of taking material out of the computer to be assembled manually as inefficient. In fact, 'full page composition' by computer is practicable though not widely used, because of the great flexibility of the paste-up process.

Half tones

From paste up the pages go for photographing by a process camera, a large copying camera, to produce transparencies from which printing plates or cylinders can be made. Black and white artwork, such as line drawings and text, need no other processing, because no tones are present (though dots and cross-hatching may be used in drawings to give an illusion of tone), but the reproduction of photographs presents a difficulty.

Black and white photographs are not all black and white, of course; they include shades of grey, and the same applies to wash and line illustrations. However, they have to be printed with black ink which has no gradations. The problem is solved by breaking a picture into dots of different sizes, large for dark areas, and small for pale ones, these dots being created, in effect, by placing a film or glass screen bearing a mesh of lines between the photograph and the film in the camera.

The screen may be fine or coarse, depending on the printing method and paper. If too coarse a screen is used when printing on glossy paper, the result will be coarse and the dots evident, while if too fine a screen is used with newsprint, the paper will not be able to cope with the smallest dots. So while newspapers generally use coarse screens of 65 or 85 lines per inch (26 or 34 lines per centimetre) many magazines use screens of 100 or 120 lpi (40 or 48 lpc) and the glossiest use fine screens of 133 or 150 lpi (54 or 60 lpc).

Incidentally, published pictures occasionally display a strange chequered pattern. This 'moiré' effect is caused by using an already screened picture, e.g. a page from a newspaper or periodical, resulting in a clash of screens. When it is necessary to reproduce such pictures, possibly in a survey of magazine covers or in a flashback to an historic issue, the best course is to proceed boldly and present the results as though the effect is intended.

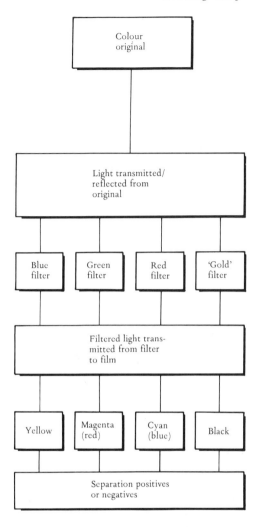

Figure 43   *The process of colour separation*

Colour separations

Colour photographs also have to be broken into dots for the half-tone process, but more work is necessary, because full colour is printed by combinations of four colours – yellow, magenta (red), cyan (blue) and black, imposed in that order – and a picture has to be separated into the four colours. This is done by the use of filters, a blue filter creating the negative for printing yellow, a green isolating magenta, a red yielding cyan and a combination yellow-orange filter giving black. The four negatives are known as 'separations', since each contains only one of the printing colours.

Colour separation and screening are done by high speed electronic 'scanners'. A transparency is attached to a drum, and an operator keys in the percentage reduction or enlargement and the screen required. The drum is then rotated at speed while a laser beam scans the image and by means of filters and a computer converts it within seconds into screened films for each of the four colours.

Sophisticated scanners will do much more. Instead of producing separations for each individual picture to be placed on a page, they scan each one, store the information digitally, and then produce one film per colour for the whole page. They can enlarge transparencies up to ten times, improve the sharpness of pictures, modify colour balance and local contrast, and crop, compress or stretch an image if, for example, it is desired to make a car look longer and sleeker or shorter and dumpier.

From the film negatives for the complete page are etched the printing plates or cylinders.

Colour proofing

The first proofs to be supplied to a magazine office are usually those of colour pictures, both because of their importance and for the longer time needed in dealing with colour. For clarity, they are often reproduced on finer quality paper than the magazine actually uses. They are examined closely in the art department, for much can be done to change colours at the proof stage. If a picture is too 'hot', the flesh tones too lurid, a filter can be used to cut the magenta. If a picture is too 'cold' it can be made warmer by using a filter to reduce the cyan.

Generally, journalists should limit themselves to telling the repro house or printer the effect required – for example, to darken green, rather than, say, asking for more cyan. It is rash to try to tell experts how to do their job, which in this case might be better achieved by reducing yellow.

Proof reading

In hot metal printing the first text proofs were traditionally galleys, showing text in long columns without division into pages. These may still be required if text is being set by a typesetting house to be pasted up as camera-ready artwork in an editorial office, but increasingly the first proofs to be supplied are page proofs, struck after paste-up assembly, with the text therefore in pages and correctly positioned headlines in accordance with the layouts supplied.

In a computerized editorial office where copy has been subbed on screen everything should fit perfectly, since the computer can give a line or word count and copy should have been cut or lengthened, if necessary, before operation of the photo-setter. Proof reading is effectively done before paste-up rather than after it.

For other subs, working on hard copy, the arrival of proofs is when they discover if they have done their work properly. If they have been skilful, and perhaps a little bit lucky, the text will fit exactly. More likely, since the tightness of setting can vary according to the compositor and the system used, a page will have a line or two of 'overmatter', which will be reproduced in a margin. Sloppy subbing can result in a considerable amount of overmatter, which will make the sub responsible unpopular, because it means more work, wastes money and time, and the magazine may need to await corrections and a revised proof before the page can be passed.

Journalists should forget stories of Victorian novelists who practically rewrote books at the proof stage. Alterations are expensive today. A printing firm can earn much money from 'authors' corrections', the name given to alterations which are not merely corrections of printers' errors, and inquiries are held when the bill for authors' corrections arrives, for the money could be better spent.

So this is not the time for rewriting. It is a time for necessary corrections and minor improvements to the look. Paragraphs may have to be transposed. Sometimes a paragraph of a feature will have been omitted or pasted in the wrong place. Punctuation may have to be altered and there may be changes of type from Roman to italic or bold, and from capitals to lower case. There will probably be deletions and insertions known as 'cuts and fills'.

To cut text to make it fit, it is preferable to remove entire paragraphs rather than a sentence here and a sentence there, and if possible they should be taken from the end rather than the middle of a feature. To fill, a sub can write in more words (casting off as accurately as possible with a character count). Again, these words are better inserted at the end of a paragraph than in the middle. A sub can also fill by creating more paragraph breaks or inserting additional crossheads or typebreakers.

Proof reading requires concentration, and it is helpful to read text with a ruler or sheet of copy paper across the page below the line being read, moving it down a line at a time, so that the eyes do not jump ahead and miss an error. Literals such as transpositions or characters in body type are fairly easily spotted; it is often harder to spot a transposed character in a headline, and the bigger the type, the easier it can be to overlook an error. Figures and spellings should be checked against the copy (returned with the proofs). It might seem natural that the proof reading should be done by the sub who handled the feature originally, but it is often better to bring a different pair of eyes and another mind to bear.

BS 5261C : 1976

UDC 001.816 : 655.255.1

Marks for copy preparation and proof correction

(extracted from BS 5261 : Part 2 : 1976)

Repères pour la préparation du manuscrit et correction sur épreuve

Zeichen für die Manuskriptvorbereitung und Korrektur der Probeabzüge

Notes on the use of the marks
(clauses **4.5**, **4.6**, **4.7** and **4.8** of BS 5261 : Part 2 : 1976)

1. For each marking-up or proof correction instruction a distinct mark is to be made:

(a) in the text: to indicate the exact place to which the instruction refers;

(b) in the margin: to signify or amplify the meaning of the instruction.

It should be noted that some instructions have a combined textual and marginal mark.

2. Where a number of instructions occur in one line, the marginal marks are to be divided between the left and right margins where possible, the order being from left to right in both margins.

3. Specification details, comments and instructions may be written on the copy or proof to complement the textual and marginal marks. Such written matter is to be clearly distinguishable from the copy and from any corrections made to the proof. Normally this is done by encircling the matter and/or by the appropriate use of colour (see below).

4. Proof corrections shall be made in coloured ink thus:

(a) printer's literal errors marked by the printer for correction: green;

(b) printer's literal errors marked by the customer and his agents for correction: red;

(c) alterations and instructions made by the customer and his agents: black or dark blue.

British Standards Institution

2 Park Street London W1A 2BS · Telephone 01-629 9000 · Telex 266933
© British Standards Institution, 1976
ISBN: 0 580 09057 4

8402-1-4k-JWD

Figure 44   *Correcting proofs – standard correction marks*

Classified list of marks (Table 1 from BS 5261 : Part 2)

NOTE: The letters M and P in the notes column indicate marks for
marking-up copy and for correcting proofs respectively.

Group A General

Number	Instruction	Textual mark	Marginal mark	Notes
A1	Correction is concluded	None	/	P Make after each correction
A2	Leave unchanged	– – – – – – under characters to remain	Ⓙ	M P
A3	Remove extraneous marks	Encircle marks to be removed	✕	P e.g. film or paper edges visible between lines on bromide or diazo proofs
A3.1	Push down risen spacing material	Encircle blemish	⊥	P
A4	Refer to appropriate authority anything of doubtful accuracy	Encircle word(s) affected	⑦	P

Group B Deletion, insertion and substitution

B1	Insert in text the matter indicated in the margin	⋏	New matter followed by ⋏	M P Identical to B2
B2	Insert additional matter identified by a letter in a diamond	⋏	⋏ Followed by for example ◇A	M P The relevant section of the copy should be supplied with the corresponding letter marked on it in a diamond e.g. ◇A
B3	Delete	/ through character(s) or ├────┤ through words to be deleted	⌀	M P
B4	Delete and close up	⁀ through character or ├────┤ through character e.g. chara*z*cter chara**bd**cter	⌀	M P

Number	Instruction	Textual mark	Marginal mark	Notes
B5	Substitute character or substitute part of one or more word(s)	/ through character or ⊢────┤ through word(s)	New character or new word(s)	M P
B6	Wrong fount. Replace by character(s) of correct fount	Encircle character(s) to be changed	⊗	P
B6.1	Change damaged character(s)	Encircle character(s) to be changed	✕	P This mark is identical to A3
B7	Set in or change to italic	──────── under character(s) to be set or changed	⊔⊔	M P Where space does not permit textual marks encircle the affected area instead
B8	Set in or change to capital letters	════════ under character(s) to be set or changed	═	
B9	Set in or change to small capital letters	════════ under character(s) to be set or changed	═	
B9.1	Set in or change to capital letters for initial letters and small capital letters for the rest of the words	══ under initial letters and ════ under rest of word(s)	═	
B10	Set in or change to bold type	∿∿∿∿∿∿ under character(s) to be set or changed	∿	
B11	Set in or change to bold italic type	∿∿∿∿∿∿ under character(s) to be set or changed	⊔⊔ ∿	
B12	Change capital letters to lower case letters	Encircle character(s) to be changed	≢	P For use when B5 is inappropriate
B12.1	Change small capital letters to lower case letters	Encircle character(s) to be changed	≠	P For use when B5 is inappropriate

Number	Instruction	Textual mark	Marginal mark	Notes
B13	Change italic to upright type	Encircle character(s) to be changed	⨆	P
B14	Invert type	Encircle character to be inverted	↻	P
B15	Substitute or insert character in 'superior' position	/ through character or ⅄ where required	⌐ under character e.g. ⌐₂	P
B16	Substitute or insert character in 'inferior' position	/ through character or ⅄ where required	∟ over character e.g. ∟₂	P
B17	Substitute ligature e.g. ffi for separate letters	├————┤ through characters affected	⌒ e.g. f͡fi	P
B17.1	Substitute separate letters for ligature	├————┤	Write out separate letters	P
B18	Substitute or insert full stop or decimal point	/ through character or ⅄ where required	⊙	M P
B18.1	Substitute or insert colon	/ through character or ⅄ where required	⊙	M P
B18.2	Substitute or insert semi-colon	/ through character or ⅄ where required	;	M P
B18.3	Substitute or insert comma	/ through character or ⅄ where required	,	M P

Extracts from BS 5261: Part 2: 1976 are reproduced by permission of BSI. Complete copies of the standard can be obtained from them at Linford Wood, Milton Keynes, Bucks MK14 6LE

Proof marks

For each correction or alteration, marks are made in the text to indicate the exact place to which it refers, and in the margin to amplify the instruction. These marks are laid down in a British standard (BS 5261) of 1976. Where there are a number of instructions relating to the same line, they can be placed in both left and right margins in that order.

Printers conventionally mark their own errors in green, though they should have already carried out all corrections they noticed were required. There was a time when printers employed 'readers', properly styled 'Correctors of the Press', who, apart from marking literals, would draw attention to grammatical errors, badly constructed and ambiguous sentences and such possible errors of fact as an incorrect date or title, but today a printer is unlikely to be concerned with anything except typographical mistakes.

Printed errors noticed in the editorial office are conventionally marked in red and there should be no charge for correcting them. Other alterations, which may be charged for, are made in blue or black, A fine tip should be used, for clarity is vital.

Different editors have different obsessions, but 'widows and orphans' are generally unpopular. A widow is the last word, or syllable of a word, which happens to fall on a line on its own at the end of a paragraph. This looks ugly, and if it happens at the foot of a column, a reader may think that the feature ends there. An orphan is a widow which occurs at the top of a column and looks even worse, particularly when it is only part of a word such as *-ed* or *-ing*. Some editors ban widows and orphans completely. Others permit those that meet certain criteria: for example, those consisting of at least three characters, provided that the column is not wider than 12 ems.

On some magazines 'running turns' are required between all columns. That means full measure lines at top and bottom and never a full point at the end of a column.

Marked proofs are returned to the printer stamped 'Passed for press', unless a sub is sufficiently unhappy about complicated amendments to call for a revised proof. When the changes have been carried out, a further set of proofs will be supplied. There should be no further changes to be made, unless necessitated by outside events, such as developments in a story or a change in a price mentioned. Unfortunately, in making corrections new errors sometimes creep in, and even what was right may become wrong. When the last page has been approved, the proofs are agreed and stamped 'As to press'; the production editor ticks and dates the final column on the progress chart and the issue is in the hands of the printer.

The working dummy

During the proofing process described, spare page proofs or photocopies of page proofs of both editorial and advertisements are usually pasted into a dummy by the production editor so that executives can view the progress of the issue. The dummy starts out with blank pages of the same number as the issue being worked on and steadily fills up.

This dummy gives a much better picture of the flow of a magazine's contents, and the strengths and weaknesses of an issue, than can be obtained from a flat plan. It makes it easy to spot too similar headlines, pictures or layouts, and any clashes between editorial and advertisements. These may include not only clashes of content but of typography and display, for an advertisement facing editorial may be so bold that it overshadows the editorial completely, and some redesign of the editorial may be needed to compete. The dummy also helps promotion and sales staff to gauge the sales potential of the issue.

In fact, owing to the overlapping of printing schedules, with colour for one issue going to the printer before mono of the previous one, there may be three dummies in different stages of completion at any time. On some big magazines, reduced size photocopies of the pages are pinned up in sequence on a notice board so that subs and artists can keep an eye on them.

Printing

The work of printing the issue gets under way. There are three main kinds of

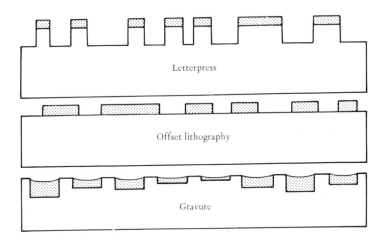

Figure 45 *How the printing image is carried in the three main processes – letterpress, offset litho and gravure*

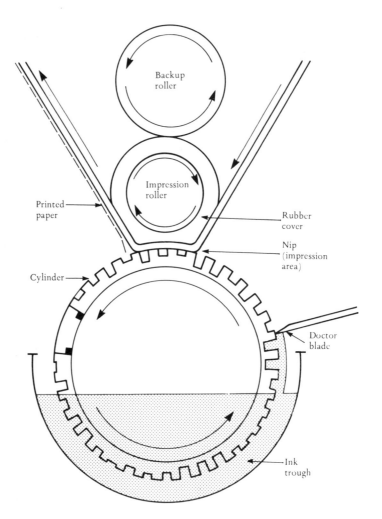

Figure 46   *How gravure works*

magazine printing: letterpress, done from a raised type surface, but obsolescent; photogravure (or gravure) from a recessed surface; and, most
common in magazines today, lithography (or litho) from a flat or only
slightly recessed surface.

In *letterpress* printing rollers ink the raised surface of a plate, which is then
pressed into contact with the paper. *Gravure* is the reverse of letterpress in
that the ink instead of being on a raised area it is in cells or tiny hollows below
the surface of a copper-plated cylinder, etched by acid to varying depths, the

darker the tones the deeper being the cells. The lower part of the cylinder is immersed in a reservoir of ink which flows over the cylinder as it rotates. As it comes out, it is scraped by a 'doctor blade' so that ink remains only in the cells. With colour a separate cylinder is used for each of the four process colours, and the main drawback is the high cost of cylinders; gravure is only economical for runs of more than 100,000 copies.

Litho prints from thin plates (a separate one for each colour) and depends on the natural antipathy of grease and water. Basically, areas to be printed are greased and the non-printing surfaces dampened; printing ink, which is oil-based, adheres to the greasy surface but is rejected by the water on the dampened part of the plate. Plates used to be made from thin metal, but they were subject to damage and breakage, and are today often surfaced with polymer, which has proved to be more durable. The image is 'burned' into the polymer under ultra violet light.

However, the common practice now is not to print from a plate but to offset the impression to a cylinder carrying a rubber blanket and from there to paper, hence the name, *offset litho*. This has the advantage that long print runs are possible without plates wearing out.

Web offset, used since the 1950s, mainly for runs of more than 20,000, is offset litho printing on a continuous web of paper from a reel as opposed to individual sheets of paper. When machines are sheet fed, one side of the paper is printed in one pass, then, after a change of plates, the paper is turned and the reverse side printed. Web-feeding (which is also used with gravure) makes it possible to run machines three times as fast while printing both sides of the paper simultaneously and also folding it. The disadvantages are the greater wastage of paper, especially at start-up, and time lost when a web breaks.

Desktop publishing

New technology has made it possible for small circulation magazines to be printed and published by a do-it-yourself process known as desktop publishing or DTP. This is basically an extension of word processing, and while it has not posed a threat to existing magazines, it allows one person at an office desk to produce an entire publication quickly and cheaply, and therefore makes possible publications which would be too expensive to produce by conventional publishing methods.

Instead of the powerful mainframe computers with many terminals used in newspaper and major magazine offices, DTP relies on domestic microcomputers coupled to laser printers. With appropriate programs an operator can keyboard type, draw graphics, produce page layouts, headings, text and rules, and insert illustrations and captions. The result can be printed out on the spot, or sent to a printer for the final version. One person has control of the whole process, which is quick, convenient and cheap.

DTP began in the mid-1980s in business offices with a need to publish reports, mailing shots, price lists, brochures, technical manuals and the like. Conventionally some were typed and photocopied (the result functional but not attractive) and others typeset and printed, with an artist employed to carry out the design work (the result attractive but expensive). Then in the mid-1980s the Apple computer company adopted a computer software program which could produce a full page of text, graphics and digitized pictures, and linked it to a laser printer.

In typesetting DTP offers a number of typefaces in Roman and italic from 4-point to 127-point. For design it can work on an A4 spread. Text from a word processor can be dropped into the page, headlines written, graphics placed and rules drawn. A mouse can move text and objects around and alter the width of columns, while windows display what is being worked on at levels of magnification from 12.5 per cent to 200 per cent actual size.

Laser printing

Unlike dot matrix and daisy-wheel word processor printers in which mechanical parts strike the paper with ink, laser printers are non-impact machines, quieter as well as four times as fast. They work on the same principle as an office photocopier, by the action of light on a photo-receptor which is charged in the dark and then selectively discharged as it is exposed to a light source. A rotating drum is scanned by a laser beam – an intense, narrow beam of light reflected by revolving mirrors – and picks up minute electrostatic charges that attract toner (a fine powder ink), which is transferred on to the paper and the image fixed by heat.

Early DTP snags, apart from the unavailability of colour, were that operators did not necessarily have design skills (and if the user has no flair for design, the results look amateurish) and laser printers did not produce text looking as sharp as professionally printed material. Nor were long runs economic. However, several of the drawbacks of conventional publishing apart from cost – the time spent waiting for page design, typesetting and proofing – were overcome.

Desktop publishing was soon being used for house magazines, then home publishing. It offered opportunities for community groups and specialist societies with low budgets to bring out fairly professional looking publications. A computer journalist who publishes magazines from the back room of his semi-detached house near London does all the design, layout and typesetting for them himself, and for short runs does the printing by laser. For longer runs, and publications needing to be folded and bound, he sends a print-out as camera-ready artwork to a conventional printing house.

With modems and 'fax' machines it is now also possible for a small magazine to be published simultaneously in several centres or countries.

Types of paper

On some small magazines the buying of paper is left to the printer. On others it is the responsibility of the production editor. But the choice is important because cheap paper looks cheap, and reproductions of pictures on it will not do them justice; on the other hand, fine quality paper is expensive.

Paper is, of course, obtained from wood – mainly conifers, such as spruce or pine – which is why the centres of the paper industry are in places with large softwood forests, such as the United States, Canada and Scandinavia. There are basically two methods of producing it. The first is *mechanical*, in which the wood is ground on stone rollers rather like milling flour; this gives comparatively short fibres. The second and more expensive is *chemical*, which gives longer fibres. The two types of pulp are frequently blended and have materials such as china clay added during the manufacture, which comprises draining, drying, reeling and rolling the pulp.

There are six main grades of paper, though many subsidiary ones, and from the cheapest to the most expensive they are:

- *Newsprint* – mainly ground wood and too coarse for good picture reproduction. Used principally for newspapers.
- *Machine finished (MF) mechanical uncoated* – also mainly ground wood but smoothed to some extent by rolling. However, it remains relatively rough and is mainly used for letterpress printing.
- *Super calendered (SC) mechanical uncoated* – contains more chemical pulp and is calendered (smoothed by rollers) to give a better surface. Used for many popular magazines including Sunday supplements.
- *Coated mechanical* – coated on both sides with a mixture of clay and binders to create a glossier paper, usually of fairly light weight.
- *Woodfree uncoated* – a misleading name, as it is all wood, but chemically produced without any mechanically ground wood. Used for many technical magazines.
- *Coated woodfree* – the same paper but coated both sides and made mainly in heavy weights for prestige monthlies.

Use of inferior paper is false economy. Some magazines incorporate two types of paper, perhaps an outer section of reasonable quality for colour and a cheaper, flimsier paper inside, but this is rarely a happy idea.

Paper is bought by publishers by the tonne in reels and by the ream (500 sheets) for sheet-fed printing. Its cost depends on weight, which is quoted as, say, 90 grams per square metre, which indicates not only weight but relative thickness. It is available in 5 gsm steps from 35 gsm to 140 gsm. Thin paper below 65 gsm is used for leaflets which are printed on one side only, because printing tends to show through on the reverse side. Paper of above 100 gsm is mainly for covers.

The main problems with paper in printing include:

- *Poor runnability*, when paper breaks in the web (sometimes due to incorrect tensions on the press).
- *Linting*, when small fibres build up on web offset blankets and cause image loss.
- *Strike through*, when ink soaks into the paper and shows through on the reverse side.
- *Creasing*, usually caused by moisture or dryness.
- *Blistering*, when ink seals in moisture which then bubbles during drying.
- *Misregistering*, due to the paper having expanded or contracted between the first and subsequent passes through a press.

Printers have shorthand codes for mishaps with paper. For example, PB/A (paper break, accidental), PB/C (paper break, creasing), PB/DE (paper break, damaged edge) and PB/W (paper break, bad winding).

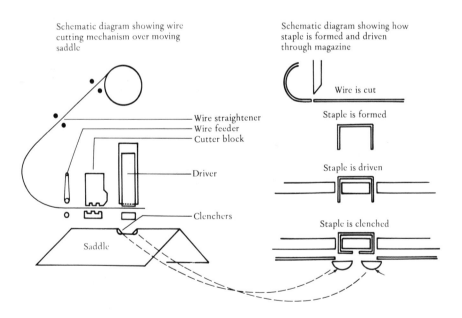

Figure 47   *Binding: the saddle stitching method*

Finishing

The processes that follow printing are known as 'finishing'. The first is folding, when sheets of paper are folded into 8, 16 or 32 page 'sections' for binding, though with web-fed offset litho or gravure this will have been done on the printing machines.

The fastest and most economical method of binding is *saddlestitching*. The sections are placed in hoppers, dropped in order over one another on a saddle or moving belt, and are stapled spine to centre. All sides except the spine are then trimmed on a guillotine by a three-bladed trimmer. When a magazine is too thick for saddlestitching, *perfect* or *adhesive* binding is commonly used. The folded sections are collated side by side, the binding edges sawn off and roughened, and glue applied to them. Then the cover is attached and the whole publication trimmed on three sides.

Copies for sale in shops go in bulk from the printer for delivery to regional wholesalers, whose orders will have been collected, and maximized, by the magazine's sales force. Weeklies are mostly distributed by rail, but monthlies by road, which is cheaper. Wholesalers distribute copies to the retailers in their area. Copies for postal despatch are inserted in envelopes, polythene sleeves or paper wrappers, already franked for the post and printed with a return address in case of non-delivery. Subscribers' addresses are normally printed on labels by computer.

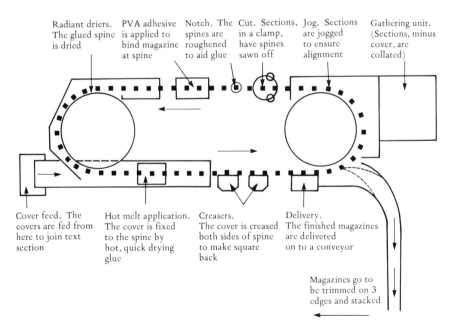

Figure 48 *Binding: the method known as 'perfect binding'*

11 POST PRODUCTION

Work on an issue is not ended when it has been printed. If it contains any noteworthy features, the promotion department may try to obtain publicity by sending tear sheets to newspapers, embargoed with the day of sale, and possibly arranging for the editor to be interviewed on television or radio. Pictures have to be filed for possible future use or sale if they are the magazine's property, or returned to their owners if they are not. Syndication will try to sell some of the features and pictures of which copyright is owned, to offset costs, sending a circular letter setting out what is on offer to other magazines which buy material.

Subbed copy should be filed for some months in case of complaints leading to disputes about the responsibility for particular words or lines. To avoid failing to make payments it is common practice for features and picture editors to go through the issue marking each item either 'Staff' or with the name of the person to be paid. This also helps them to monitor their own departmental budgets. There may be competitions to be judged, winners notified, and arrangements made for presentations, perhaps by a celebrity at a dinner for the winners.

But most post-production work is concerned with reaction to the issue.

Correspondence

Reaction is made known mainly by readers' letters, all of which should be acknowledged in the interests of goodwill. Much reaction is predictable. 'I have been a loyal reader of your journal for 20 years but your comments on x in the latest issue disgusted me, and I am cancelling my subscription.' A certain number of these is inevitable if a magazine is not entirely bland. People are more ready to write complaining than to write in agreement or praise, but too many such letters suggest a miscalculation.

Letters are a useful gauge of reader reaction. For example, a diary editor on a show business weekly introduced a policy of running a sexy picture of a girl every week. Another executive expressed some concern but the diary editor, convinced his policy was right, delighted with the pictures and encouraged by photographers who were enjoying themselves immensely, went ahead until he was brought a pile of letters, all complaining about the pictures, which were clearly offending a huge number of women readers. The diary editor had no option but to concede, and the pictures were dropped.

Sometimes readers' letters will contain gifts of money or presents to be passed to the subject of a feature whose story has moved them. Insufficient thought is often given to the effect of such stories, which can bring as big a response as an overt appeal on behalf of a cause. In one case, concerning a handicapped child, many readers sent dolls and money which a writer undertook to deliver personally. Finding the child's father was a ne'er do well, eager to get his hands on the gifts and convert them into drinking money, the writer gave the child her choice of several of the dolls and, taking advice from a solicitor, put all the money into an account for the child which the father would be unable to touch. The legality might be questionable but the idea was well meant and intelligent; however, magazines should foresee such problems.

Market research

For more reaction magazines also commission surveys. Members of the public are shown a copy and asked what they like and dislike about it, and whether they buy, or would consider buying, or would never buy it. Journalists are often scornful of this kind of research, which tends to confirm what they believe instinctively. For example, research will find that the readers' letters page and the diary are the two best read features, or have 'the greatest page traffic', as researchers put it. This is normal because many readers like short pieces and 'busy' pages.

Editors in particular are dismissive of research. 'I know my public', they like to claim, and the good ones do. But an editor is only one of a publication's management team. Marketing executives want ever more research in order to sell advertising and justify the rates charged. Circulation figures, even when certified by the Audit Bureau of Circulations, are not enough. Advertisers expect to be told not merely how many thousand people they are reaching for their money but who those readers are. For this purpose readers are divided into six social grades which are (with typical occupations of heads of household in brackets):

A, Upper middle class (higher managerial, administrative or professional).

B, Middle class (intermediate managerial, administrative or professional).

C1, Lower middle class (supervisory or clerical, and junior managerial, administrative or professional).

C2, Skilled working class (skilled manual workers).

D, Working class (semi-skilled and unskilled manual workers).

E, Lowest level of subsistence (state pensioners and widows, casual and lowest grade workers).

A magazine marketing manager likes to have a profile of a typical reader, his or her age, marital status, size of family, type of house and car, level of income and education. Research will provide statistics on the number of readers who own dishwashers, car telephones, swimming pools and budgerigars; how many swim and play tennis and cards, drink lager and use power drills; and how many buy clothes off the peg and how many have them made.

Marketing executives want to know more still, such as how long buyers spend looking at a magazine, how many others see the same copy, and how they all rate it. One of their tools is an index known as MXP (for Magazine Page Exposure), set up by a number of leading magazine houses in 1986 on the premise that some magazines are looked at more often and over a longer period, and are in a home longer than others. In the first measurement, a sample of several thousand people was interviewed about the number of days on which the magazine was read, the percentage of pages read and the number of separate issues in the house at the time. These figures were multiplied together and the results weighted to balance the sample by sex, age, social grade and working status. The most publicized finding was that TV programme guides scored highly compared with Sunday newspaper colour magazines, which any journalist would have expected, since a TV magazine can be bought several days before the start of the week with which it is concerned, and is going to be in a home for at least the duration of that week.

Pressure groups

More reaction comes from pressure groups. For example, the National Union of Journalists has an Equality Council which campaigns against such thoughtlessness as references to doctors, lawyers and even motorists as male. They argue, why write 'The motorist . . . he' when it is just as easy to write 'Motorists . . . they', or 'policemen' when it is as easy to write 'police officers'?

They also campaign against the stereotyping of women as featherbrained blondes, pretty mums, battling grannies and elderly spinsters. Some publications are remarkably crass. For example, some motoring columns declare patronizingly, 'The ladies will find this little car a joy with its easy-to-use controls and pastel colours'. Some articles on sporting activities suggest, 'Why not take the little woman along? Wives come in handy for minding equipment and cutting sandwiches and they will have time for a good natter about shopping bargains'. It seems inevitable that in an interview with a woman astronaut, a major concern will be whether she carries a lipstick and scent into space. Curiously, this sort of stuff is not written solely by men.

It is not only women whose stereotyping causes offence. It happens also to pensioners, ramblers, football fans, homosexuals, immigrants, the mentally handicapped, union members and many others, and the interests of nearly all are championed today by pressure groups which will protest at ill-chosen words or illustrations.

The Press Complaints Commission

Any organization or member of the public can complain to the Press Complaints Commission about unethical behaviour by a newspaper or magazine. The Commission came into being in 1991 to replace the Press Council, established in 1953. It is a voluntary body funded by the industry, with 7 of its 16 members being editors or ex-editors, and the others, including the chairman, drawn from other fields.

When a reader complains, and he or she need not have been personally named or injured, the complaint is sent to the editor of the publication with an invitation to try to reach a settlement. If the editor cannot, or will not, there is a hearing of both sides and an adjudication is issued. The Commission has no other powers. Publicity given to its rulings is its sole sanction. Publications do not have to report findings against themselves, though they usually do, if only because rival publications may draw attention to them.

Most complaints, which are more often about newspapers than magazines, concern failure to correct errors or to allow a reply to biased comments, distortion and sensationalism in headlines or presentation, payment of money to relatives or friends of criminals for information, and invasion of privacy to obtain information.

Libel

More worrying can be communications from lawyers threatening libel actions. Libelling persons means defaming them by lowering them in the estimation of society, or bringing them into hatred, ridicule, contempt or dislike. Publication of a libel can bring a civil action for damages against those responsible – writer, editor, printer, publisher, and even distributors, who can hardly be expected to vet every issue of every magazine they sell. There are some who welcome an opportunity to try to win a tax-free prize in the courts, and whether a magazine fights or settles (and most actions are settled out of court), libel cases are almost invariably time-consuming and expensive, with legal costs capable of exceeding any damages awarded. What follows relates to the law of England and Wales, though Scotland's is similar.

Plaintiffs have to establish that the matter was published by the defendants, refers to themselves and is defamatory. It is not necessary for a magazine actually to have named them; the test is simply whether plaintiffs are identified or indicated to those who read the piece. To say all journalists fiddle their expenses is so wildly sweeping an accusation, considering there are about 41,000 in Britain, that it does not give any individual journalist a cause of action, but if one says that all the journalists on a certain small magazine with a staff of perhaps half a dozen are corrupt, they would each have a right to sue because they have been identified individually.

There is an obvious risk of a libel action in accusing a jockey of throwing a race for money, or a surgeon of killing a patient through incompetence, but it is also possible to libel innocently and unknowingly. The subject of an interview introduces a woman as his wife, and a magazine may publish her picture and describe her as such, having no reason to disbelieve him. Unfortunately, she may be a mistress, and if the man's legal wife lives elsewhere, it is not unknown for the legal wife to sue on the grounds that the story implied that she was not the man's wife as she has given acquaintances to understand, and lowered her in their eyes.

A magazine published a friendly, well intentioned diary story saying how pleasant it was to see a certain actor back on television in a comedy series after a heart attack, and that it was a tribute to his professionalism that the series had been undertaken, considering that he was still only allowed to work half days. A writ alleging libel arrived claiming that the statement that he could work only half days was financially damaging because he considered himself capable of working fully, and the reason the unit was working only half days was to suit the convenience of others. After it was decided to fight the case and solicitors obtained an affidavit from the producer of the series that half days were being worked on the advice of the actor's doctors, the action was dropped, though, as a friendly gesture some months later, the magazine ran pictures of the actor demonstrating his complete return to fitness in games on a beach.

Even fiction can bring writs. People have brought actions charging that they were represented and misrepresented by characters in stories, in which they recognized themselves, and friends recognized them, despite fictional names.

The defences

The main defences to libel actions are:

- **Justification**, which means proving that what was written was true. This is a complete defence, but the truth may be difficult to substantiate in court, and attempting to do so, and failing, may result in having to pay higher damages.
- **Fair comment**, which applies only when what is complained about is a statement of opinion rather than one of fact. It has to be an expression of honestly held opinion made in good faith (which means without malice) on a matter of public interest.
- **Privilege**, which gives absolute protection from the consequences of fair, accurate and contemporaneous reporting of cases in law courts and, with some qualifications, proceedings in parliament and at council and company meetings, tribunals, public inquiries and the like.
- **Innocence** (under Section 4 of the Defamation Act 1952), which offers a defence where the publisher did not intend to refer to the plaintiff, or did not know of circumstances which would make what was published defamatory, exercised all reasonable care, and swiftly offers amends, including the publication of a correction and apology and payment of the plaintiff's legal costs.

When an action is indefensible, it is wise to offer an apology immediately rather than prevaricating, but journalists, including editors, should never take it on themselves to make decisions. Any threat of legal action should always be referred to the company's lawyers without delay.

Should a case come to court, it will normally be heard by a judge and jury, with the jury deciding the amount of any award, which is intended to compensate plaintiffs for injury to their reputations; there is no need for them to prove actual financial loss. On top of this a jury may award 'aggravated' damages if it thinks the defendants behaved malevolently or spitefully, and 'exemplary' or 'punitive' damages where the financial rewards of having published might otherwise outweigh any sum awarded against the defendants. On the other hand, damages can be merely 'nominal' or 'contemptuous' if the jury finds the libel trivial or the plaintiff unsavoury.

Less serious than a libel action, and more unusual, is one for *malicious falsehood*, which covers the publishing of an untrue story, an action that is upsetting but not defamatory: for example, stating wrongly that a book is being withdrawn from circulation, the launch of a product postponed or the size of food portions in a chain of restaurants reduced. In order to succeed, plaintiffs have to prove that the words were false, malicious and likely to cause financial loss.

Proposed reform

The present state of libel litigation is generally unsatisfactory. On the one hand, it is almost impossible for anyone other than a rich person or company to pursue a case against a publication, because legal aid is not available. On the other hand, a millionaire complainant could hound and ruin a small magazine because legal aid is not available for defence either. Cases can take years to resolve and costs can be astronomical, while no one can predict a jury's assessment of damages. For this reason many magazines insure against libel, the premiums varying according to the nature of the publication, with magazines that specialize is scandal stories having to pay considerably more than hobby or trade magazines.

Reforms that have been suggested include abolition of jury trials, the hearing of cases in county courts instead of the High Court, making legal aid available to both plaintiff and defendant, and giving judges power to order the publication of a correction and apology without awarding damages unless a libel was calculated or indefensible.

Another proposal which has been discussed is a Media Arbitration System under which each side would choose an arbitrator from the Chartered Institute of Arbitrators, and they in turn would choose a chairman from a list of specialist libel barristers. The three would receive written submissions from both sides on the meaning of the words complained about and the defendant would prepare a defence of justification, fair comment or privilege – or apologise.

Both sides would be able to present their cases at a hearing, at which there would be no jury, and rules of evidence would be relaxed. Damages would be limited to a fixed sum, with another, two and a half times greater, if special damage was proved. No costs would be awarded unless it was shown that a plaintiff had refused a reasonable offer of compensation, or either side had behaved unreasonably. The arbitrators' fees would normally be paid by the defending publication, though a plaintiff could be ordered to do so if the defence succeeded. Such a scheme would make litigation cheaper and more accessible.

Criminal offences

A libel can also be a crime in certain circumstances, and those responsible can be punished by fines or imprisonment for up to 2 years, though this is a survival from earlier centuries when prosecution was a weapon of censorship. The offence was created in 1275 to protect 'the great men of the realm', and is rarely met today. This is fortunate for journalists, because in criminal prosecutions truth alone is not a defence, as it is in civil actions. A defendant has also to prove that publication was in the public interest.

Other criminal offences include publishing sedition, obscenity, incitement to racial hatred and blasphemous libel.

- **Sedition** is criticism of the sovereign, government or laws of the land expressed in a manner likely to incite persons to insurrection, civil commotion or violence.
- **Obscenity**, under the Obscene Publication Act 1959, is matter which, taken as a whole, is liable to deprave and corrupt (rather than merely to shock and disgust) persons likely to read or see it. A defence is to prove that publication was justified by being in the interests of science, literature, art or learning, and expert witnesses can be called to this effect.
- **Incitement to racial hatred** is threatening, abusive or insulting matter which, irrespective of the intention, is likely to stir up hatred against any group in Great Britain distinguished by colour, race or ethnic origins (an offence under the Race Relations Act of 1976).
- **Blasphemous libel** is vilifying the Church of England or its ceremonies, or making outrageous (as opposed to merely critical) comments about the Anglican faith.

Official secrets

These are not, by any means, the only laws of which journalists can fall foul. For example, the Forgery and Counterfeiting Act of 1981 makes it an offence to reproduce any British banknote without permission from the Bank of England, and even if permission is sought and obtained, the notes have to be reproduced at a different size from genuine ones and shown at an oblique angle, and the Chief Cashier's signature must be obscured or obliterated. There are, happily, no restrictions on depicting coins.

A major concern though is secrecy. British bureaucracy's obsession with secrecy is indicated by the fact that there are altogether some seventy different statutes – such as the Atomic Energy Act and the Rehabilitation of Offenders Act – which bar civil servants from disclosing certain types of information. The most notorious is the Official Secrets Act, which exists to stop civil servants leaking official documents to the press and need not concern espionage. 'It is an official secret if it is in an official file', a Whitehall mandarin told a committee, and though the Act has been discredited, it can be used against an official for communicating secrets and a journalist for receiving them.

D notices advise publishers and editors of categories of information which are secret. They are issued by the Defence Press and Broadcasting Committee, consisting of representatives of the armed forces, the Civil

Service and the media. No responsible journalist would wish to publish information damaging to the security of the country but secrecy can be invoked in bizarre circumstances. One writer was solemnly warned against publishing a paragraph about self-heating cans of soup on the grounds that they had been developed for the army for use in cold climates and cold climate military equipment was covered by a D notice. However, D notices have no legal force and can be disregarded when absurd.

Breach of confidence

Information cannot be kept secret merely by marking it 'Confidential'. A magazine which obtains it has not broken any confidential relationship, though, of course, the person who gave it to the publication may have done. An action for breach of confidence could be brought in such circumstances by a person or organization to whom the confidence is owed, and an injunction which would stop publication might be obtained. There is however a 'public interest' defence to breach of confidence: the media can publish if they reveal information of public importance, though how important it has to be is arguable.

Another pitfall in gathering information is that under the Prevention of Corruption Act of 1906 it is an offence to offer a bribe to employees for doing something in relation to their employers' business. Payments to extract information to reveal a scandal, however, would not be corrupt.

Journalists should, of course, protect confidential sources, and this can bring them into conflict with the law, for they can be compelled by subpoena to give evidence to a court or tribunal and may be ordered by a judge to disclose sources to police investigating a suspected crime. It can become a matter for a journalist's conscience whether or not to obey.

Contempt of Court

Refusal could put a journalist in contempt of court for disobeying a court order. It is also contempt to make a 'scandalous' attack on judges (as opposed to reasonable criticism of them), or to publish the secrets of a jury room, telling how a jury reached its verdict.

Generally, however, contempt of court is connected with impeding or prejudicing the outcome of a court case. The law relating to contempt is intended to prevent trial by the press, and if a magazine deliberately sets out to influence public opinion during a trial, or runs pictures of defendants when identification is an issue, the editor could be subjected to an unlimited fine and up to 2 years in jail, and this is understandable. But it is also possible to fall foul of the law innocently: for example, by running a feature on a series of country house robberies, written when the police had few clues, but appearing in print after someone has been arrested.

Copyright

Complaints alleging breach of copyright are commonplace. Copyright is intended to prevent unauthorized copying of published work. It does not cover facts – though copyright exists in the way they are presented – so to take a statistic from a reference book is normally permissible but to lift word for word a writer's interpretation of that statistic is not. Copyright does not cover ideas, though if they are of commercial value, have been set down on paper and marked 'Confidential,' they may be protected under a law of confidence. Nor does it cover a joke, though copyright exists in the way a cartoonist draws it or a humorist tells it.

In the United Kingdom no formalities such as registration are necessary; as soon as a page of copy is written or recorded in any way, a drawing made, or a photograph taken, copyright exists under the Copyright Act of 1988. It covers any published work as long as some skill and labour has been employed in its composition, which is why football fixture lists, television programme schedules and opinion poll results are protected.

Work has to be original but it does not need to be novel. Two photographers standing side by side at a function will produce almost identical pictures; both will be copyright; and while dictionaries and directories are covered by copyright, one can, of course, produce similar works. There is infringement only if one has copied earlier volumes. However, the title of a story is not normally protected, being regarded as too short to be treated as a literary work (though a 'passing off' action is possible if a title is taken and used in order to mislead).

The person protected is the author, the person who has actually written the words or drawn an illustration, though when the work is done by a staff employee for the purpose of publication in a magazine, the employer owns the copyright so far as that publication is concerned. However, a freelance who has been working for a periodical under a particular pen name and ceases to contribute should be entitled to use the pen name elsewhere; it does not belong to the periodical except by agreement.

Photographers are in a more complex position, and have been protesting about it for years. Copyright in commissioned pictures belong to whoever commissioned them (for example, the sitter), otherwise to the owner of the film on which the pictures were taken, which will probably be a magazine if the photographer is a staff employee.

Infringements

Normal copyright exists until 70 years after the author's death, but a separate copyright exists in every published edition of a work and lasts 25 years. It is infringed by reproducing any substantial part of a work without permission, infringements being determined by a detailed comparison of similarities. However, quoting for purposes of criticism or review is permitted, providing it is 'fair dealing' and accompanied by reasonable acknowledgement.

The overriding principle is that one is not entitled to rip off and exploit another person's work. Therefore, when journalists come into possession of secret documents, they will not be in breach of copyright if they summarize the contents in their own words; what they cannot do without risk is publish them verbatim. Author, publisher and printer are equally liable in the case of an infringement. A copyright owner can get an injunction – a court order – restraining them from repeating it, and can also obtain damages. These damages, based on evidence of loss suffered or the fee the owner might reasonably have charged, may be increased by 'exemplary' damages, depending on the flagrancy of the infringement and the money obtained by it.

The Copyright Act applies only within the UK, including Northern Ireland, other countries having slightly different codes, but there are two major international conventions according reciprocal protection in member countries for a minimum term of the life of the author and 25 years after. Different national formalities are satisfied if published material bears the symbol © accompanied by the name of the copyright owner and year of first publication.

Rights agreements

Copyright ownership occasions much wrangling. Freelance writers and illustrators automatically own the copyright of their own work – and photographers may do – and control the publication of it by granting licences. An editor acquires only those rights intended by both parties at the time of the commissioning, and if not specified, this is usually taken to mean first rights only.

- **First British rights** allow a magazine to reproduce material for the first time in one issue only. The contributor keeps the copyright, but cannot offer the material elsewhere for earlier publication within the circulation area of the magazine without its permission, though the magazine must use it within reasonable time.

- **One use** allows publication of the material once in one issue, the contributor keeping the copyright.
- **All rights** means the company acquires complete world copyright and can syndicate the material if it wishes. The National Union of Journalists recommends that the fee for all rights should be at least a first-use fee plus 150 per cent.

Publishers sometimes try to assume further rights than they have bought by paying fees with cheques requiring the freelance's signature on the back below a statement relinquishing all rights. The National Union of Journalists advises members not to accept this. Publishers have also been known to syndicate material from freelances without telling them and without making any additional payment. Freelances who have retained their copyright should be paid whenever their material is put to further use than was originally agreed and, if they allow it to be syndicated, the NUJ recommends that they should claim at least 50 per cent of the gross sales.

Editors may also seek to gain employer status over a contributor to obtain control of copyright. A freelance commission is technically a contract *for* services and not a contract *of* service (which is employment) and editors should not ask freelances to sign contracts of service unless they are prepared to grant full staff conditions and benefits.

The journalist's code

The Code of Conduct of the National Union of Journalists, to which all members are required to adhere, sets out the following rules, which, if always observed, would reduce complaints greatly:

1 A journalist has a duty to maintain the highest professional and ethical standards.
2 A journalist shall at all times defend the principle of the freedom of the Press and other media in relation to the collection of information and the expression of comment and criticism. He/she shall strive to eliminate distortion, news suppression and censorship.
3 A journalist shall strive to ensure that the information he/she disseminates is fair and accurate, avoid the expression of comment and conjecture as established fact, and falsification by distortion, selection or misrepresentation.
4 A journalist shall rectify promptly any harmful inaccuracies, ensure that correction and apologies receive due prominence and afford the right of reply to persons criticised when the issue is of sufficient importance.

5   A journalist shall obtain information, photographs and illustrations only by straightforward means. The use of other means can be justified only by over-riding considerations of the public interest. The journalist is entitled to exercise a personal conscientious objection to the use of such means.

6   Subject to justification by over-riding considerations of the public interest, a journalist shall do nothing which entails intrusion into private grief and distress.

7   A journalist shall protect confidential sources of information.

8   A journalist shall not accept bribes nor shall he/she allow other inducements to influence the performance of his/her professional duties.

9   A journalist shall not lend himself/herself to the distortion or suppression of the truth because of advertising or other considerations.

10 A journalist shall not originate material which encourages discrimination on grounds of race, colour, creed, gender or sexual orientation.

11 A journalist shall not take private advantage of information gained in the course of his/her duties before the information is public knowledge.

12 A journalist shall not by way of statement, voice or appearance endorse by advertisement any commercial product or device, save for the promotion of his/her own work or of the medium by which he/she is employed.

12 A CAREER GUIDE

There are broadly three groups of recruits to magazine journalism. Firstly, there are experienced journalists, most of them from newspapers, who seek a less hectic life, or opportunities for more creative or specialized work. Secondly, there are those with experience in other occupations which can be turned to account in journalism: for example, engineers who join motoring magazines and chefs who become cookery editors. The third group consists of new entrants.

About 80 per cent of newcomers to British magazines are graduates or have had at least some full-time education beyond A-levels, it is estimated by the Periodicals Training Council, which organizes and monitors training. Non-graduates normally need a minimum of two A-levels, one of them preferably in English. It also helps to have had some work published – in a school magazine or a local newspaper. To become a freelance, of course, one need have no qualifications of any kind – just talent.

There are three major differences between starting on magazines and on newspapers. Firstly, there are local newspapers in every town of any size in the country, but most magazines are London-based. Secondly, though there is no national agreement on magazine salaries, periodicals tend to pay better than newspapers in the early stages but comparatively less well later. Thirdly, magazines offer more opportunities than newspapers to specialize, for a journalist who wants to work in, say, motor sport or fashion can seek work on an appropriate publication.

Training for periodical journalism in Britain became formalized only in the 1980s, monitored by the PTC, which is backed by the main companies employing 85 per cent of magazine journalists. Competition to enter magazine journalism is keen. The PTC receives about 5000 letters a year seeking information about careers, about 40 per cent of the boys wanting to be sports writers and 40 per cent of the girls wanting to be fashion writers. The PTC estimates that the number actually finding jobs every year in normal circumstances is between 200 and 225, but this applies only to staff jobs. In addition to the 5000 who staff mainstream magazines there are probably as many freelances working for magazines to some extent.

There are two main options open to would-be magazine journalists. The first is to try to get accepted on a pre-entry training course, though there are only about 160 places yearly, and there is competition for them. The second is to find a job on a magazine and learn in-house. The most comprehensive training is a pre-entry course at a university, and for graduates the best advice is to try to find a place on one. There is no guarantee that a job will follow, but the courses are well regarded, and those who complete them generally find worthwhile posts.

Pre-entry courses for graduates

The main centres for pre-entry courses for graduates are City University in London and University College, Cardiff, in Wales, both of which offer 1-year diploma courses. The older established is Cardiff, which pioneered practical journalism in British universities. Its Centre for Journalism Studies was the first of its kind at a British university when it was set up in 1970 by Sir Tom Hopkinson, former editor of *Picture Post* and the African magazine *Drum*.

All students start the year with a common core course concerned with news values, news gathering and writing, and then go on to specialize in magazines, newspapers or broadcasting. Students who have chosen the magazine course will spend some weeks on attachment to different periodicals. At other times they will work in an office atmosphere, with closed circuit television being used to teach interviewing skills. They learn to use tape recorders and are sent out to cover stories. They also learn subbing and combine to produce their own periodicals.

Professional studies on the course include the practice of journalism, the organization and administration of publications, and the relationship between journalism and society. Background studies include the legal system as it affects journalism, and the structure of local government. Assessment by the staff – all of them journalists – is continuous, but students also sit an examination and have to write a series of feature articles suitable for a periodical on a chosen subject.

About 600 apply for the 60 places every year. From their application forms the most promising candidates are sent a written test, and from their replies a short list is chosen for interviewing during the Easter vacation. All students must be able to type before arriving and be prepared to reach 100 words per minute in Teeline shorthand quickly.

The Centre is part of the largest college of the University of Wales, which has 5000 students, and accommodation is not easy to find; the college has only a limited number of hostel places. However, grants covering tuition fees and subsistence are available from local education authorities. Students from other countries may be able to obtain grants from the British Council, UNESCO, the Commonwealth Press Union, the EEC, Rotary International, the Muslim Institute or an overseas government.

Diploma courses at City University in Clerkenwell are similar, and also engender ten times as many applications as there are places. There are also 13-week postgraduate courses at the London College of Printing at the Elephant and Castle, providing the basic skills of periodical journalism and including a week in a magazine office. These courses start twice yearly in September and January and are about three times oversubscribed.

All three centres offer a number of other courses, such as Master's degrees in journalism studies and MEd degrees in media studies, but these are mainly for experienced journalists.

Post A-level courses

For the would-be magazine journalist without a degree the choice of courses is smaller. The London College of Printing offers a 1-year post A-level full-time pre-entry course in periodical journalism (ten times oversubscribed) and a 2-year pre-entry Higher National Diploma business studies course which includes journalism.

Two large magazine companies, Reed Business Publishing and Emap, offer courses of 17 and 20 weeks respectively, which, although set up as in-house training schemes, are now open to selected external applicants on a fee-paying basis. These students are not promised jobs with the companies after training, but some have in fact been taken on.

The editorial training scheme

The second option for the would-be magazine journalist is to find a job and learn journalism in-house. There is no indenture or apprenticeship scheme on magazines, but some publishers accept trainees, who must undergo a programme of tuition in basic journalistic skills and knowledge lasting some 2 years. Since 1992 the PTC has backed the registration of trainees for National Vocational Qualifications (NVQs).

There are more than 2000 different NVQs in industry and commerce, controlled by a quango, the National Council for Vocational Qualifications. Magazine NVQs are based on workplace experience and assessments rather than examinations, trainees being required to gain a number of units, each representing competence in a specific skill such as interviewing, feature writing, subbing or layout. An assessor (usually an editor) decides when the requirement for each unit has been met, whereupon a certificate is issued; an NVQ is earned when all the relevant units have been accumulated.

Initially there was a certain lack of enthusiasm for NVQs among publishing companies, but in 1995 the PTC set out to build more support for them.

Block release courses

Some companies send trainees on block release courses held at the London College of Printing. Between 3 and 9 months after starting work is considered the best time to take them, though the timing is flexible. Trainees must be at least 18, have a minimum of four O-levels, including English language, and be able to type.

The courses, which last 4 weeks, divided into two fortnightly periods, are held daily at the College (though enrolment is through the Periodicals Training Council). Students should not be required to do any work for their employers while on a course. The courses cover:

(a) *Interviewing and reporting.*
(b) *Writing copy*, both news and features.
(c) *Subbing copy* and preparing it for printing.
(d) *Printing processes*, including typesetting, platemaking, binding, folding and trimming.
(e) *Law for journalists*, including libel, copyright and consumer law.
(f) *Organization of the industry*, and of editorial departments, and the role of advertising.
(g) *The journalist's role* in industry and society.

In addition, a number of independent companies now exist solely to provide short training courses for journalists – both juniors and seniors – sent by their employers.

Other courses

It will have been noted that all the training courses mentioned in this chapter are mainly concerned with those who work with words, such as potential writers and sub-editors. There are no equivalent magazine-oriented pre-entry courses for photographers and artists and they are not often recruited for training in-house, though at least one senior magazine photographer started work as a darkroom assistant in the office for which he still works. However, most photographers working for magazines are freelances.

For would-be designers and photographers the best plan is to learn art or photography at a college of art or polytechnic, or in a photographic or art studio, before applying for a job on a magazine. There is a 1-year press photography course approved by the National Council for the Training of Journalists, which controls training for newspapers, and this is held at Richmond College in Sheffield, but the competition is intense; only twelve to fifteen students a year are accepted because there are not enough jobs available to justify more places.

It is also possible for writers and subs to enter magazines by first becoming reporters or subs on newspapers, which offer more openings than magazines. But training under a national scheme administered by the NCTJ is obligatory and normally lasts three years, which means a late entry into periodicals.

A word of warning: there are correspondence courses promising to teach pupils to become successful writers of fiction and features, and the reputable schools do their best, setting exercises and offering intelligent advice and criticism. They can be of value, but they are really aimed at teachers, civil servants and others who already have careers and are looking for paying hobbies. They are limited in their scope and are no substitute for on-the-job training or full-time pre-entry courses, and, of course, there are fees to pay and no grants on offer.

Job hunting

Finding a job on a magazine is never easy for a novice. Saturday is the best day for looking for one, because the chief sources of job advertisements are *The Guardian* on that day and *UK Press Gazette*, which also appears every Saturday. A letter in response to an advertisement should be brief. State as crisply as possible the job for which you are applying (with the reference number if one is given, for a company may be advertising different jobs at different levels). If the advertisement calls for particular skills or enthusiasms or knowledge (such as youth, or fluency in French, or enthusiasm for sailing), claim whichever of them you can, but do not write more. All other relevant information, such as age, education details and references should be included in a *curriculum vitae*, or CV, which should be attached. Make sure there are no spelling or grammatical errors in the letter, which should be typed if possible. The accompanying CV, which should be equally fault-free, should *always* be typed.

The curriculum vitae

For anyone with access to a word processor, it is useful to put a CV on disc because it is then easy to tailor it for a particular publication. If applying for a job on a sports magazine, one can give greater prominence to sporting associations (captain of football team, crewing a sailing boat) and omit or play down such hobbies as knitting and embroidery. It also means a crisp clean CV for each application. Anyone with any special claims for attention, such as experience of working on a magazine, should introduce them at the beginning, rather than starting with details of schooling: for example, '18 years old, currently a researcher on *Blank* magazine'. Otherwise a CV should be set out like this:

NAME
ADDRESS and telephone number.
AGE (with date of birth in brackets).
SCHOOLS ATTENDED (name and town). From . . . to . . .
COLLEGES OR COURSES ATTENDED (name and town). From . . . to . . .
ACADEMIC QUALIFICATIONS (name of examination, subject and grade).
FURTHER EDUCATIONAL PLANS, if any.
JOBS HELD
OTHER WORK EXPERIENCE
INTERESTS AND ACTIVITIES
REFERENCES (names, addresses and telephone numbers).

Always ask permission from those whose names it is intended to give as references. This is only polite; fail to do so and a reference may be less enthusiastic than if courtesy had been shown. Add any other relevant information, e.g. a driving licence held or a foreign language spoken.

Of course, it is not necessary to wait for a job to be advertised to make application. Some magazines rarely advertise; they can fill vacancies without doing so. *Benn's Media Directory* lists magazines by subjects with their addresses. Study magazines on which you would like to work. (Use of a public library's reading room can keep down the cost.) The stock reply goes something like, 'Thank you for your letter. Unfortunately we have no vacancies at the present, but will file your name and will contact you should a suitable opening occur'. It is just possible they will do so, and nothing is lost by trying. One may just pick the right time.

Women in magazine journalism

Opportunities are at least as great for women as for men. There are many magazines, not merely those intended for women, where they outnumber men. In 1987 IPC Magazines employed 177 male journalists and 264 females. There are women at all levels – editors, chief subs and picture editors, as well as writers and artists – and many men work for women executives. It is probably still harder for a woman to win acceptance as a specialist in sport, industry or politics, but there are few barriers encountered today. Most secretaries are still girls, though at least one woman editor recently employed a male secretary, and most printers have been male because hot metal printing required muscle; but there is no physical reason why women should not operate new technology. With most battles for equality in pay and status won, women journalists are campaigning for more part-time work and job-sharing, parental leave and childcare facilities.

Job interviews

If asked for an interview, prepare for it. Study the magazine and write an analysis of it. At whom is it aimed? (Men, women, what age groups, what kind of income level?) What does it try to do? How does it go about it? How far does it succeed?

Try to devise some ideas for suitable features. On the day of the interview, if you have to travel, get the train before one that should arrive in time. If the town or area of the city is unfamiliar, allow time for finding the office. Be prepared to wait. Any editor can mistime. Another interview may have overrun, the proprietor may have been on the phone. A junior job applicant is not the most important person in the editor's day, but staff should be courteous and, at least, offer a seat, a magazine to read and coffee. To be left standing for half an hour does not suggest a well run office.

Be smart. Magazine offices are not dressy places. Subs and others who rarely go out of the office may wear shirts and jeans. Normally only executives and writers and photographers who may have to meet people dress formally, and then not always. But you are not yet one of the team; you are applying for a job and employers expect candidates to dress for an interview. A suit is appropriate for males. If you think that casual clothes are more appropriate, ensure that they are scrupulously clean. Wear clean shoes, and have clean fingernails. There are people who judge by such things.

If you have any cuttings of features you have written, for a school or college magazine or local newspaper, take them with you – or, rather, take photocopies. Never let magazines have originals, they will lose them.

Smile and look the interviewer in the face. Do not smoke without an invitation to do so. If a cigarette is offered, it is up to you whether to take it, but you may find yourself embarrassed by the lack of an ash tray. It may be better not to light up until after the interview. Favourite opening questions are, 'What did you think of our latest issue? and 'How do you think the magazine is looking?' Be ready with some intelligent comments. Be prepared to criticize something, to show you are not a sycophant, but make sure it is not too fundamental. For example, you could say, without giving offence, that you preferred the cover the previous week, because it had action while the latest one is static. Anyone is entitled to such a view. It is not tactful to compare the magazine unfavourably with a rival or to say that you think it is too downmarket. Do not mumble. Answer what is asked. Do not be monosyllabic but do not ramble on. Do not worry about pauses. The interviewer is in charge.

Other questions likely to be asked are the following. What made you decide on this as a career? What made you apply for this particular job? What makes you think you would be good at it? How would you like your career to develop? How does this job fit into the picture? When asked about your hopes for the future, there is nothing against showing ambition. If you would like eventually to write a regular column for the magazine or to edit it, or one similar, there is no harm in saying so, but on no account tell the interviewer that what you really want to do is to write a great novel. It suggests a lack of enthusiasm and respect for the job on offer. You may regard it as a mere stepping stone but try and appear interested in it.

Have some ideas for features in your mind. Sooner or later you will be asked for ideas, either on the spot or to be sent within a few days. It is good to show that you have ideas already, but be realistic. Anyone can suggest an interview with the Queen's personal maid or an 'at home' with an Old Bailey judge. It is no good suggesting either unless you know how it can be got.

You should be asked if you have any questions. Do not invent ones for the sake of it, but you should have been told the salary, starting date, working conditions, holiday entitlement, pension rights, and promotion prospects. If not, ask.

Contracts of employment

If a job is offered and accepted, an employeer is obliged to provide written details of the contract. These should include the job title and description, salary, and when and how payment will be made (weekly or monthly, by cheque or transfer to a bank account). Salaries are commonly structured in bands or grades, agreed with union negotiators, the lowest being grade one. Top salaries in one band will be roughly equal to the lowest in the band above. Some companies have as many as eight grades, but a simple structure may be like this:

Grade 1: writers, photographers, artists and sub-editors without special responsibilities.

Grade 2: deputies such as deputy picture editor, deputy features editor, deputy chief sub and others with special responsibilities.

Grade 3: departmental heads such as features editors, picture editors, chief sub-editors.

Off-grade: assistant editors and other senior executives whose salaries are individually negotiable.

Contracts or letters of appointment should also cover hours of work, meal breaks, holiday entitlement and pay, sick pay, maternity leave, length of notice (on both sides), redundancy arrangements, disputes, grievance and disciplinary procedures, pension rights, union recognition and status, and any requirement to join one. The agreement may also state whether journalists are allowed to do other work. Sometimes all outside work is banned; in other cases journalists are allowed to undertake work as long as it is not for direct rivals or publications of a similar nature.

Other matters which may be covered include expenses, such as allowances for car mileage, meals when working late, telephone and newspaper bills, insurance while working, any requirement to operate new technology, and any provision for paid or unpaid leave for study or research. Some companies grant sabbaticals. These may be merely extra holidays – 5 weeks off after every 4 years, in one case. On other magazines a committee of members of management and staff considers requests for time off to undertake research projects, such as studying the wine industry in France or the establishment of salmon farms in Scotland, and grants a small number every year.

A copy of the agreement should be kept safely. It may be valuable if the company seeks to change the nature or hours of work or a title.

Early days

The first few days of a new job on a magazine are usually spent in 'induction', which means learning how the mail and telephone systems operate, how to use the library, the peculiarities of the office, and who is who. Magazines usually run on first names, but do not think this means everyone will always be friendly or long-suffering. The fact that senior executives are addressed by their first names does not mean that they are necessarily easy-going people; they may be unpleasant and ruthless.

Specializing is to be recommended as early as possible. On a general magazine identify some area of interest you enjoy, from gliding to country and western music. On a specialist one make a particular corner in some area: for example, on a photographic magazine in darkroom tricks, on a show business magazine in soap operas. One gains respect by having an area of expertise, it enables one to bring authority to one's work and it may be of help when moving on. Apart from anything else, a long working life might as well be spent doing what one enjoys most.

The expenses system

The generosity of expenses varies between magazines. Normally staff travel first class on trains, tourist on planes, and stay at good hotels, partly because it is bad for a magazine's image to have its staff staying in seedy ones, but also because if one is working, one may need the facilities of better hotels, such as night service, telephone messages, and secretarial help. On all but the smallest publications, taxis are used liberally, because time is more important than money. One may also be able to entertain contacts to moderately expensive lunches. Credit cards with generous limits make life easier. Unfortunately, it can be hard to switch from a free-spending attitude while working to having to economize at other times.

Some journalists abuse the system. It may be that a features editor signs expense sheets without even appearing to read them, but accounts departments have been known to run checks on restaurant bills and taxi fares. Writers have also come to grief by charging a lunch for a person who was in fact having lunch with the editor on the day concerned. Other journalists rely on expenses for additional income, and will therefore travel second class and charge first, if travel warrants are not provided by the company. This is stupid. Travelling first, one has a chance to think about a feature, making plans on the outward journey, roughing out a feature on the return. This may be impossible when travelling in a compartment packed with football rowdies, foreign students or families with small children.

Union membership

There are two well-established unions for journalists in Britain — the

National Union of Journalists, which has much the greater number of members, and the older Institute of Journalists. In 1992 they were joined by the new British Association of Journalists. In some offices members co-exist, but others have 100 per cent NUJ membership. Whether one should belong to a union is most often a matter of inclination and conscience, though in some offices NUJ membership is expected. Unions negotiate salaries, holiday entitlement and working conditions, and help if a member is badly treated; but union membership also brings obligations which can sometimes be onerous, e.g. being instructed to take industrial action against one's own wishes and the wishes of many other members.

13 THE ROLE OF THE FREELANCE

Magazines make great use of freelances – understandably, for there is no need to provide them permanently with expensive office space or to pay them during illness. Compared with newspapers, magazines do not normally have the same need for staff to be available around the clock to be dispatched to far-off places at a moment's notice, and it would be costly for general magazines to employ experts in all the subjects they cover; whereas freelances can be called on as required, and a glance through the NUJ's *Freelance Directory* shows their range. Farming and forestry, immigrant organisations, crime, education, retailing, chemicals, construction, antiques, gardening, food and wine, quizzes, crosswords and the law are just some of the specialities listed.

Freelances are particularly useful to cover for staff during illness or holidays but there are many other reasons for using them. Staff become stale. After a certain age they may stay only for their pensions and because they will not find better jobs elsewhere. By using freelances the magazine can recruit enthusiastic newcomers and develop new talent, and if freelances become unreliable or temperamental, or their copy becomes dull, they can be dropped without compensation, apology or even explanation. There is every advantage in using freelances from the management point of view.

The word 'freelance' (and there is no justification for 'freelancer', despite its frequent use in trade publications) is as all-embracing and meaningless as 'model'. Some freelances are among the country's busiest writers or photographers, earning more than staff journalists; others who call themselves freelances may be pensioners who write occasional verses for religious magazines or snap pastoral scenes for county magazines, happy to earn a few hundred pounds a year as a hobby. Staff journalists will often commiserate when told a former colleague is freelancing, for they regard it as a euphemism for being out of a job – which sometimes it is.

In fact freelancing is the best possible way of life for the successful, able to pick and choose their jobs and their working hours. It is the worst possible life for the unsuccessful, having to take whatever comes along, no matter how they despise it, and forever worrying about the next cheque. Free-lancing requires discipline. A freelance may have too much work, but be reluctant to turn any down for fear of being out of work shortly. Yet when freelances meet quiet patches, they can seldom bring themselves to relax until business picks up again; they start scratching around for work, no matter how ill paid or unattractive, and then find they are overworking again – if they are lucky.

Those trying unsuccessfully to break into freelancing sometimes allege there is a magic circle of insiders. There is, but it is not a closed circle. Anyone with talent can break in. It is perfectly natural for editors to use freelances they have worked with before, knowing their reliability, strengths and weaknesses, and equally to exclude those who have let them down, perhaps on another publication. However, it is certainly hard, and not to be recommended, for an unknown to start as a freelance. No one commissions unknowns. The most a beginner can hope for is to be told a feature will be considered. The established freelance can, of course, win a commission from an idea.

The truth of the old saying about being nice to people you meet on the way up, because you may meet them again on the way down, is never more true than in journalism. A colleague snubbed years ago may reappear as an editor or publisher.

The good and the bad

The good side of freelancing is that you cannot be ordered to be in Port Talbot by nine on a Monday morning if you don't want to go – and who would? However, turn down too many jobs and they may cease to be offered. Freelances can avoid commuting to city centre offices. It is possible to work at home, in the middle of the night if you wish, and in the garden on summer days. ('I have a mental picture of you sitting on your patio at home wondering who to favour with your next contribution', a publisher told a freelance, who was, as it happened, desperately in need of work at the time.) As the use of computers and modems grows, it becomes even less necessary to visit offices, for copy can be input from home. Unfortunately freelances can miss the exchange of ideas, the camaraderie and gossip. Work is completed and dispatched, accepted and paid for, but one is deprived of any further part to play.

There are compensations. Freelances can get to keep more of their earnings, because they can claim as expenses against tax a proportion of the rent, rates, lighting and heating of their homes when used as offices, and of bills for their cars, telephones, newspapers and reference books. However, that is not necessarily comparable with the perks of staff, which may include company cars, health plans, bonuses, profit shares, free newspapers and periodicals, cheap TV rental, luncheon vouchers and expenses for entertaining contacts.

The bad side is that while features editors want copy yesterday, there is rarely the same urgency when it comes to paying for it. Staff, who are commonly paid a month in advance and will complain loudly to the accounts department if their monthly cheques do not reach their banks on the first of every month, will leave freelances' invoices in their in-trays for weeks awaiting initialling. It only needs a junior in an accounts department to be ill and freelance contributors may have to wait even longer for already overdue payments.

Most magazines claim to pay on publication. Unfortunately, allowing a 6-week production schedule and then time for a features editor to mark up a printed copy for payments (and even assuming the piece is scheduled immediately and not held over for some weeks), it can often take 3 months. Pursuing executives and the accounts department makes a freelance unpopular.

A better system is payment on acceptance. An invoice is sent to the accounts department when the work is delivered. Better still is payment on commissioning. A contributor will still usually have handed in the work before a cheque arrives, but may on occasion get it before the work appears in print rather than weeks afterwards.

A freelance has to work much harder than an employee to earn the same kind of living. The staff man or woman envies the freelance, who may get more for one feature than a staff wage for a week, but freelances are rarely offered such a feature every week, and would not be able to cope were it to happen. A staff writer may produce a feature every 3 weeks, whereas a freelance who spent 3 weeks on one would starve. Freelances do not get holidays, sick pay, pension contributions or company perks, which is why the rate for a day's work should be at least a quarter more than the equivalent staff pay for a day.

Freelances need to be grafters, as well as talented. They also need to be healthy. The pay of staff will continue when they are ill, but freelances who do not work do not earn, and they must make their own arrangements for pensions or they will have an impoverished old age.

Freelances have to be more responsible. Staff, possibly talented at one time, may become lazy and careless, but it is impossible for a firm to get rid of them except after a long drawn out procedure of written warnings. Freelances may be allowed only one mistake. In fact no mistake is necessary. The editor tires of the style or the face or the clothes or the voice. There is no need to fire freelances; they just get no more work, and there is no obligation to explain the reason. One contributor's work for a publication was ended because an executive was irritated by the habit of the man's wife of acknowledging telephoned messages with 'Righty ho-ho', which may or may not be a sound reason.

When there are economy waves, which are annual events on many publications, the first casualties are freelances. Department heads are told to cut down on the use of them and get more work out of the staff. This seldom lasts; the dependence on freelances is too great.

Freelances' time is wasted by staff. They may be asked to visit the office to discuss a feature. There is a conference in progress, which goes on to lunchtime. Freelances cool their heels; if they are taken to lunch, that will be seen as adequate compensation, though it is more unpaid time expended. A freelance who has come in from the country can waste half a day waiting for a briefing; the fee will never take account of that half day, though it should.

Freelances also become used to having their brains picked without payment. Staff telephone wanting information on subjects they are knowledgeable about or they ask for contacts' numbers and this is regarded as friendly help. Such information should be paid for, as much as copy.

When there is a dispute at a publication, freelances are the first to suffer and can be the hardest hit. The staff may go on strike. If management try to bring out the publication, freelance contributors will be asked by the editor to supply copy. If they do, they will win the temporary goodwill of the editor but the enmity of the staff. If they refuse, they will have the temporary appreciation of the staff but may lose work from the editor in the future. A freelance always loses income during a strike, but rarely wins any benefit from it. When the strike is settled, the volume of freelance work may be cut back to pay for rises won by the staff.

Of course, freelance pay should be linked to staff salaries automatically; it is in the interests of the staff to see that freelances are not undercutting them. Yet this is not universal practice. The truth is that few love freelances. Staff are envious of their freedom and unions regret being unable to organize them like staff.

Setting up as a freelance

It is essential to have some money in the bank before becoming a freelance; it may be some months before any cheques come in, and having to borrow money when one would not need to do so if firms paid promptly is worrying as well as expensive. A room which serves purely as an office is desirable; it is difficult to work when paperwork has to be put away (and is lost) when the room is used as a bedroom.

Essential pieces of equipment are a telephone and a typewriter, or preferably a word processor. A telephone answering machine is also a good investment. Commissioning editors, unable to get a reply and unsure if a freelance is on holiday or out working, tend to move on rapidly to another. A fax machine is also desirable. It is worth having business cards and headed notepaper printed, because scribbling one's telephone number on a page from a notebook and typing letters on copy paper does not look professional or suggest success. Some writers have their paper headed 'Author and journalist, contributor to ...', but this does not impress editors.

Be prepared to invest in some reference books. It is not worth spending a lot on ones that will soon be out of date, and can be consulted in any public library or magazine office, but inexpensive ones will save journeys to libraries. Most important is to set up a system for filing cuttings. Clip anything which might be useful, or which sparks an idea. Fill a notebook with ideas for features, writing them down as they occur, for tomorrow they may have been forgotten. File them later. Successful freelances will have dozens of ideas on file, and with luck will never get around to many of them. There will be too much work on offer.

Arrange a personal pension plan. Premiums are variable, so in a bad year contributions can be reduced, but it is important to start making some provision early or retirement will be bleak. It is wise to find an accountant before getting into problems over income tax, because it is easier to stay out of trouble than to get out of trouble. Good accountants generally save a client as much as they charge, and their fees are tax-deductible anyway. They will provide some peace of mind and confidence that one is neither missing out on expenses that might be allowable, nor in danger of the Inland Revenue's displeasure.

Get a reputable accountant. There are unqualified self-styled accountants on the fringes of newspaper and magazine circles who will do the job cheaply and with few scruples. One such man was threatened with imprisonment for contempt of court when he failed to produce documents as ordered by a judge, and then disappeared, leaving at least one freelance client without his records and in difficulties with the Inland Revenue.

Unless freelances have more work than they can handle, they do not need an agent. Why give away a percentage of a modest income? On the other hand, if a freelance is highly successful an agent can be worthwhile, finding outlets for work that the freelance did not know existed, and talking up fees in a way the freelance would be embarrassed to attempt personally. As it happens, well established agents will not want to know a struggling freelance; they have enough work servicing their successful clients. Fortunately, the best agents for freelances are newly established ones who are still hungry.

Freelance routine

No one commissions unknowns. A freelance starting out has got to be prepared to work 'on spec'. Study markets. There are market reports for freelances, which may be helpful, but they cannot supplant detailed study of magazines for which one would like to write. Send in a feature. Attach a brief covering note, offering it at the magazine's usual rates, and setting out any special circumstances that show it is not just a rehash of cuttings. For example: 'This feature is the result of an expedition I made to the North Pole this year', or 'The information in this feature is based on a long interview with the Chancellor of the Exchequer, who is my godfather'.

Unknown contributors are usually advised to send a stamped and self-addressed envelope for the return of unwanted contributions, which seems hard, given that the magazine has more money. However, it may ensure that if the work is rejected, it is returned – though it cannot be guaranteed. Magazine offices lose a great deal, and nothing should be sent to one without making a copy. A copy may also be of value if words are altered and it is necessary to prove that one was not responsible for an offending phrase. The cheapest way of obtaining a copy, when one has become known in an office, is to use its machine when delivering material.

In the case of speculatively offered material the editor should tell the freelance within a month whether it is accepted or rejected. An acceptance letter should set out the fee offered and the rights required. A rejection need have no details, and it is a mistake to write back demanding to know the reasons for rejection. It is not an editor's job to advise freelances or suggest other markets, though a word of encouragement softens rejection and is always pleasant.

An editor who needs further time than a month for consideration should negotiate a holding fee. If there is no response after a month, a freelance should write politely saying that he or she is proposing to offer the material elsewhere. But it should not be submitted elsewhere without such warning, and should never be sent to more than one publication at a time. This annoys editors. After a few sales to a magazine a freelance should be able to be able to submit ideas to that publication and get commissions, but, again, the same idea should never be submitted to more than one magazine at a time.

It is important to keep on putting up ideas. Some journalists have worries about this, fearing that ideas will be poached. It would be naive to claim this has never happened, but it is not a common problem. The suspicion may arise because it is not unusual for the same idea to occur to a number of journalists. Given a noteworthy anniversary, any number of freelance writers will suggest features to mark the occasion, and some of the suggestions will be almost identical. It is also possible for features editors to produce, without any intention of unfair dealing, ideas which they believe to be original but which actually sprang from an otherwise forgotten conversation or something read weeks or months earlier.

Keep records of all material produced, whether or not it is sold. Enter all work done in a book such as a desk diary, along with a rough assessment, in days or half days, of the time spent on it, payment agreed and when made. It helps in evaluating the better payers.

Money matters

The biggest magazines and the highest payers are not necessarily the best at paying. Some magazines pay well but commission infrequently, expect a lot for their money and have a high nuisance factor, ringing with trivial queries, asking for additional information, and then losing or altering copy and introducing mistakes. There are small magazines where, while it is low, payment is prompt, because their editors value contributors and have problems finding good ones for the kind of money on offer. There may be a case for doing some low-paying jobs, provided they do not require too much labour, but it is sensible to aim to work for the better payers.

Circulation alone is not a reliable guide to a publication's rates of payment. There are many controlled-circulation professional magazines which have small readerships but high advertising revenue and can pay accordingly, so the NUJ, in a guide for freelances, bases desirable levels of payment largely on advertising rates for a page. It divides publications into bands, with Group A consisting of those with the highest advertising rates, and Group E of those which carry no advertising or charge little. Rates in Group A are about three times as high as those in Group E, and Group A publications should pay the highest fees to contributors. Examples cited by the Union include:

A   *Woman, Woman's Own, Woman's Realm, Reader's Digest, Radio Times, TVTimes.*
B   *Cosmopolitan, Chat, Family Circle, Good Housekeeping, Vogue, Smash Hits.*
C   *Living, Options, She, Over 21, Ideal Home.*
D   *Tatler, New Statesman, The Face, Country Life, Practical Photography.*
E   *Waterways, Woman's Story, Labour Research, Judy, Everywoman, Acorn User.*

Some magazines, particularly special interest ones, pay abysmally. They can do so because they use enthusiastic amateurs. A successful barrister was an expert on railways, eager to write for any railway publication on his hobby. Magazines were happy to take his work because they got the knowledge and enthusiasm of a lifetime, and as he was highly paid as a lawyer, he was unconcerned about the fee. He would probably have been prepared to pay the magazine to see his work in print. Full-time freelances who accepted the same fees would soon be bankrupt.

Apart from undercutting other professional journalists, accepting low fees is a road to ruin; even working flat out it will be impossible to make a decent living from them. It is all too easy to jog along, occupying yourself pleasantly, but spending a week on a job that pays only the equivalent of 2 days' money. Freelances should calculate the daily rate they need to earn. It will not be achieved every day, of course, for some days will be spent researching or travelling, but with some higher than usual payments it should average out over a period. When it does not, a reappraisal of working practices and ambitions is necessary.

Freelances need to drive themselves. It is too easy to daydream, re-reading published work, doing accounts, filing cuttings, using all the time until a deadline to rewrite and polish material. A press junket to some establishment is a pleasant day out for staff writers who are using the company's time, but freelances are spending their own. If there is no possibility of earning money from it in the near future, they should forget it. Their need is to keep working. When the problem is finding time to do the non-earning though essential chores, such as keeping accounts and filing, then they have no real problems.

They should avoid putting all their eggs in one basket, i.e. becoming totally dependent on one publication. There may be a change of editors and a new editor will bring in a new team of contributors. The publication may fold or there may be a strike or a freelance may simply fall from favour. It is desirable always to have at least two sources of income, more if possible.

Try to work only for established magazines. The problem with new ones is that while it may seem a good idea to get in on the ground floor and become part of the team, too often new magazines never actually reach the bookstalls, or fold after a couple of issues, leaving freelances unpaid, or being asked to accept a fraction of the agreed payment.

When an editor offers an attractive sounding commission, it is easy to accept it without even asking about money, but one may regret it later. Never put pen to paper without establishing the fee and the rights required for it. Check also whether expenses will be paid. This is of no importance if the research comprises only a few telephone calls, but if the job means travelling and nights in hotels, be sure that expenses will be met or they will make a hole in the fee. Most useful is to be able to charge to a magazine the cost of lunching any contacts, because entertainment is not deductible against tax (unless entertaining foreign clients). If possible, get an advance towards expenses. Alternatively, get a magazine to provide tickets and arrange for hotel bills to be sent to it. This saves being out of pocket until the magazine settles.

Contracts

A commission is a contract in law, and, following normal business practice, terms should be agreed and confirmed in writing before the work is delivered. The editor or commissioning agent – and freelances should be sure that the person commissioning has the authority to do so – should always specify at least the minimum rate that will be paid, state the length of the feature (or minimum time for a photographic commission), provide an adequate briefing on what is expected, and make arrangements for reimbursement of expenses.

If a commission demands an immediate start, and features are usually wanted 'yesterday', agree the terms verbally and ask for written confirmation. A verbal contract is legally binding, but can be difficult to prove, particularly if the executive who commissioned the work leaves the company or becomes ill. If written confirmation does not arrive promptly, send your own letter of confirmation, setting out the arrangement as you understand it and saying that you will regard this as agreed unless any point is queried. If no firm publication date has been given, specify that payment should be by a certain date, such as a month ahead.

Incidentally, companies should insure commissioned freelances against injury or illness as a result of their assignments on the same level as staff journalists, and should indemnify freelances against damages for libel.

Once a freelance has delivered as specified, the company is legally bound to fulfil its side of the contract and payment should be made in full within a month. Do not rely on a company paying automatically when the work has been completed and delivered. It may not. Submit an invoice with the feature, or send one within a day or two. Freelances, as individual self-employed workers, suffer even more severely from bad payers than do companies. When commissions consist of work over a long period of time, freelances should be paid an immediate advance on the total fee, and if a commission is cancelled before the work is completed, a fee of at least 50 per cent should be paid.

If the editor chooses not to publish the material immediately, or not at all, that is not a matter for freelances who have fulfilled their contractual obligations. However, editors sometimes try to negotiate lower fees when circumstances, which are in no way the fault of the freelance, make the copy unusable. For example, a freelance works for a trade magazine on an advertising-backed supplement about an industrial company; on the eve of publication the managing director of the company is changed and the company decides it no longer wants to finance the supplement. That is not the freelance's fault, yet a magazine will commonly try to halve the fee or withhold it until such time as the supplement may be published – if it ever is. The National Union of Journalists has a good record in dealing with recalcitrant publishers.

Regular contributors should have written contracts for services, and in the view of the NUJ those hired full-time for 3 months should be offered staff jobs, unless the work is for a specified limited period (for example, covering for a member of staff on sabbatical leave), in which case a freelance should be given a contract. Freelances who have worked regularly for a publication or publishing organization for more than a year should be compensated for redundancy on the same terms as staff journalists.

Tax problems

Freelances pay income tax as self-employed persons under Schedule D. They can claim for the use of home as office and will normally be allowed a proportion of the rates, rent, heating, and lighting, the proportion being related to the size of the house and whether the room used as an office is reserved exclusively for that purpose. The tax inspector may similarly allow a percentage of the costs of running a car, based on the respective mileages covered for work and on pleasure. Telephone bills, newspapers, magazines, union membership, postage, stationery, and travelling can also be charged. However, a record should be kept of any expenses paid by magazines; the Inland Revenue may ask for details and will not allow them twice over. For example, travelling expenses cannot be set against income if they have been refunded by a magazine.

However, the tax authorities can be strict about freelance status. Freelances who operate without supervision from their own offices or homes, and who work, or are prepared to work, for several publications and are free to accept or reject commissions are unlikely to have problems over this. Those who sell their services by the day or week rather than by the feature or job, and do their work in magazine offices, can find themselves in a different position. This applies particularly to subs and designers, who usually have to work in a magazine office during office hours in order to do the job. They may also regard themselves as freelances, in that they are not staff employees, but tax inspectors regard them as part-time or casual employees, and this means tax is deducted at source under PAYE arrangements.

There are other effects: whereas freelances can charge expenses for travelling to magazine offices (because their homes are their offices and they are therefore travelling in the course of their work), casuals cannot (because they are held to be travelling to reach their place of employment). Freelances may find it convenient to do some work in magazine offices – for access to cuttings, for example – but should make it clear that this is their own choice. They will often find it convenient to work out what fee to ask by calculating the time a job will take, but they should then ask for the money in the form of a fee for the job, not a daily payment, or they may find tax and national insurance deducted.

If freelances are successful and reach a certain level of income, they are obliged to register for VAT. This is generally to be avoided. It means adding the VAT tax (currently 17.5 per cent) to fees, which make them look high; there are sometimes problems in collecting VAT, and the journalist does not get to keep it, for it has to be paid to Customs and Excise. There may be some advantages for a photographer who does his or her own processing and has to buy expensive printing paper, chemicals and equipment and can save paying the VAT content of the price, but there is little in it for a writer, whose outgoings may be less.

Treatment of freelances

This code of practice was adopted at the 1986 annual conference of the National Union of Journalists as official policy for the treatment of freelances, and members are supposed to observe it.

1 Staff journalists hiring freelances have a duty to see that these freelances are treated reasonably.
2 Conditions and rates of pay should be established clearly when the work is accepted or commissioned, preferably in writing.
3 Freelances shall be paid in all cases for providing background information, tips, research material, expertise, etc.
4 Work commissioned or accepted should be paid for at a date agreed at the time of commissioning or acceptance, which should normally be no more than one month after delivery.
5 Staff journalists shall check that the right payments are made at the proper time to freelances they hire, and mistakes in payment should be rectified immediately.
6 Work, including photographs, should be bylined or credited on the same basis as for staff unless the contributor has agreed that this should be omitted.
7 Copyright should remain with the freelance unless a specific signed agreement to transfer it has been made with the freelance in each case.
8 Artwork and photographs should remain the property of the freelance

unless a specific signed agreement is made transferring ownership, and should be returned to the freelance after use.

9   Freelances should be paid expenses on at least the same basis as the staff, and preferably these should be advanced before expenditure is incurred.

10   Freelance work should go to freelance members of the NUJ and not moonlighters.

'Moonlighters' are staff employees who take on additional regular work on other publications, or sometimes, for extra money, on the ones that employ them. They are thereby depriving freelances of opportunities and are often prepared to undercut normal rates, since the work – sometimes done in their employers' time and using their employers' facilities – is merely an additional source of income and not their main one.

GLOSSARY

ABC Audit Bureau of Circulations, a body that authenticates the circulations of newspapers and periodicals.

Acetate A transparent plastic sheet used as an overlay for artwork.

Ad An advertisement.

Add An addition to copy already written.

Adhesive binding, see **Unsewn binding**.

Advance copies Limited number of printed copies of a new issue delivered to a magazine for checking before the main print run.

Advertising agency An organization that buys advertising space for clients, and prepares and delivers copy for them.

Advertorial Advertising-sponsored material presented to look like editorial.

A4 A sheet of paper 297 × 210 mm (11.6 × 8.2 in).

Agony column A feature offering advice on personal problems.

Alignment The correct levelling of the characters in a line of text, or of text and pictures.

Artwork (or **A/W**) Illustration of any kind suitable for printing.

Ascender The part of a lower case letter rising above its body: for example, the upper limb of a 'b' or 'd'.

As to press Proofs showing final positioning of colour material.

Author's corrections Alterations made by the editorial department on proofs, other than those necessitated by printers' errors.

Back margin The margin of a page nearest to the spine.

Back numbers Previous issues of a publication.

Back of the book Pages after the centre spread of a periodical.

Back-up copy Duplicate of a computer disc, made in case of accidental damage to the original.

Bad break Unattractive breaking and hyphenating of a word between two lines.

Banner A headline extending the full width across the top of a page.

Bastard measure A non-standard width of text.

Binder A folder designed to hold collected issues of a magazine or part-work.

Black Originally a carbon copy, now more likely a photocopy. Also used to refer to bold type.

Blanket cylinder The component of an offset press that applies ink to paper.

Bleach-out A photograph deliberately overdeveloped to render it black and white without any tones, sometimes used as a logo.

Bleed The part of an illustration extended beyond the type area to reach any outer edge of a printed page.

Block A zinc or copper plate on which is etched or engraved a line or halftone illustration.

Blow-up An enlargement of part or all of a picture.

Blurb Copy designed to sell a publication: for example, an announcement of what will be in the next issue.

Body type Main typeface in which features are set, usually between 8 and 12-pt.

Bold Thick black type for emphasis.

Box A piece of text segregated from other matter by rules or borders on all four sides, or by the use of a colour tint.

Bromide In photography a print from a negative; in printing a proof from photocomposition.

Bucket Three rules, two vertical and one horizontal, forming a bucket shape or a box without a top, commonly used to house a caption beneath a picture.

Bulk Thickness of a printed publication, measured in pages per inch.

Buster A headline too long for the space available.

Byline The name of a writer on a feature.

© Copyright mark recognized by the Universal Copyright Convention.

Calendering Process which glazes or smooths the surface of paper.

Camera-ready Material such as copy and pictures, set out on a page exactly as they are to appear in the magazine and ready to be photographed for printing.

Caps   Capital (upper case) letters.

Caption   Words accompanying a picture or graphic, printed above, below or beside it.

Cast off   A count of the number of words or characters and spaces in a piece of copy to estimate the space it will occupy when set in type.

Catchline   Identifying word, not for publication, placed with folio number at the top of pages of typed copy and galley proofs.

Cathode ray tube (CRT)   Electronic tube used as light source to transmit characters on to film in photocomposition.

Centre spread   The two facing pages in the middle of a magazine, printed on the same sheet of paper, allowing them to be treated as a single unit. Also known as a **centrefold** or **natural spread**.

Chapel   An office branch of the National Union of Journalists.

Chapter   An office branch of the Institute of Journalists.

Character count   The number of characters in a piece of copy to be set.

Cicero   Unit of measurement used in France and Germany, roughly equal to an em.

Classifieds   Small advertisements, commonly for jobs or property, which appear in alphabetical order.

Clean proof   One practically free from errors.

Clicker   Foreman compositor who receives and distributes copy for setting.

Clips   Abbreviation for clippings; Americanism for cuttings from news-papers or magazines.

Close quotes   Punctuation mark or marks at the end of quoted words.

Close up   Instruction to reduce space between characters, words or lines of text.

Coated paper   A quality paper to whose surface a mineral coating has been applied to render it glossy.

Cold type   Method of typesetting such as photocomposition in which molten metal is not used, as opposed to **hot metal** type.

Collating   Assembling printed sections of a magazine in order ready for binding. Also known as **gathering**.

Colour   Descriptive writing.

Colour cast   Unwanted tinge of colour in a picture, sometimes caused by reflection from a wall or garment.

Colour code   Set of bars on four-colour proofs showing the strength and registration of the colours.

Colour correction   Adjustment of colours at proofing stage.

Colour positives   A set of positive colour separations.

Colour separation   Division of colours in a picture into yellow, magenta, cyan and black for separate printing by the four-colour process.

Composing room   Premises where type is set.

Composite   A sheet of assorted pictures of a model, offered for reference purposes.

Comps   Abbreviation for compositors who set copy in type.

Condensed   A type style in which the letters are narrower than normal.

Contact   A same-size photographic print made by direct contact between negative (or another positive) and paper.

Copy   Matter to be reproduced in type.

Copy fitting, see **cast off**.

Copy paper   What copy is written on.

Copywriter   One who writes copy for advertisements.

Credit   A byline on a story or picture; sometimes the payment for it.

Cromalin   A pre-proof made swiftly by the use of powder instead of ink.

Cropping   Trimming a picture to exclude unwanted areas.

Crosshead   A subsidiary heading, usually in bold type, centred on its own line and with extra spacing above and below.

Cross-reference   Words directing readers to turn elsewhere in a publication for further relevant information.

Cursor   A flashing spot on a computer screen; an indicator used when manipulating text.

Cut off   A rule cutting off one feature from another.

Cut-out   A picture treated to remove everything but the main subject.

Cuttings   Material cut from newspapers and magazines and housed in office libraries. A **cuttings job** is a feature based on such material.

Cyan   The shade of blue used in four-colour printing.

Daisy wheel   Good quality, but slow, computer printing system in which characters are arranged at the ends of 'petals'.

Database   Information stored in the memory of a computer.

Dateline   A line over a feature indicating where it was filed: for example, Los Angeles, 1 January. More common in newspapers than magazines.

Deadline   The time or day by which a piece of work must be delivered.

Descender   The part of a lower case letter below its body, such as the tail of 'p' or 'y'.

Didot point   Continental type size unit measuring 0.0148in., slightly larger than the Anglo-American point.

Direct input   The keyboarding of material into a computer by writers for editing and setting.

Dirty proof   One bearing numerous corrections and amendments.

Disclaimer   A paragraph explaining that a previously published story has no connection with another person or organization of the same name.

Display advertisement   One of a size to demand attention, as opposed to a **classified** or **small**.

Display type   Type for headings, larger than that used for the text of features – usually 14-pt or upwards.

D-notice   An official warning that a subject is secret and nothing about it should be published.

Dot matrix   Cheap, quick, computer printer system forming letters from dots.

Double columns   Across two columns.

Double page spread   A feature or ad occupying two facing pages.

Drop cap   A large initial letter at the start of a piece of text, descending alongside indented lines of type below.

Dummy   A mock-up of an issue of a magazine, to show the design for a new publication or the progress of an issue being worked on.

Dupe   Duplicate, usually of a colour transparency.

Editorial   Any matter which is not paid-for advertising. *Not* a leading article.

Ellipsis   Omission of words, indicated by three dots.

Elite   Smaller kind of typewriter type, giving 12 characters to an inch.

Em   Printers' standard unit of measurement equal to the width of a 12-point letter m; in fact, a sixth of an inch.

Em rule   A dash one em in length, also a ruler marked in ems.

Embargo   A ban on publication until a nominated time of material supplied in advance.

En   Unit of measurement half the width of an em; a twelfth of an inch.

En rule   A short dash commonly used to replace the word 'to', for example in *1939–1945*.

Engraving Design or lettering etched on a plate or block.

Exes Expenses.

Expanded (or **extended**) **A style of type in which letters are wider than normal.**

Facing matter (FM) Position for an advertisement facing editorial matter.

Fair copy Text which is free from corrections.

Father of the Chapel (FoC) The chairman of an office branch of the National Union of Journalists. **MoC** stands for Mother of the Chapel.

Fax Facsimiles of pages, or a machine that can transmit them by means of a telephone line.

Filler A short paragraph used to fill a space.

Filmset Photo-set type.

Fine rule A thin rule, but not as thin as a **hairline**.

Finishing The operations following the production of printed sections, e.g. binding.

Fixed costs Expenses which remain the same irrespective of the number of copies printed, e.g. typesetting.

Flat artwork, see **camera-ready**.

Flat plan Diagrammatic representation of the pages of a magazine, used in planning the positions of features and advertisements.

Flop To reverse an image, left to right.

Floppy disc Disc for storing computer information. **Hard discs** hold more.

Flush left Unjustified setting lined up flush to the left.

Foldout A wider than normal magazine page that has to be folded back on itself.

Folio A page of copy.

Follow copy Instruction to compositor to set exactly what is written, despite apparent errors (for example, deliberate mis-spellings).

Foot margin The margin at the bottom of a page.

Forme Type and blocks assembed in pages and locked in position for letterpress printing.

Fount (or **font**) A complete set of all the different characters and punctuation marks in any one size and style of a particular typeface: for example, 10-pt Times italic.

Four-colour process Method of printing full colour by separation into yellow, red, blue and black.

Free sheet   A newspaper or magazine given away to readers and financially dependent on advertising.

Full out   Instruction to compositor to make a line run from margin to margin without any indent.

Galley   In printing, a metal tray used for assembling a column of type; used editorially to mean a proof in single column form.

Ghostwriter   A journalist who writes a feature or book on behalf of a celebrity.

Gravure, see **Photogravure**.

Gsm   Grams per square metre, the measurement of weight and thickness of paper. Also written as G/M^2.

Grot   Abbreviation for Grotesque, a family of sans serif type.

Gutter   The unprinted margins where two facing pages meet.

Hairline   The finest rule in printing.

Half tone   Photographic method of representing variations in light and shade by breaking up the tones into black dots of different sizes; also the block made by this process.

Half up   Artwork prepared half as big again as it will be in a magazine. This calls for one-third reduction.

H and J   Hyphenate and justify. A computer instruction. See **Justification**.

Handout   A press release.

Hanging indent   The reverse of a normal indent; a number of lines in which the first line is set full measure and the following lines are indented.

Hard copy   Computer term for a document on paper, as opposed to being on disc or on screen.

Head   Abbreviation for headline, also the top margin of a page.

Heavies   Quality newspapers such as *The Financial Times* or *Guardian*.

Hot metal   Typesetting in which the characters are cast from molten metal.

Imposition   The arrangement of pages for printing, so that after folding they will be in numerical sequence.

Imprint   Name and address of publisher and printer, required by law to be included in a magazine, usually placed in small type at the back.

Indent   Instruction to set back the beginning of a line from the margin at the start of a paragraph.

Insert   An additional piece of copy to be included in the body of a feature already written.

Inset   A page or pages included in a publication, but not part of the normal pagination.

Intaglio Processes that print from an image recessed into a plate, e.g. a photogravure plate.

ISSN International Standard Series Number, a unique reference number allotted to and identifying individual periodicals, similar to the ISBN given to every edition of a book.

Italic Type with forward-slanting letters.

Journalese Pejorative term for cliché-ridden writing.

Justification Adjusting lines of type by inserting spaces to create lines of equal length, fitting flush with both left- and right-hand edges of the print area.

Kerning Reducing space between letters so that one overlaps the next.

Key number A figure inserted by an advertiser in a coupon, to identify the publication and issue date after the coupon has been cut out and mailed.

Kicker A story made to stand out from the rest of a page by the use of different type and setting.

Kill To scrap material such as a feature, picture or section of type.

Laminate A glossy protective coating given to paper or card, such as a cover, by the application of transparent plastic material.

Layout Design for a page or feature, sent to the printer to show positions of text and illustrations.

Lead Pronounced 'leed', the main item at the top of a page.

Leading Pronounced 'ledding', extra white space between lines of type, so called from the practice in hot metal setting of inserting blank slugs to achieve it.

Leg Any length of type on a page.

Letraset Best known range of self-adhesive dry-transfer lettering used for display purposes.

Letterpress Relief printing in which the impression is made on paper by inking a raised surface.

Letter space Space the width of an average letter in the type being used.

Letterspacing The insertion of space between the letters of words to improve appearance.

Lift In editorial offices, to take from another issue or publication; in printing, to make use of matter already in type.

Ligature Joined letters such as *fl*

Light Type of lighter weight than standard.

Light box A glass-topped box lit from inside, used for viewing negatives and transparencies.

Line block   Zinc or copper printing plate consisting of solid areas and lines, made from line drawings or other illustrations without tones.

Line drawing   Artwork composed of solid black lines, without wash or tones.

Linotype   Typesetting machine casting whole lines (slugs) of metal type.

Literal   A typing or printing error.

Lithography (litho)   Printing from a flat, or only slightly recessed, surface of a metal plate, using the antipathy of grease to water, the non-printing areas being dampened and therefore ink-repellent.

Logo   Abbreviation of logotype, a trade mark or identifying house symbol.

Lower case   Small letters as opposed to capitals. When type was set by hand, printers kept it in two cases, capitals in the upper and small letters in the lower.

Low key   Photograph having predominantly dark tones.

Mainframe   A large computer system which can be accessed by terminals consisting of a keyboard and VDU and can perform several functions simultaneously.

Magenta   The shade of red used in four-colour printing.

Make up   The arrangement of type, pictures and headlines to form pages.

Mark up   Place instructions on copy or overlays to indicate required type sizes, degrees of reduction and the like.

Masthead   The title block or logo identifying a publication.

Matrix   A mould from which type characters and pages are cast in hot metal printing.

Measure   The width of any setting.

Mechanical   A camera-ready page of printed text and artwork, on a board with instructions, ready for processing.

Medium   Standard weight of type, neither light nor bold.

Merchandising   Information about prices and availability of products.

MF (abbreviation of **more follows**)   Used at the foot of a page of copy to indicate that it is not the end.

MFL (more follows later)   Used at the end of a feature when it will be some time before the add is available.

Micro   Abbreviation for microcomputer, a small computer of the type used for word processing.

Milk   To extract information from another publication.

Modem (abbreviation of **modulator demodulator**)   A device enabling computer information to be transmitted by a telephone line.

Monochrome A print of a single colour, usually black on white.

Monotype Hot metal typesetting machine casting characters individually.

Morgue Section of a library to which are relegated files about the long since dead, and others unlikely to be often wanted.

Mug shots Head and shoulders portraits.

Must A feature or paragraph that *must* go in a publication for legal reasons or because the editor has decreed it.

Neg A photographic negative.

Newsprint Cheap paper used for printing newspapers on.

NMI Abbreviation for **Next Month's Issue**.

Nose The intro or starting point of a feature.

Offset litho Printing system in which litho plate and paper do not touch, the impression being offset to a rubber-surfaced cylinder and from there to paper.

On line under the control of, or in communication with, a computer. **Off line** is the opposite.

Open quotes Punctuation mark or marks placed before the start of quoted material.

Origination Typesetting, colour separation, blockmaking or any other first step towards readying original material for printing.

Orphan A single word or syllable standing alone on the first line of a column; the worst form of **widow**.

Overlay A transparent sheet covering artwork and bearing instructions to the printer, or additional colour to be incorporated.

Overmatter Copy which has been set but for which there is no space on the page.

Overrun Copies of a publication in excess of the number ordered.

Padding Overwriting; unmerited wordage.

Page proofs Following galley proofs, these show text after it has been arranged into pages.

Pagination The numbering of pages, also the number of editorial and advertising pages to be contained in an issue.

Panel Text enclosed in rules or borders, also known as a **box**.

Par A paragraph.

Part-works Non-fiction publications sold like magazines but with a prearranged number of issues, intended to be stored in binders.

Pass for press Final authorization after proofing to proceed with printing.

Paste-up   A dummy page or issue made from proofs.

Pay off   The last par of a feature, particularly one containing a final twist.

Perfecting   Printing both sides of paper in one pass through a press.

Photocomposition   Setting text by means of characters photographed on film.

Photogravure (or **gravure**)   Method of printing mass circulation magazines, using a cylinder etched to varying depths, and holding ink in the pits.

Pica   In typewriting, the type giving ten characters to the inch. In printing, 12-point type.

Pix   Pictures.

Plagiarism   The unauthorized use of another person's copyright material without acknowledgement.

Play down   Minimize an aspect of a feature. To **play up** is to maximize it.

Point   A measure of type size equalling 0.01383in.; for practical purposes there are 72 points to an inch.

Print order   The number of copies of a publication ordered to be printed.

Print run   The number of copies of a publication produced.

Process engraving   Hot metal printing method of transferring a photographic image to a metal plate by etching with acid.

Progressives   A set of proofs in colour printing, each showing one colour to be imposed on the previous one.

Proportional spacing   A method of spacing characters, taking account of the different widths of letters.

Puff   A blatant free plug for a person or product.

Pull   A proof, so called because of the way a roller is pulled over paper in letterpress printing.

Pull-out   A section of a magazine, such as a stitched-in supplement, designed so that the pages can be pulled out and kept.

Quire   Newagents' measurement of quantity; usually 26 copies of a publication.

Qwerty   A standard keyboard layout, the name derived from the first six letter keys on a typewriter.

Ragged right   Copy set unjustified at the right-hand edge.

Range left   An instruction to position unjustified lines of unequal length so that all are flush with the left edge of the print area; **range right** commands the opposite.

Rate card   Comprehensive list of a publication's charges for advertising spaces and positions.

Reader   A proof reader at a typesetting house.

Readership   The total number of readers of a publication, which may be two or three times as great as the circulation (number of copies distributed).

Ream   A quantity of paper, usually 500 sheets.

Register   In printing, the accurate positioning of one colour on another.

Register mark   Usually a cross in a circle, placed on film to aid positioning of negatives in register.

Rejig   To change the sequence of a feature already written.

Repro house   A firm specializing in colour separation and blockmaking.

Reverse left to right   Instruction to printer to alter a picture to its mirror image.

Reverse out   To print letters in white on a black background, or sometimes yellow on blue.

Revise   A new proof supplied after corrections have been carried out.

Roman   Normal, upright type, as opposed to *italic* or **bold**.

Rough   A preliminary sketch of a design.

Round up   A feature incorporating reports from a number of places or sources.

Rules   Vertical or horizontal printed lines that separate columns of type or features.

Run on   In subbing, an instruction to make text continue without paragraphing; in printing, an instruction to produce additional copies beyond the original order.

Running costs   Those expenses additional to fixed costs which relate directly to the number of copies required: for example, printing and binding.

Running headline   The title and issue date at the top of magazine pages. A **running foot** is when they are at the bottom.

Saddlestitching   Binding system in which inset sections of paper are stitched through the spine. If staples are used, this is sometimes known as **saddle wiring**.

Sale or return (SoR)   Distribution system in which the publisher agrees to take back any copies unsold by the retailer, commonly adopted for the first issues of a new publication before sales can be predicted confidently.

Sans (abbreviation of **sans serif**)   Typefaces without tailstrokes.

Save　Instruction to computer to move data from the memory on to disc for storage.

Scaling　Process of establishing the depth of a picture after enlarging or reducing its width.

Scalpel　Razor sharp tool used in art departments for cutting, lifting and moving material.

Scamp　A first rough sketch or 'visual' produced by an artist to meet a brief.

Schedule　List of proposed features for an issue; also a list of dates on which material is due for processing or printing.

Scheme　To plan the design of a page.

Screamer　An exclamation mark.

Screen　The pattern of dots by which half-tone pictures are reproduced.

Second deck　A subsidiary headline.

Section　A printed sheet which, when folded and trimmed, makes up part of a magazine.

Separations　Film for making plates for colour printing, produced by isolating the four process colours.

Serif　A short bar or cross line at the end of a main limb of a printed character. **Sans serif** are typefaces without them.

Set and hold　Instruction to printer to set a feature in type and retain until further instructions.

Set solid　Instruction to set type without leading between lines.

Sheet-fed　Printing with single sheets of paper as opposed to a reel.

Shoulderhead　Subheading, usually in italic or bold, ranged left or indented slightly, but not on a separate line. (The text runs on.)

Sidebar　Complementary text placed alongside a main feature.

Sidehead　A subheading, usually in italic or bold, ranged to one side on its own line with extra spacing above it.

Sign-off　The name of a writer at the foot of a feature.

Slip　A page, which may be advertising or editorial, solely for a particular circulation area, and only in issues for sale in that area.

Slugline　Americanism for catchline.

Small caps　Capitals of approximately the same size as lower case characters, mainly used for a list of decorations and degrees after a person's name.

Smalls　Classified advertisements.

Snatch　To take a photograph without the subject's consent and possibly knowledge.

Spike In newspaper offices a device on which subs impale rejected copy. Though spikes are not normally seen in magazine offices, unwanted copy is said to be 'spiked'.

Spine The bound edge of a magazine, visible when on edge in a bookcase.

Splash The main front-page story in a trade magazine or other with news on the cover.

Spot colour A colour applied to a page during the run of press.

Spread Two facing pages in a magazine.

SS (abbreviation for **same size**) Used as instruction when artwork is not to be enlarged or reduced.

Standfirst Introductory paragraph before the start of a feature.

Stet Instruction meaning 'let it stand', used to countermand a deletion.

Stock Paper for printing.

Strap Strapline, an introductory headline, usually above the main one.

Stringer A local correspondent, not on the staff, commonly abroad.

Strip in To replace a line with a new one when preparing camera-ready text, or to overlay lettering or type on artwork.

Super calendered Paper smoothed and given gloss by heated rolling.

Supplement Self-contained section, a mini-magazine bound into, or otherwise given away with, a periodical.

Swash Florid italic lettering or type.

Take back Instruction placed on proof when words are to be moved back to the preceding line or paragraph. **Take over** means the opposite.

Tear out Picture with a simulated torn edge, as though ripped out of a newspaper or periodical. Also known as a **rag out**.

Transparency A colour slide, a positive photographic image on film.

Trimming Cutting a magazine on three edges after binding.

Turn Continuation of a feature on a later page.

Twice up Artwork prepared at twice the size at which it will be published.

Type area The part of a page, surrounded by margins, used for the main body of material.

Typo Americanism for a typographical error, or literal.

U/Lc Abbreviation for 'upper and lower case'.

Unjustified Text of uneven line length, ranged left or right.

Unsewn binding (also known as **perfect binding**) Method in which the binding edge is trimmed, separating the leaves, the spine is coated with adhesive, a cover is attached and the magazine trimmed.

Update   To incorporate new information in a feature, making it more timely.

Upper case   Capital letters.

VDU   Visual display unit (a television screen) used with computer.

Vignette   An illustration without a border, fading into white at the edges.

Web   A continuous reel of paper (as opposed to sheets).

Web offset   Offset litho printing from a reel of paper.

WF   Wrong fount; proof mark to indicate a character or characters in the wrong size or style.

Widow   A line of type containing only one word or syllable.

Wire machine   Device for transmitting pictures.

Wirestitching   Stapling, the cheapest method of binding.

Word break   Splitting a word at the end of a line and ending it on the next.

Word count   Assessment of the number of words in a piece of copy.

x height   The height of letters without ascenders or descenders, such as an 'x'.

BIBLIOGRAPHY

Barnard, Michael, *Magazine and Journal Production*, London, Blueprint, 1986.

Craig, James, *Designing with Type*, New York, Watson-Guptill Publications, 1980.

Davis, Anthony, *Working in Journalism*, London, Batsford, 1979.

Derrick, John and Oppenheim, Phillip, *The Word Processing Handbook*, London, Kogan Page, 1984.

Fincher, Terry, *Creative Techniques in Photo-journalism*, London, Batsford, 1980.

Graham, Walter, *The Beginnings of English Literary Periodicals*, New York, Oxford University Press, 1926.

Graham, Walter, *English Literary Periodicals*, New York, Thomas Nelson, 1930.

Hammond, Ray, *The Writer and the Word Processor*, Sevenoaks, Coronet Books, 1984.

Hooper, David, *Public Scandal, Odium and Contempt*, Sevenoaks, Coronet Books, 1986.

Hutchings, Ernest A. D., *A Survey of Printing Processes*, London, Heinemann, 1970.

Langford, Michael J., *Professional Photography*, London, Focal Press, 1974.

McLean, Ruari, *The Thames and Hudson Manual of Typography*, London, Thames and Hudson, 1980.

Monk, Barry, *The Freelance Photography Handbook*, London, Ebury Press, 1983.

Partridge, Eric, *Usage and Abusage*, Harmondsworth, Penguin Reference Books, 1963.

Peterson, Theodore, *Magazines in the Twentieth Century*, Urbana, University of Illinois Press, 1956.

Robertson, Geoffrey and Nicol, Andrew G. L., *Media Law*, London, Sage Publications, 1984.

Rogers, Geoffrey, *Editing for Print*, London, Macdonald, 1986.

Sanders, Norman, *Graphic Designer's Production Handbook*, Newton Abbot, David & Charles, 1984.

Sellers, Leslie, *The Simple Subs Book*, Oxford, Pergamon Press, 1985.

Smith, Anthony, *Goodbye Gutenberg*, New York, Oxford University Press, 1980.

Strunk, William Jr and White, E. B., *The Elements of Style*, New York, Macmillan, 1979.

Thomas, Donald, *A Long Time Burning: The History of Literary Censorship in England*, London, Routledge & Kegan Paul, 1969.

Tunstall, Jeremy, *The Media in Britain*, London, Constable, 1983.

Waterhouse, Keith, *Daily Mirror Style*, London, Mirror Books, 1981.

White, Cynthia L., *Women's Magazines 1693–1968*, London, Michael Joseph, 1970.

White, Cynthia L., *The Women's Periodical Press in Britain 1946–1976*, London, HMSO, 1977.

Winsbury, Rex, *New Technology and the Press*, London, HMSO, 1975.

Wood, Frederick T., *Current English Usage*, London, Macmillan, 1962.

Writers' and Artists' Year Book (annually), London, A & C Black.

USEFUL ADDRESSES

British Association of Journalists, 97 Fleet Street, London EC4Y 1DH.

British Standards Institution, 2 Park Street, London W1A 2BS.

City University, St John Street, London EC1V 4PB.

Emap Training, 57 Priestgate, Peterborough PE1 1JW.

Institute of Journalists, Suite 2, Dock Offices, Surrey Quays, Lower Road, London SE16 2XL.

Institute of Trade Mark Agents, Canterbury House, 2–6 Sydenham Road, Croydon CR0 9XE.

London College of Printing, Elephant and Castle, London SE1 6SB.

National Council for Training Journalists, Latton Bush Centre, Southern Way, Harlow, Essex CM18 7BL.

National Union of Journalists, Acorn House, Grays Inn Road, London WC1X 8DP.

Periodicals Training Council, Imperial House, 15–19 Kingsway, London WC2B 6UN.

Reed Business Publishing, Quadrant House, The Quadrant, Sutton, Surrey SM2 5AS.

University College, Cardiff, 69 Park Place, Cardiff CF1 1XL.

APPENDIX: CODE OF PRACTICE FOR THE PRESS

The Press Complaints Commission Code of Practice for the Press

The Press Complaints Commission are charged with enforcing the following Code of Practice which was framed by the newspaper and periodical industry and ratified by the Press Complaints Commission in 1993.

All members of the Press have a duty to maintain the highest professional and ethical standards. In doing so, they should have regard to the provisions of this Code of Practice and to safeguarding the public's right to know.

Editors are responsible for the actions of journalists employed by their publications. They should also satisfy themselves as far as possible that material accepted from non-staff members was obtained in accordance with this Code.

While recognising that this involves a substantial element of self-restraint by editors and journalists, it is designed to be acceptable in the context of a system of self-regulation. The Code applies in the spirit as well as in the letter.

It is the responsibility of editors to cooperate as swiftly as possible in PCC enquiries.

Any publication which is criticised by the PCC under one of the following clauses is duty bound to print the adjudication which follows in full and with due prominence.

1 Accuracy

(i)   Newspapers and periodicals should take care not to publish inaccurate, misleading or distorted material.

(ii) Whenever it is recognised that a significant inaccuracy, misleading statement or distorted report has been published, it should be corrected promptly and with due prominence.

(iii) An apology should be published whenever appropriate.

(iv) A newspaper or periodical should always report fairly and accurately the outcome of an action for defamation to which it has been a party.

2 Opportunity to reply

A fair opportunity for reply to inaccuracies should be given to individuals or organisations when reasonably called for.

3 Comment, conjecture and fact

Newspapers, while free to be partisan should distinguish clearly between comment, conjecture and fact.

4 Privacy

Intrusions and enquiries into an individual's private life without his or her consent including the use of long-lens photography to take pictures of people on private property without their consent are not generally acceptable and publication can only be justified when in the public interest.

Note - Private property is defined as any private residence, together with its garden and outbuildings, but excluding any adjacent fields or parkland. In addition, hotel bedrooms (but not other areas in a hotel) and those parts of a hospital or nursing home where patients are treated or accommodated.

5 Listening devices

Unless justified by public interest, journalists should not obtain or publish material obtained by using clandestine listening devices or by intercepting private telephone conversations.

6 Hospitals

(i) Journalists or photographers making enquiries at hospitals or similar institutions should identify themselves to a responsible official and obtain permission before entering non-public areas.

(ii)   The restrictions on intruding into privacy are particularly relevant to enquiries about individuals in hospital or similar institutions.

7   *Misrepresentation*

(i)   Journalists should not generally obtain or seek to obtain information or pictures through misrepresentation or subterfuge.
(ii)   Unless in the public interest, documents or photographs should be removed only with the express consent of the owner.
(iii) Subterfuge can be justified only in the public interest and only when material cannot be obtained by any other means.

8   *Harassment*

(i)   Journalists should neither obtain nor seek to obtain information or pictures through intimidation or harassment.
(ii)   Unless their enquiries are in the public interest, journalists should not photograph individuals on private property without their consent; should not persist in telephoning or questioning individuals after having been asked to desist; should not remain on their property after having been asked to leave and should not follow them.
(iii) It is the responsibility of editors to ensure that these requirements are carried out.

9   *Payment for articles*

(i)   Payments or offers for stories, pictures or information should not be made directly or through agents to witnesses or potential witnesses in current or criminal proceedings or to people engaged in crime or to their associates — which includes family, friends, neighbours and colleagues — except where the material concerned ought to be published in the public interest and the payment is necessary for this to be done.

10   *Intrusions into grief or shock*

In cases involving personal grief or shock, enquiries should be carried out and approaches made with sympathy and discretion.

11   Innocent relatives and friends

Unless it is contrary to the public's right to know, the Press should generally avoid identifying relatives or friends of persons convicted or accused
of crime.

12   Interviewing or photographing children

(i)   Journalists should not normally interview or photograph children
       under the age of 16 on subjects involving the personal welfare of the
       child, in the absence of or without the consent of a parent or other
       adult who is responsible for the children.
(ii)   Children should not be approached or photographed while at school
       without the permission of the school authorities.

13   Children in sex cases

(1)   The press should not, even where the law does not prohibit it, identify
       children under the age of 16 who are involved in cases concerning
       sexual offences, whether as victims, or as witnesses or defendants.
(2)   In any press report of a case involving a sexual offence against a child—
(i)   The adult should be identified.
(ii)   The terms 'incest' where applicable should not be used.
(iii) The offences should be described as 'serious offences against young
       children' or similar appropriate wording.
(iv)   The child should not be identified.
(v)   Care should be taken that nothing in the report implies the relation-
       ship between the accused and the child.

14   Victims of crime

The press should not identify victims of sexual assault or publish material
likely to contribute to such identification unless, by law, they are free to
do so.

15   Discrimination

(i)   The press should avoid prejudicial or pejorative reference to a
       person's race, colour, religion, sex or sexual orientation or to any
       physical or mental illness or handicap.

(ii)   It should avoid publishing details of a person's race, colour, religion, sex or sexual orientation, unless these are directly relevant to the story.

16   Financial journalism

(i)   Even where the law does not prohibit it, journalists should not use for their own profit financial information they receive in advance of its general publication, nor should they pass such information to others.
(ii)   They should not write about shares of securities in whose performance they know that they or their close families have a significant financial interest, without disclosing the interest to the editor or financial editor.
(iii) They should not buy or sell, either directly or through nominees or agents, shares or securities about which they have written recently or about which they intend to write in the near future.

17   Confidential sources

Journalists have a moral obligation to protect confidential sources of information.

18   The public interest

Clauses 4, 5, 7, 8 and 9 create exceptions which may be covered by invoking the public interest. For the purposes of this code that is most easily defined as:

(i)   Detecting or exposing crime or a serious misdemeanour.
(ii)   Protecting public health and safety.
(iii) Preventing the public from being misled by some statement or action of an individual or organisation.

In any cases raising issues beyond these three definitions the Press Complaints Commission will require a full explanation by the editor of the publication involved, seeking to demonstrate how the public interest was served.

Comments or suggestions regarding the content of the Code may be sent to the Secretary, Press Standards Board of Finance, Merchants House Buildings, 30 George Square, Glasgow G2 1EG, to be laid before the industry's Code Committee.

INDEX

THE DILEMMA OF QUALITATIVE METHOD

The dispute over the value of qualitative versus quantitative approaches to social research originated in nineteenth-century debates about the relationship between the methods of history and natural science. Within sociology, this dispute first arose in the United States during the 1920s and 30s, between adherents of 'case study' and 'statistical' methods. One of the main advocates of case study was the Chicago sociologist, Herbert Blumer. His influential writings on methodology provide a link between this earlier controversy and the debates of the 1960s, 70s and 80s. However, Blumer's arguments for qualitative, or 'naturalistic', method retain a central ambivalence: does that method share the same logic as natural science, or does it represent a different form of inquiry characteristic of history and the humanities? That issue continues to underly discussions of qualitative method, and provokes fundamental questions about the procedures employed by qualitative researchers.

The Dilemma of Qualitative Method is a stimulating guide to this key area of social research methodology. The author sketches the historical context of the dispute and provides a detailed account and systematic analysis of Blumer's methodological writings, including his doctoral thesis. The strategies for qualitative research advocated by Blumer and others within the Chicago tradition are closely assessed. The author's conclusions about the current state of qualitative...